MONEY MATTERS

4TH EDITION

4TH EDITION

Englisch für Bankkaufleute

von
Susan Lau
Freya Preuß
Rosemary Richey
Margit Soll
Isobel Williams

in Zusammenarbeit mit der Verlagsredaktion

Cornelsen

Yeliz Günes

Verfasserinnen:	Susan Lau, Hamburg Freya Preuß, Essen Rosemary Richey, München Margit Soll, Passau Isobel Williams, Berlin
Verfasser KMK mock exam:	Manfred Thönicke, Hamburg
Beraterinnen:	Freya Preuß, Essen Margit Soll, Passau
Verfasserinnen KMK Aufgaben:	Irene Eckhart, Flensburg und die Autoren
Beraterin KMK Aufgaben:	Petra Schappert, Stuttgart
Projektleitung:	Shaunessy Ashdown
Redaktionelle Mitarbeit:	Christine House, Ingrid Raspe und Georg Raspe (Wörterverzeichnisse)
Bildredaktion:	Meike Kolle und Christina Scheuerer
Gesamtgestaltung und technische Umsetzung:	vitaledesign, Berlin
Titelfoto:	Shutterstock / Image Wizard

Erhältlich sind auch: **Handreichungen für den Unterricht mit DVD-Extra und Audio-CD**
ISBN 978-3-06-451011-1
Online-Ergänzungen unter
www.cornelsen.de/matters

Soweit in diesem Lehrwerk Personen fotografisch abgebildet sind und ihnen von der Redaktion fiktive Namen, Berufe, Dialoge und Ähnliches zugeordnet oder diese Personen in bestimmte Kontexte gesetzt werden, dienen diese Zuordnungen und Darstellungen ausschließlich der Veranschaulichung und dem besseren Verständnis des Inhalts.

www.cornelsen.de

Die Webseiten Dritter, deren Internetadressen in diesem Lehrwerk angegeben sind, wurden vor Drucklegung sorgfältig geprüft. Der Verlag übernimmt keine Gewähr für die Aktualität und den Inhalt dieser Seiten oder solcher, die mit ihnen verlinkt sind.

1. Auflage, 2. Druck 2017

Alle Drucke dieser Auflage sind inhaltlich unverändert und können im Unterricht nebeneinander verwendet werden.

Druck und Bindung: Livonia Print, Riga

ISBN 978-3-06-451009-8 (Schülerbuch)
ISBN 978-3-06-451010-4 (E-Book)

PEFC
PEFC/12-31-006

PEFC zertifiziert
Dieses Produkt stammt aus nachhaltig bewirtschafteten Wäldern und kontrollierten Quellen.

www.pefc.de

VORWORT

Money Matters – 4th Edition ist die komplett aktualisierte Neubearbeitung des bewährten Lehrwerks für angehende Bankkauffrauen und Bankkaufmänner und wurde für die Ausbildung in den Berufsschulen sowie die innerbetriebliche Aus- und Weiterbildung konzipiert. Es basiert auf den Lehrplänen der Bundesländer für die Berufsschulen und bei der Aufgabenerstellung ist ein besonderes Augenmerk auf die Erfüllung der unterschiedlichen Anforderungssituationen und deren Zielformulierungen gelegt worden.

Money Matters ist auf Lernende zugeschnitten, deren Englischkenntnisse dem Niveau eines mittleren Bildungsabschlusses bzw. eines durchschnittlichen gymnasialen Grundkursabschlusses entsprechen (B1/B2). In der Rubrik *Extra Material* ist für die Lernenden mit fortgeschrittenen Englischkenntnissen anspruchsvollerer Lernstoff enthalten. So wird eine kontinuierliche Förderung aller Zielgruppen gewährleistet.

Neu an dieser Edition ist die durchgängige Vorbereitung auf die KMK-Zertifikatsprüfung in Englisch (Stufe II und III). Dies geschieht anhand von authentischen, prüfungsbezogenen Aufgaben zu den unterschiedlichen Kompetenzbereichen. Jede Unit enthält mindestens zwei Aufgaben, die den KMK-Richtlinien entsprechen. Zu Beginn des Buches werden Aufgaben der Stufe II angeboten. Ab Unit 6 entsprechen die angebotenen Übungen zur Vorbereitung der Stufe III der KMK-Fremdsprachenzertifikatsprüfung. Alle Übungen sind jeweils mit dem KMK-Symbol gekennzeichnet. Am Ende des Buches findet sich ein KMK *mock exam* der Stufe III.

Besonders hinzuweisen ist auf die authentischen Videos, die in mehreren Units angeboten werden. Sie setzen sich mit den in den Units behandelten Themen auseinander und ermöglichen den Lernenden eine andere Perspektive hinsichtlich des Inhaltes und Abwechslung hinsichtlich des Mediums.

Selbstverständlich können Units je nach Bedarf getauscht und auch ausgelassen werden, da jede Unit in sich abgeschlossen ist. Aufgrund des inhaltlich ansteigenden Schwierigkeitsgrades und dem kontinuierlichen Aufbau des Fachvokabulars empfehlen wir jedoch, die Reihenfolge einzuhalten.

Das Lehrwerk zielt in erster Linie darauf ab, kommunikative Kompetenzen zu vermitteln. Die Lernenden sollen in die Lage versetzt werden, mit englischsprachigen Kunden ein Beratungsgespräch führen zu können. Das zuvor eingeführte notwendige Fachvokabular wird dafür trainiert und gefestigt. Außerdem werden das Lese- und Hörverständnis sowie das eigenständige Verfassen englischsprachiger Geschäftskorrespondenz (E-Mail und Brief) eingeführt und geübt.

Neben der Aufarbeitung des Fachvokabulars und der spezifischen Redemittel werden auch berufsbezogene Grundlagen der Grammatik zur Wiederholung angeboten und geübt.
Die Lehrer-DVD enthält ein breites Spektrum an Zusatzmaterialien zur Erweiterung der Arbeit mit dem Schülerbuch.

Money Matters – 4th Edition vermittelt die Grundlagen, die für ein sicheres Auftreten und korrektes Handeln in der Bank und bei Bankgeschäften mit englischsprachigen Kunden unverzichtbar sind. Wenn die Lernenden sich dabei mit Vergnügen der englischen Sprache bedienen, hat dieses Werk sein Ziel erreicht.

2 Dialog bzw. Hörtext auf der Audio-CD

KMK Übungen zur Vorbereitung auf die KMK-Zertifikatsprüfung

WEBCODE MMU02 Die Webcodes weisen auf Zusatzmaterial zur selbstständigen Weiterarbeit hin und können unter **www.cornelsen.de/matters** abgerufen werden.

TABLE OF CONTENTS

UNIT 1

Working in a bank

- Making a professional impact
- Describing your branch
- Talking about your training

1 Warm-up

A Discuss these photos. What kind of impression would these employees make? Explain why.

a neat and tidy appearance • serious • smartly dressed • overdressed • underdressed • (in)appropriately dressed • (un)acceptable • too casual

B An American bank is planning a brochure on dress code for its staff. In small groups, brainstorm more topics to include. Each group should then choose one topic, find a good heading and write the brochure text.

clothes | shoes | make-up (incl. nail varnish) | jewellery | hair | piercings & tattoos

Dress to impress – Banking success!

Whether you are a bank teller, a customer service representative or an investment adviser, it is essential to dress in a professional and appropriate way. These tips and guidelines will help you dress to impress customers and colleagues alike.

2 Making a professional impact

Working in a bank not only requires a presentable appearance but also good people skills.

A Read through the points made by a careers adviser in a seminar for bank trainees on making a professional impact. Choose the two that you think are the most important and explain why.

1 Building good rapport is essential for working with colleagues and customers. Without it there can't be any trust in communication.

2 You have to be excellent at follow-through with any banking request. Customers expect you to handle their finances in a thorough, complete way.

3 Bank employees have to be meticulous. Our business can't afford to let any details slip by.

4 Customers count on reliable advisers for all their account needs. Whatever they ask, you need to show them you are competent and trustworthy.

5 No matter how complicated a request from one of your colleagues may be, be patient. This is crucial to create a cooperative working atmosphere.

6 Courteous language is a must for positive communication with both colleagues and customers.

7 And last but not least, remember that we bankers are actually selling just one product: it's called trust.

B Find words or phrases in A that are similar in meaning to the following.

polite, showing respect for others • belief in the honesty of sb • dependable • very careful about small details • extremely good • a polite demand for sth • deal with • extremely important • agreement and understanding

C Now complete the words in the sentences below. The first letter has been given. Look back at A and B if you need help.

1 Our colleagues expect us to be c… and help each other whenever we can.
2 Advisers need to have good r… with customers to maintain their loyalty.
3 It is c… to be meticulous when dealing with other people's money.
4 All questions and r… need to be handled in a competent and friendly way.
5 Good at f…- … is essential, not leaving anything unfinished for the customer.
6 My staff must be completely r… because I depend on them to get all the necessary documents from the customers in order to process their loans.
7 We need to take time and always be p… so that we can solve any problem a colleague or customer may have.
8 Bank advisers should always be honest and t… when dealing with customers.
9 Employers want staff who are meticulous, t… and pay close attention to detail.

D Now create a profile for yourself. Think about the following:

- why the skills are important when working in a bank.
- the importance of dress code and being well presented.
- which qualities you can bring to a trainee programme and why they are important.

E Discuss and compare your profile with a partner.

CULTURE

Training in banks: UK, USA and Germany

In Britain and the USA people who work in banks train on the job, learning by doing. In the UK basic requirements for an entry level banking position are excellent interpersonal skills and keen business awareness. Relevant degrees in business are helpful, but the person must be highly competent with figures.

In the USA applicants interested in going into banking should have at least a high school diploma or an equivalent certification for most entry-level positions. A college degree in accounting, finance, business or another maths-related field, such as credit analysis or insurance will assist the job applicant not only when initially hired, but also when seeking promotion within the banking industry.

In the UK and the USA there is no standard 'dual system' of *Ausbildung* like there is in Germany and so there is no direct translation for the word *Bankauszubildende/r*. Like many UK and US banks, this book uses the word 'trainee' to describe people training to work in a bank. 'Traineeship' means *Ausbildung.*

3 An email about training in a bank

Robert Schmidt, a trainee with a Hamburg bank, sent this email to a friend in the USA.

A Read the email and find the expressions which mean the following.

Gehalt • Filiale • Privatkunden • Firmenkunden • Abteilung • Berater/in • Darlehen • Geldanlage • Schalter • Zentrale

An: Sarah25@mailUSA.com

Betrifft: Greetings from Germany!

Von: Anlage(n):

Hi Sarah

Thanks for your news. I'm pretty busy too right now because I started my traineeship at the bank on August 1. For the first week we had a course at head office, but now I'm working in a branch. I was a bit nervous at first, but my colleagues are really nice and help me a lot.

My bank has got about 180 branches in and around Hamburg, but I'm staying at the same one during my training. The branch is open from 9 a.m. till 4 p.m. on weekdays except on Thursdays when we are open till six. We have to be at work by 8 a.m. each day. It's a long day, but the time goes quickly because there's so much going on. My branch is near the university, so most of the personal customers are students, but quite a few wealthy people have accounts there too, and there are business customers as well.

Some of the foreign students can't speak much German so we serve them in English.

I'm working on the counter at the moment – we call it the service desk. My bank doesn't have different departments for things like loans or investments because every adviser sells all the different banking products. I'll learn about them during the next two and a half years.

I'm trying to save part of my salary to fly over to see you next summer. But first of course, I'm looking forward to seeing you here in Hamburg next month. Not long now!

Take care

Robert

B Compare Robert's bank and traineeship with your own. What are the similarities and differences?

C Write an email to an English-speaking friend about your work.

4 Inside the branch

2

A When you started your training, who showed you round the branch and who were you introduced to?

B When Sarah comes to Germany, Robert shows her round his branch. Listen and note the three jobs mentioned in the dialogue.

C Listen again and say what each of the points 1–9 on the floor plan refers to.

Floor plan of Robert's branch, ground floor

Robert … so you can use your bank card to get into this lobby even when the bank is shut. Here on the left we've got two cash machines …
Sarah Cash machines? Is that what the Americans call ATMs?
Robert ATMs?
Sarah Automated teller machines – for taking money out of your account.
Robert That's right. In Britain they also call them cashpoints.
Well, nowadays many of these machines handle both withdrawals and deposits. And opposite them on the right there's the statement printer near the door, and the self-service terminal is beside it on the left.
Sarah I can see cameras everywhere. Security is a really big issue everywhere, isn't it?
Robert Absolutely. Let's go inside and the first thing you see are our service desks.
Sarah Wow, why are so many people standing in line?

Robert They're queuing at the tills to get assistance from the cashiers. Normally, the queue is not that long actually.
Sarah Then why don't they just go to the ATMs?
Robert The cashiers do a lot of special transactions that can't be done at the machines like selling currency or dealing with cheques. Or, for example, yesterday I had a customer who needed to fill in a special form to make an international transfer.
Sarah Oh, I get it. By the way, we call cashiers tellers in the States. Would you like to be a teller when you finish training?
Robert I'm not sure yet. I think it's a big responsibility since the person has to work on all kinds of services for the customers.
Sarah Hmm, true … Hey, where do those steps go?
Robert Down to the basement. That's where the strongroom is.
Sarah How fascinating! We call it a vault in the US. So can I go and take a look at it?
Robert Only if you rent a safe deposit box. Even then you can't go alone.
Sarah Ah, we use almost the same word: safety deposit box. Oh, well, whatever name we use, pity we can't have a quick look. Anyway, where are you working right now?
Robert I'm training at the service desk this month. This week I'm learning how to take care of lost cards and how to order a new PIN.
Sarah That sounds interesting. Could you open an account for me or give me a loan?
Robert Not if I'm on the service desk, no. People always come to us first, but when we see that they need advice – say, if they want to borrow money or invest some capital, we make an appointment for them with one of our generalists or advisers. They handle personal accounts and business customer accounts.
Sarah I imagine they all have their offices hidden away upstairs?
Robert No, they don't actually. Their desks are over there on the right. The private banking department for wealthy customers is on the first floor – the stairs are next to the lift – and corporate clients are looked after at our head office. Our headquarters are not here, though, they're in Frankfurt.
Sarah Um, if you'll excuse me, I'm just going to that room next to the elevator …
Robert No, hang on, don't go in there! That's the bank manager's office! The toilets are downstairs. I'll show you where they are. But be quick – because we're having lunch with some of my colleagues at 12.30, OK?

> **!** head office = headquarters (always with an 's' at the end!)

5 My branch

Draw a simple plan of the branch or bank where you work. Use it to tell your partner where to find the different services. Use expressions from the language box below.

Example: *The statement printer is in the lobby on the left when you come in.*

LANGUAGE

Giving directions

It's	in the lobby / basement / on the ground floor / first floor.
	opposite / in front of / behind the …
	beside / next to / near the …
	straight ahead / on the left / on the right.
	upstairs / downstairs.

Turn left / right.
It's the first / second door on your left / right.

6 Who does what

Write sentences about the jobs mentioned in the dialogue using the phrases below. Then write two more about other jobs in your bank.

be in charge of • be responsible for • deal with • handle • look after • take care of

7 A new trainee at a branch

KMK

Im Rahmen Ihrer Ausbildung bekommen Sie die einmalige Gelegenheit, für eine längere Zeit in einer Filiale Ihrer Bank in Großbritannien zu arbeiten.

Führen Sie das Rollenspiel durch.

LANGUAGE

Using polite language

Could you tell me …?
May I ask …?
I'd like to know about …
What about …?

I wonder if you could give me …?
I'd be glad to help/show you …
I'll help you …
Would you like …?

Partner/in A

Sie arbeiten schon länger in der englischen Filiale und kommen nun mit einer weiteren Auszubildenden aus Spanien ins Gespräch. Es ist ihr erster Tag in einer Bank überhaupt, da das Praktikum im Ausland ganz am Anfang der Ausbildung stattfindet. Stellen Sie sich vor. Lassen Sie die unten stehenden Punkte in Ihr Gespräch einfließen.

- Bieten Sie eine Führung durch die Filiale an.
- Nennen Sie zwei wichtige Bereiche der Filiale und beschreiben Sie diese.
- Geben Sie zwei gute Tipps für den Umgang mit Kunden/Kundinnen.
- Sprechen Sie über die Arbeitsbereiche folgender Mitarbeiter/innen:
  - Filialleiter/in
  - Kundenberater/in
  - Kassierer/in
- Beantworten Sie weitere Fragen, die Ihre Gesprächspartnerin haben könnte.
- Gehen Sie angemessen darauf ein, dass sich Ihre Gesprächspartnerin am Ende des Gespräches bedankt.

Partnerin B

Sie haben in Spanien Ihre Ausbildung begonnen und gleich am Anfang die einmalige Gelegenheit bekommen, in einer Filiale Ihrer Bank in London ein Praktikum machen zu können. Sie kennen sich noch nicht gut aus und sind daher froh, dass Sie auf eine/n andere/n Auszubildende/n treffen, der/die aus Deutschland kommt und in derselben Situation ist wie Sie – allerdings mit mehr Erfahrung. Sie kommen ins Gespräch.

- Stellen Sie sich vor.
- Danken Sie Ihrem/Ihrer Gesprächspartner/in dafür, dass er/sie Sie herumführt.
- Erkundigen Sie sich, wo Sie wohl zuerst eingesetzt werden. Fragen Sie nach den bisherigen Einsatzgebieten des/der anderen.
- Fragen Sie nach Tipps im Umgang mit Kunden/Kundinnen.
- Bitten Sie darum, dass Ihnen erklärt wird, wie die Arbeitsbereiche der anderen Kollegen/Kolleginnen aussehen.
- Stellen Sie ein paar allgemeine Fragen, z. B. wann und wo Mittagspause gemacht wird.
- Bedanken Sie sich für die Informationen.

8 American and British English

A **Complete the table below. If you need help, you will find the words in the dialogue on pages 9–10.**

vault	…
line	…
restrooms	…
ATM	…
…	lift
first floor	…
…	safe deposit box
teller	…

B **Choose words from the list to complete the sentences below.**

British customers:

1 get in a … to wait for the cashier for special transactions.
2 use a … to store their valuables.
3 keep their safe deposit boxes in the … .
4 use the stairs or take the … to the meeting rooms on the second floor.
5 will find the men's and women's … next to the meeting rooms.

American customers:

6 wait in … at the service desk for their banking services.
7 want a … where they can keep their important documents.
8 can make withdrawals or deposits at an … .
9 ride the … to the executive offices on the tenth floor.
10 will find reception when they enter the headquarters on the … .

C **Now choose four words from the list and write four sentences of your own.**

GRAMMAR

Present tenses

1 Cashiers **assist** customers every day. simple present
2 The adviser normally **makes** phone calls to customers. simple present
3 **Does** your bank **change** foreign currency for tourists? simple present
4 The adviser **is phoning** an American customer at the moment. present-continuous
5 She **is saving up** to buy a new car.
6 What time **is** the new customer **seeing** the bank adviser this afternoon?

- The simple present is for actions which happen regularly (1, 2) or which are generally true (3).
- Signal words for the simple present are: *always, normally/usually, often, sometimes, seldom, never, every day/week,* etc.
- The present continuous is used for actions which are happening at the moment (4), take place over a limited period of time (5) or describe a future arrangement (6).

trends = present progressive

9 Practice

A **Look back at the dialogue on pages 9–10 and write down four examples of present tenses. Explain which tense is used and why.**

B **Complete these sentences with the correct form of the verbs in brackets.**

1. The investment department … (handle) real estate and shares.
2. The adviser … (deal with) a special investment fund this week.
3. I normally … (work) in a branch in the centre of Munich.
4. Rich customers usually … (keep) gold or cash in safe deposit boxes.
5. The cashier … (assist) a customer with a lost credit card at the moment.
6. We sometimes … (call) the headquarters in Frankfurt about special transactions.
7. Right now our branch manager … (phone) an investment bank in Houston.
8. This month I … (work) in Frankfurt on a special project.
9. In their day-to-day work, cashiers … (assist) customers with general enquiries.
10. The new customer … (see) an adviser tomorrow to discuss an investment fund.

10 Your training at the bank

KMK

Beschreiben Sie Ihre Ausbildung bei der Bank. Sprechen Sie dabei folgende Punkte an:

- die Dauer Ihrer Ausbildung
- einen typischen Arbeitstag
- die Arbeitsfelder/Projekte/Abteilungen, in denen Sie für längere Zeit eingesetzt sind
- die Aufgaben, die Ihnen bisher am meisten Freude bereitet haben und Gründe dafür

11 Working with words

A **Find words or expressions from this unit to complete these sentences.**

1. Cashpoints are usually called … in America.
2. A person who borrows a fixed sum from a bank gets a … .
3. If you wish to invest capital, you should speak to an … .
4. The safe deposit boxes in the bank are usually kept in the basement in the … .
5. The place where the cashier works is called the … .
6. For anyone who wishes to use the bank's services, they will have to open an … .
7. If you want to check payments made this month, you can print a … .
8. Many banks have their main office or … in Frankfurt, which is the banking centre of Germany.

B **Choose the correct prepositions to complete these sentences.**

1. Would you like to speak (*at/to*) one of our advisers?
2. The investment department is (*in/on*) the second floor.
3. The cash machines are in the lobby (*at/on*) the right.
4. I started working here (*at/on*) September 1.
5. The branch opens (*at/on*) 9 a.m. and stays open (*by/until*) 4 p.m.
6. Student customers have to spend their money (*for/on*) books.
7. I work (*at/by*) Horizons Bank.
8. My boss wants this job to be done (*by/until*) Friday.
9. The customer wanted to invest (*in/into*) stocks and shares.
10. Let's have a look (*at/on*) these figures.

12 Hörverstehen

3

Ein britisches Radioprogramm informiert junge Leute jede Woche über verschiedene Berufe und Berufsfelder. Sie interessieren sich für ein Praktikum in einer britischen Bank. Daher hören Sie den Informationen über die Arbeit eines Kassierers aufmerksam zu.

Machen Sie sich Notizen auf Deutsch zu den folgenden Punkten:

- *Beschriebener Beruf:*
- *Erforderliche Fähigkeiten:*
- *Karriereaussichten:*
- *Vier Tätigkeiten eines Kassierers:*
- *Die wichtigsten Aspekte folgender Arbeitsbereiche:*
  - *Kundenberatung*
  - *Pflege von Kundenkonten*

13 Interaktion

Julia/Jake Stone macht ein dreiwöchiges Praktikum in Ihrem Kreditinstitut. Ein/e Auszubildende/r stellt die Bank vor und informiert über Tätigkeiten, die gemacht werden müssen.

Erstellen Sie in Partnerarbeit einen Dialog mithilfe der folgenden Rollenkarten.

Partner/in A

Sie sind Julia/Jake Stone.
Sie stellen sich vor und erzählen:
- woher Sie kommen
- welchen Schulabschluss Sie haben
- warum Sie das Praktikum absolvieren.

Sie bieten an, sich mit dem Vornamen ansprechen zu lassen.

Kreditinstitut
Sie möchten wissen:
- wie groß das Kreditinstitut ist
- wie viele Mitarbeiter/innen es gibt
- wie die Öffnungszeiten sind.

Fragen Sie nach dem Arbeitsplatz.

Service
Sie fragen nach Tätigkeiten, die ein/e Auszubildende/r zu erledigen hat.

Partner/in B

Sie sind der/die Auszubildende/r des Kreditinstituts.
Sie stellen sich vor und berichten über:
- Ihren Schulabschluss
- Ihre Berufsschule
- Ihre Ausbildung.

Kreditinstitut
Sie informieren darüber, dass es neben der Hauptstelle noch fünf Zweigstellen in Ihrer Stadt gibt.
Sie teilen Julia/Jake Stone die Arbeits- und Öffnungszeiten mit.
Sie zeigen ihr/ihm den Kundenraum.

Service
Sie nennen einige Ihrer Tätigkeiten.

14 'Mobile' banking

Read this text and discuss the questions below with a partner or in a small group.

1 What are the benefits and drawbacks of mobile banking? Can you add any other points?
2 Do you think this trend should continue? Why / Why not?

Money on wheels: Banking gets seriously mobile

23 April 2014
By Brian Milligan Personal Finance Reporter, BBC News

For the UK's urban-dwelling, short-of-time majority, mobile banking is something that usually comes in the shape of a smartphone app.

But ever since crofters on the Isle of Lewis first encountered it in 1946, mobile banking has also had another manifestation, in the form of a bank on wheels. At that time the crofters found it hard to reach the main town, Stornoway, as they were too busy weaving tweed. Instead the bank would travel to them. But nearly 70 years on, as the popularity – and the affordability – of High Street branches dwindles, mobile banks could be coming into their own. So when Royal Bank of Scotland (RBS) announced the closure of 44 branches earlier this month, it also announced it was buying five new mobile branches. It is adding three new routes for the vans, two in Scotland and one in Wales. [...] So do mobile banks provide an additional level of customer service, or are they just the excuse that banks need to close further branches?

'Proper branch'

For two hours every Thursday, an RBS mobile branch pulls into the market square in the town of Moffat in Dumfries and Galloway. At the wheel is Jim Russell, who has been driving the van for 14 years. He and his colleague, Audrey Murphy, provide their regulars with a special level of service. 'If customers are ill, and cannot come down, if they're not far off route, we'll drive to their houses,' says Jim. If regulars do not turn up, they may get a text to check if they are OK. The older ones might even get the snow swept off their doorsteps. Local customers certainly appreciate the service, although they bemoan the lack of a proper bank. 'I'd prefer it if there was a branch in Moffat,' says local butcher Scott Wallace. 'But I like it. It's a lot easier than going to Lockerbie, which is 16 miles away,' he says. Anne Murray would otherwise have to travel 39 miles to her branch in Selkirk. 'Yes, I would prefer a proper branch, but it's not going to happen, is it?' she says. [...]

Community service

But RBS, like other banks, insists that branch closure decisions are all taken on a case-by-case basis, according to how many people use them. Only then does it consider alternative facilities, such as a mobile branch. Nevertheless, it says that branch transactions have fallen by 30% since 2010. And it says the new mobile vans – in which it is investing £600,000 – will provide a more personalized service to its customers. 'It's about being where the customers want us,' says Jane Paterson, who is in charge of rolling out the new fleet of RBS mobile branches. The existing RBS and NatWest vans already drive more than 7,000 miles a week, and reach 357 different communities.

'Two customers'

The new vans will provide a much more practical service than the existing fleet. Because they are equipped with satellite dishes, they can connect directly with the network, and a customer's account. In the existing vans – as crewed by Jim Russell and Audrey Murphy – staff have to make a note of each transaction, and then update the accounts when they get back to base. Or they have to make a phone call to the customer's branch, to check their balance. But Jim and Audrey have plenty of time for paperwork, as clients can be a little thin on the ground. Indeed some mobile vans have fewer customers than the branches they supposedly replace. 'In Lamington, our next stop, we have just two customers,' says Mr Russell. 'So we park between their doors.'

http://www.bbc.com/news/business-26993637

UNIT 2

Excellent service

- Using polite language
- Practising telephone language
- Looking at digital channels

1 Warm-up

Three of these people are bank customers, two are bank employees. Read what the speakers say and decide what sort of communication they usually use and probably prefer to use. Justify your choice.

face-to-face communication • communication over the telephone • communication via digital channels

1 I work as a salesperson in a large company and so I have to travel quite a lot. Last week, for example, I had to fly to Hungary and on to the United States. There is always the question of foreign currency. So, I just gave my bank a ring. Luckily, they had the currencies in their safe.

2 I retired last year and unfortunately had to have a knee operation six months later, which means I am not so good on my feet these days. But what has come in very handy is the iPad my wife gave me for my birthday. I'm not the fastest on the keyboard either – walking to the bank was always quicker, I reckon! But I'm getting better with my new toy and enjoy the convenience.

3 I graduated from university at 30 and have worked as an IT specialist in southern Germany ever since. Being a bit of a technology freak and sitting at my screen all day can really make you feel lonely. I welcome a break when I can go out for a bit of a walk and see the real world. And, anyway, answering machines and call centres are not my cup of tea.

4 My name is Cathy, I like dealing with different customer requests and I'm always particularly happy whenever I manage to handle a complicated situation. But sometimes you get a difficult customer and then if things get really awkward, you can always say "Sorry, I'll have to check your file first, I'll get back to you in half an hour."

5 In my job, I really like talking to customers. I enjoy trying to find out what their personal needs are and then seeing if I can find the right banking product for them. I listen to all sorts of stories – the customers are all so different that my work is never boring. And of course it's great seeing the children bringing in their money boxes. I always put a little something in – you can't start advertising too early, can you?

2 What went wrong?

4

Michael Lange works as customer service officer at a bank in Nuremberg. He started his traineeship two months ago. Unfortunately communication is not his strong point.

Listen and write down the mistakes that Michael makes.

3 Structuring a conversation

Michael's line manager knows how important communication is, so she has sent him on a training seminar to improve his skills. The first talk was about structuring a conversation.

A Put the headings in what you think is the most logical order.

- **a** Arranging a follow-up
- **b** Expressing thanks and saying goodbye
- **c** Getting down to business
- **d** Giving advice
- **e** Greeting the customer
- **f** Introducing yourself
- **g** Offering help
- **h** Offering refreshments
- **i** Repeating the key facts
- **j** Starting with small talk

B Compare your order with a partner.

C Read these sentences that an adviser at a bank could have said and put them into one of the categories a – j above.

- Good morning/afternoon/evening Mr/Mrs/Ms … I hope you enjoyed your holiday.
- Could we set up / fix an appointment on … (day) at … (time) to …?
- Would you like to take a seat for a moment and I'll see if … is available.
- Have you considered …?
- Nice to see you again – I hope you've been keeping well?
- How can I be of assistance to you?
- I see what you mean, but perhaps we can …
- I look forward to seeing you again soon.
- I would recommend …
- If I were you, I would …
- Why don't we meet next week on … (day) at … (time) to sign …?
- To sum up the main points …
- Thank you very much for coming in.
- So, if I have understood this correctly, the basic situation is …
- My name is Ian Flemming. I'm in charge of customer service. Nice/Pleased to meet you.
- Let's get down to business, shall we?
- Dreadful weather, isn't it?
- May I take your coat?

4 Serving a dissatisfied customer

5

The following day, a student from Dublin, Ryan Leigh, approaches the service desk of his bank in the centre of Nuremberg. Michael has just gone out for lunch, so his colleague Susan Stadler welcomes Mr Leigh.

A Hören Sie das Gespräch und vervollständigen Sie die Tabelle auf Deutsch. KMK

Grund der Beschwerde	…
Mögliche Konsequenz des Kunden wegen Beschwerde	…
Aktueller Anlass für Beschwerde	…
Kontonummer des Kunden	…
Name des Kunden	…
Beteiligte Partner der „Cash Group“	…
Vorteil der „Cash Group“	…
Anzahl der Geldautomaten der ▪ „Cash Group“ ▪ Sparkassen-Finanzgruppe ▪ Volks- und Raiffeisenbanken	 … … …
Vorschlag der Kundenberaterin	…
E-Mail-Adresse des Kunden	…

B Now read the dialogue and do the following tasks.

1 Note down the phrases of apology Susan uses in her conversation with Ryan Leigh.
2 Compare your answers with a partner.

Ryan Hello, I'd like to speak to Mr Lange, please.

Susan Good afternoon, sir, I'm very sorry, but I'm afraid Mr Lange's out at lunch at the moment. Maybe, I can help you?

Ryan Hmm, I'm not sure. Well, let me explain the situation to you. I have a complaint to make: I'm very disappointed with the bank. You see, Mr Lange told me that cash withdrawals are free of charge, but I have to pay an extra fee every time I withdraw money at an ATM. And, to be quite honest, I'm seriously thinking about switching my current account to another bank which offers a better service.

Susan Oh dear, yes, that is frustrating. And I'm sorry about this, but could you give me an example of when and where you recently withdrew cash?

Ryan OK, yes, let's take last weekend when I was in Leipzig. I wanted to invite my girlfriend out for dinner and had reserved a table in a nice restaurant. I needed to get some money from a cash machine, but unfortunately, didn't see any of your branches in the centre of town. So, after walking round in the freezing cold for about half an hour and worrying about my table reservation, I ended up going to the next best bank and had to pay a charge of five euros. But luckily, our table in the restaurant hadn't been given away.

Susan Oh, I apologize for this inconvenience. That certainly wasn't the best way to start a nice evening, was it? Could you tell me your account number and I'll get your details up on the screen.

Ryan Of course, it is triple 3, 456 double 0, Ryan Leigh from Dublin.

Susan Sorry, but could you spell your name, please?

Ryan Of course. It's R–Y–A–N L–E–I–G–H.
... What was particularly annoying for me was the fact that I chose your bank for the very reason that I wouldn't have to pay any bank charges! That was what I was told when I opened my account.

Susan Yes, I fully understand, Mr Leigh. I can only repeat that I am extremely sorry for what has happened. ... Ah, yes, here I can see your current account has been debited with the extra charge of EUR 4.95. Did my colleague not tell you about the so-called Cash Group?

Ryan The cash what?

Susan The Cash Group. You see, if you bank with Deutsche Bank, Commerzbank, Postbank and a couple of other big national banks, you are part of the Cash Group, which means that these banks do not charge a fee when you go to any of their cash machines. So, if you had gone to one of their cashpoints, you would not have been charged anything.

Ryan Well, that doesn't really help me now, does it?

Susan No, it doesn't, I'm afraid. Perhaps I can explain the situation to you. There are three main banking groups in Germany: the Cash Group, which you are in, secondly, the Volksbanken and Raiffeisenbanken and thirdly the Sparkassen or, more accurately, the association of Sparkassen. So, if a customer goes to an ATM not in their group, he or she will pay a service charge. And this is exactly what happened to you.

Ryan OK, I see. But I couldn't see a branch of my bank anywhere. In fact, I get the impression there are more Sparkassen cash machines than Cash Group ones. Is that the case?

Susan Actually, yes, you're right. The association of Sparkassen has about 25,000 cashpoints. Next come the Volksbanken and Raiffeisenbanken with about 20,000 and then our Cash Group is third. We have got just under 10,000.

Ryan Oh, really? It sounds like I'm with the wrong bank, then, doesn't it?!

Susan No, no. And to prove that you are with the *right* bank, Mr Leigh, I'll tell you what I suggest. It looks like it was partly our fault that we may not have explained the whole business of the Cash Group to you, so I will credit the service fee you were charged to your account.

Ryan Oh, excellent, that's very kind of you. Thank you.

Susan And let me email you the full list of the Cash Group so you have it. Could you give me your email address?

Ryan Yes, sure. It's ryan.leigh@mywebsite.co.uk, that's r–y–a–n–dot–l–e–i–g–h–@–m–y–w–e–b–s–i–t–e–dot–c–o–dot–u–k.

Susan Fine, I've got that. And again, please accept our apologies for any inconvenience this misunderstanding may have caused.

Ryan That's fine, no problem. Thank you very much for your help.

Susan You're welcome. That's what we are here for – always happy to help. Have a nice afternoon. Goodbye.

Ryan Bye.

5 Telephoning with a smile

6 Michael's friend Anja works for Horizons Bank. As she speaks such good English she has been asked to deal with all the English-speaking customers.

A Listen to the recording and make notes about each call. Note the name of the caller, his/her number, email address and the message, if any.

B Listen to the telephone conversations again. How would you say this in English?

1. Kann er Sie zurückrufen oder möchten Sie eine Nachricht hinterlassen?
2. Mit wem möchten Sie sprechen?
3. Möchten Sie lieber warten oder soll ich sie bitten, Sie zurückzurufen?
4. Würden Sie das bitte noch einmal wiederholen?
5. Es tut mir leid, da kann ich Ihnen nicht helfen.
6. Ich stelle Sie zu Frau Sommer in der Kreditabteilung durch.
7. Sie ist zurzeit nicht erreichbar. Sie hat den ganzen Vormittag Sitzungen.
8. Ihre Leitung ist besetzt. Möchten Sie dranbleiben?
9. Könnten Sie das bitte noch einmal langsamer wiederholen?
10. Bitte sprechen Sie lauter, die Verbindung ist sehr schlecht.

LANGUAGE

Expressions for telephoning

Identifying your firm and yourself
Shipley and Partners, Jim Brown speaking, can I help you?
Yes, speaking (= *am Apparat*), can I help you?
This is … *oder* My name's …
(*nicht*: ~~Here is~~ …)

Asking to speak to somebody
Could I speak to someone about …, please?
Could you put me through to …, please?
Could I have extension 123, please?

Asking for identification and the reason for the call
Who's speaking, please?
Who shall I say is calling?
May I ask the reason for your call?

Giving details
It's in connection with …
I'm calling to ask about …
I'm ringing about …

Making a connection
Just a moment, please. I'll put you through.
Trying to connect you.

Explaining that somebody cannot take the call
I'm afraid … isn't available at the moment.
I'm sorry, she's in a meeting.
She's on holiday until …, I'm afraid.
I'm afraid his line is engaged.

Alternative action
Can I take a message?
Would you like to leave a message?
Do you want to hold?
Can she call you back?

Leaving a message
Could you give her a message, please?
Please can you ask him to call me?
Tell her I'll call back later.

Saying thank you
Well, thank you very much for your help.
You've been most helpful. Thank you.

Responding to thanks
Not at all.
You're welcome.

Ending the call
I look forward to seeing / hearing from / meeting you.
Thank you for calling.

TIP

Saying telephone numbers

Say each digit separately, except for double digits.
e. g. 01233 4567899 = oh (AE zero) one two double-three, four five six, seven eight double-nine.
You usually say all of the numbers in a country code separately.
e. g. 0044 = oh oh four four (or) zero zero four four

country code = *Ländervorwahl*
(dialling) code (AE area code) = *Vorwahl (einer Stadt)*
extension (number) = *Durchwahl*
mobile phone (AE cell phone) = *Handy*
landline = *Festnetz*

LANGUAGE

Saying email addresses

When calling people in foreign countries, it is often necessary to spell unfamiliar names, addresses, email addresses, etc.

It is also very helpful to have English words or names at your fingertips in case you have to spell something over the phone, for example B for Britain, G for Germany or S for sugar. These letters often cause problems for German speakers: e, g, h, i, j, q, r, v, w, y, z.

Note the expressions: capital letters (or: upper case) for ABC, etc. and small letters (or: lower case) for a, b, c, etc.

For ä, ö, ü, you can either say “a, o, u Umlaut” or “a with two dots”, etc.

But for an email address, you say ae, oe, ue.

Email punctuation

.	dot
/	(forward) slash
\	backslash
–	hyphen/dash or minus (rarely used in GB but it would be understood)
_	underscore

6 Saying email addresses and names

A With a partner practise saying and writing these email addresses and names.

1. yvonne.gilfort@rosworth-products.com
2. Jilcraigh@bosworth_solutions.biz
3. Vanessa_williams@tulsonsteelpipes.co.uk
4. John Cougar McCarthy
5. Dorothee Raynleigh
6. Dörthe Grünemeyer

B Now invent more two names and email addresses and dictate them to your partner.

7 Role-play: on the phone

KMK

Sie arbeiten in der Auslandsabteilung einer internationalen Bank. Da eine Kollegin krank ist, bittet man Sie, den Telefondienst zu übernehmen.

Führen Sie ein höfliches Telefonat auf Englisch mit einer Partnerin/einem Partner. Partner A übernimmt die Rolle des Kundenberaters, Partner B die Rolle der Kundin Kim Shackleton aus Kanada.

gold coins • to deposit safely • to depend on the size of • to be insured • a savings book

Bank adviser

Melden Sie sich mit dem Namen Ihrer Bank und Ihrem eigenen Namen.

Caller

Stellen Sie sich als Kim Shackleton vor.

Fragen Sie, wie Sie helfen können.

Bitten Sie darum, den Kundenberater Herrn Petersen zu sprechen.

Bitten Sie den Anrufer, seinen Namen zu buchstabieren.

Buchstabieren Sie Ihren Namen.

Fragen Sie, worum es geht.

Erklären Sie, dass Sie seit drei Monaten in Nürnberg leben und vor kurzem ein Konto bei Herrn Petersen eröffnet haben. Sie haben nun Goldmünzen im Wert von 1.500 Euro von Ihrer Großmutter zu Weihnachten geschenkt bekommen und möchte diese in einem Schließfach der Bank sicher aufbewahren.

Bitten Sie um etwas Geduld und sagen Sie, dass Sie den Anruf durchstellen werden. (*kleine Pause*) Entschuldigen Sie sich dafür, dass Sie den Anruf nicht weiterleiten konnten, da Herr Petersen den ganzen Morgen Termine mit Kunden hat.

Sagen Sie, dass dies schade ist. Erklären Sie, dass Sie nur gerne wissen wollen, wie viel das Mieten eines Schließfaches kostet.

Teilen Sie mit, dass dies auch abhängig von der Größe des Schließfaches ist. Ein kleines Schließfach zur Hinterlegung eines Sparbuchs kostet bspw. eine jährliche Gebühr von 25 Euro.

Danken Sie für die Informationen und fragen Sie, inwieweit die Schließfächer versichert sind.

Sagen Sie, dass Sie damit nicht vertraut sind. Bieten Sie an, einen Termin mit Herrn Petersen zu vereinbaren. Fragen Sie, ob es möglich wäre, Herrn Petersen heute Nachmittag gegen 16:30 zu besuchen.

Sagen Sie, dass Ihnen dies zusagt.

Verabschieden Sie sich freundlich.

Verabschieden Sie sich ebenfalls.

LANGUAGE

Making an appointment

Would it be possible for you to meet me on Tuesday afternoon?
Certainly. I'll be there on Tuesday.
Would Thursday suit you?
How about next Thursday? Would that be convenient?
I'm afraid. I'm fully booked on that day.
I'm free all morning on 3 May.
I'm afraid, I've got an appointment at that time.
Could we switch the appointment to the following morning, say, at 9:30?
That would be all right with me.
What about postponing the meeting to the first week in February?
OK, fine, then'll see you on 2 February at 3 p.m.

8 Working with words

A Find the nouns for the following verbs.

to apologize • to apply for • to complain • to describe • to penalize • to prove • to regret • to reply • to request • to suggest

B Find the opposite of these adjectives and the corresponding nouns.

Adjective	Opposite	Noun
patient	…	…
favourable	…	…
convenient	…	…
satisfied	…	…
polite	…	…

C Complete these sentences with a word from A or B above. In some cases you will need to use the plural form.

1. If you have good service, you will have happy and … customers who won't want to change banks.
2. I'm sorry for keeping you waiting so long. Thank you for your … .
3. Just fill in the … form in order to open a current account.
4. Please accept our … for any inconvenience caused.
5. It is best to calm … customers down in a polite and friendly way.
6. We take all … seriously – they are actually positive things and show us where our bank needs to make an improvement.
7. My … would be to refund the fee and credit your account accordingly. Is this OK?
8. … is the key to any successful sales conversation. And don't forget to smile – even if you are on the telephone!

GRAMMAR

Future forms

1 We **are going to design** a new advertising campaign to help us win more customers.
2 Everything has been cancelled – she **is not going to do** a work placement in London.
3 Look at the bills that need paying – you **are going to go overdrawn** this month.
4 I **will (won't) credit** the amount to your current account.
5 Oh, I forgot to phone that new customer – **I'll do** it now.
6 **I'll get** your details up on the screen.
7 I think the meeting **will take** about three hours.

- The *going to* future is used when we have already decided or planned to do something (1, 2) or when there are clear signs that something is going to happen (3).
- The *will* future is used when we decide to do something at the time of speaking (4–6) or for predictions and assumptions (7).

9 Expressing the future

Use the verbs in brackets in the appropriate future form to complete the sentences.

1 OK, I … you back first thing in the morning and let you know. (call)
2 I'm afraid I … on time for the meeting because of the early-morning traffic jams. (not arrive)
3 What time … phone me tomorrow? (you / be able to)
4 I … her that you called and ask her to call you back as soon as she's free. (tell)
5 Please tell him that I … later this afternoon. (call back)
6 I am in a meeting all morning, but I imagine it … over at lunchtime. (be)
7 I'm not sure if she's available. I … (have to) check.
8 Oh dear, it's already 4 p.m. We … late for the appointment in the branch. (be)

10 Introducing new digital services

VIDEO 1

A **Watch the video and fill in the missing information opposite about the Royal Bank of Scotland.**

Founded in:	...
Headquarters in:	...
Industry they are in:	...
Number of employees:	...
Cost of digital services:	...
Advertising slogan for RBS digital services:	"Manage ... "
Advice Sarah Evans gives to other decision-makers:	...

B Decide whether the following statements are true or false. If false, give the correct answer.

1. Sarah Evans, Head of Webchat & Social Media at RBS says that customers want to bank online, on the move and twenty-four seven.
2. Digital services are offered by their key brands: RBS, NatWest, HSBC and Lloyds Bank.
3. The headquarters of RBS is in Exeter, UK.
4. According to Sarah Evans, webchats can be a direct replacement for telephone banking.
5. Hayley Smith, an RBS customer, mentions that changing one's address and ordering a credit card can be done via digital channels.
6. Sarah Evans says that customers are educating their bank so that the bank will offer them digital services.
7. She also points out that customers prefer using digital channels rather than being contacted by phone.
8. RBS bank staff also offer help via social media like Twitter.

C Explain the underlined expressions in your own words.

1. Customers want to bank on the move and twenty-four seven.
2. Sarah Evans mentions the function of educating the customers.
3. For us as a business it means a lower-cost channel.
4. Manage your account safely from your sofa.

D What are the advantages or disadvantages regarding this trend? Compare the strategy of RBS with your bank.

E Give your personal opinion on digital channels. Would you agree with RBS that banks have to educate their customers?

11 Mediation

KMK

Ihre Bank ist sehr daran interessiert, neue Zielgruppen mit Hilfe digitaler Medien zu erreichen.

Lesen Sie den Text „Digital is crucial in addressing changing customer behaviour" von PricewaterhouseCoopers und fassen Sie für Ihren Vorgesetzten die wichtigsten Inhalte bezüglich verändertem Kundenverhalten auf Deutsch zusammen.

Digital is crucial in addressing changing customer behaviour

Today, a successful digital offering in banking implies the provision of high quality online and mobile banking access. We find that the new digital feature set can be used to meet the increasing demands of the customer.

There are four main considerations for a bank to invest in a robust digital offering:

1) A number of factors are changing customers' attitudes and behaviours.
2) Preference for digital is globally pervasive.
3) Generation Y, who are now at the point of choosing their primary financial services provider, cite digital as an important factor in this decision.
4) Digital itself, is evolving: the new set of features of the latest round of digital innovation is proof enough.

We believe that there are five key aspects of changing customer behaviour

Customers...				
...expect more	*...trust their peers*	*...are informed*	*...have choices*	*...have a voice*

Expectations are being shaped by experiences outside of the banking industry where content, interactions and features are richer, delivering a more engaging and rewarding experience for the consumer.	The role of banks as the financial expert has been replaced by 'word of mouth' peer conversations, or independent influencers. The rapid emergence of social media in parallel with the rise of mobility has seen customers increasingly turn to their peers for information and advice, rather than to financial experts in banks.	Financial consumers are more savvy today, due to the easy access to research, data and 'expert' views. This has also exposed the lack of differentiation between different providers' banking products. As more financial services customers become 'self-directed', they are coming to rely less upon traditional sources of financial advice.	Comparison and purchase of alternative financial products and services online is now straightforward and widespread. It has opened up a wide range of choices for consumers, some outside the boundaries of traditional banking services, such as peer-to-peer lending.	The rise of social media platforms has allowed a single consumer voice to be amplified to a tremendous degree, and consumers have not been shy about raising it. Stories of bad customer experiences rapidly spread through these media and often cause irreparable damage to associated brands.

Irate Customers: Learn How to Handle Them – And Look Like a Hero

by John Tschohl on January 9, 2012

Irate customers. No matter how good you are at what you do, what business you are in, or where it is located, you will at some point find yourself facing an irate customer. Maybe a product was flawed, a delivery was late, or a charge was inaccurate. How you deal with that customer not only will determine how he or she feels about your organization, but how you feel about yourself.

When you are able to turn an irate customer into a satisfied customer, you will gain confidence in your ability to diffuse a volatile situation and to evoke a positive outcome. You also will gain the respect of your co-workers, and you will get the attention of your supervisors. And, who knows, you might even get promoted.

When most people come in contact with an irate customer, their first instinct is to turn and run. Dealing with a customer who has a problem and is upset about it, can be more than a little daunting. With the proper perspective, however, you will see that the customer's complaint is actually an opportunity for you and your organization to put your best foot forward.

Customers who have complaints are a blessing in disguise. They are letting you know where you and your organization have flaws – and providing you with the opportunity to correct them. When you do, you will realize increased customer loyalty, revenues, and profits. It's a win/win situation. [...]

Customer service is key to success of any business. And dealing with irate customers and solving their problems is a critical element of that service. When dealing with an irate customer, take these steps:

1. Listen carefully and with interest to what the customer is telling you.
2. Apologize without laying blame, regardless of who is at fault.
3. Put yourself in the customer's place, and respond in a way that shows you care about his or her concerns. Use phrases such as, "I understand that must be upsetting", or "I don't blame you for being upset; I would feel the same way".
4. Ask pertinent questions in a caring, concerned manner, and actively listen to the answers.
5. Suggest one or more alternatives that would address the customer's concerns.
6. Solve the problem quickly and efficiently, or find someone who can.

Using these steps will quickly calm most unhappy or angry customers and allow you to address and solve their problems. Patience and tact are key.

It's important that, even if a customer is making outrageous statements and, in essence, throwing a fit, that you remain calm. Do not take those statements personally. Apologize, take the blame, and empathize with the customer, then solve the problem. [...]

When you successfully handle irate customers and their complaints, you will be rewarded with a satisfied customer – and a customer who will be loyal to you and your organization. That loyalty will have a positive impact on your organization's bottom line – and make you look like a hero.

http://www.investopedia.com/financial-edge/0512/wild-incentives-for-opening-a-bank-account.aspx

12 Understanding the text

A Match the highlighted words in the text with their German equivalents.

belohnt • einschüchternd/entmutigend • empörend/schockierend • explosiv • sachdienlich • Schwachstellen • zornig/wütend

B Find a short title for each paragraph.

C Work with a partner and discuss how you (would) deal with irate customers. Does your bank have a policy on this? Share your results with the other members of your class.

UNIT 3

Current accounts

- Looking at what current accounts offer
- Opening a current account
- Setting up online banking

1 Warm-up

A Look at this home page and compare it with the home page of the bank where you work.

B Now go onto the home page of a British bank (such as Lloyds, Barclays, HSBC, Standard Chartered, etc.) and compare that.

C Prepare a short talk on the differences and similarities.

2 Managing your finances

VIDEO 2

You are going to watch a video about Jaynee Faulks, a young student who is renting her own flat for the first time. Jaynee has a current account to help her manage her finances.

A **Before you watch the video, work with a partner and make a list of the items you think Jaynee will have to pay for.**

B **Now watch the video and check your list. Which services does Jaynee use to pay for her various expenses and why?**

3 Confirming a meeting to open a current account

Jaynee's sister, Catherine, has just moved to Germany. She wrote an email to Horizons Bank about opening a current account.

Read the bank's reply and choose the best alternative to complete the email.

An: C.Faulks@emailworld.uk

Von: g.schmidt@horizonsbank.com

Dear Ms Faulks

Many / many[1] thanks for your email about opening a current account *by / with*[2] Horizons Bank. I would be very pleased to assist you with our bank services.

I can confirm our meeting *at / on*[3] 9 September *at / on*[4] 10 a.m. Could you please *bring / take*[5] your passport and residence registration? These are required for opening an account. We *make / will make*[6] copies here at the bank for our records.

I have *attached / enclosed*[7] some *information / informations*[8] on how to reach us via navigation link. Should you have any questions, please do not hesitate to contact me.

I look forward to *meeting / meet*[9] you.

Best regards, / Best regards[10]

Gerhard Schmidt

Berater/Personal adviser
Horizons Bank
Tel: +49 89 99 458 6732
Email: g.schmidt@horizonsbank.com

4 Looking at what a current account offers

At their meeting, Catherine shows Gerhard Schmidt a printout from her UK bank about current accounts.

Match the features to the right description.

a allows you to take more money out than is actually in your account

b enables you to choose between an account in your name only or together with another person

c allows you to set up fixed payments which we transfer regularly for you on an agreed date

d gives you the flexibility to withdraw money at a cash machine or to pay for shopping

e offers purchasing convenience in addition to your debit card with the advantage that the money is not debited from your account immediately

f enables another person/company to collect regular (often variable) payments from your account

g enables you to check your balance (deposits and withdrawals) and do transactions from home, the office or on the go

h offers an additional way of paying for goods or services and is particularly useful for paying tradespeople

BARSTONE BANK

Barstone Bank offers current accounts with maximum customer convenience:

✓ Sole account or joint account
✓ Cheques
✓ Debit card
✓ Credit card
✓ Online banking
✓ Direct debit
✓ Standing order
✓ Overdraft facility

5 Opening a current account

7 **A** **Read and listen to the conversation as Gerhard Schmidt opens a current account for Catherine. Which banking service did Gerhard Schmidt talk about which is not mentioned in the Barstone Bank list above?**

Catherine … Thanks for going over the various features of the account. Now, I have another question about cheques in Germany. What happens if I get a cheque from the UK? Would you accept it?

Gerhard Yes, we would, but please be aware there is a hefty service charge for processing and clearing cheques. It's better to stay away from accepting cheques and presenting them to the bank if at all possible.

Catherine OK, fine, I'll remember that. How about debit and credit cards? Are they combined in the same card as some are in the UK?

Gerhard No, they're not. We issue the cards separately, not two in one.

Catherine All right, that's clear now. And standing orders and direct debit?

Gerhard They work exactly the same here as in the UK. For the standing orders, you just provide us with the information about which payments should be set up and on what dates. And direct debit is authorized at your end for those things that usually vary in amount but you want to pay for on a regular basis.

Catherine These are really convenient ways to take care of bills, aren't they?

Gerhard Absolutely! Right, then, are you ready to open the current account now?

Catherine Yes, indeed, I am!

Gerhard Great! Let me just bring up the form on my screen. I'll need various pieces of information from you to complete the form online. First, do you have your passport with you?

Catherine Yes, here it is.

Gerhard OK, I'll get the number from that. And I will need a copy of the information page at the back of the passport. Do you have a permanent address in Germany?

Catherine Yes, I got settled in last week.

Gerhard Good. Did you bring the certificate from the residents' registration office?

Catherine Yes, I did. Here you are.

Gerhard Oh, thanks. I'll get the details from it. And now I need to inform you about SCHUFA and how it deals with your bank accounts.

Catherine SCHUFA? Sorry, I don't know what that means.

Gerhard Let me explain. SCHUFA is the credit reference agency for banks in Germany. Any time you want to borrow money in the form of an overdraft or loan, the bank may ask the agency to run a credit check on you. I'm ticking the box that indicates I've informed you of that and you agree.

Catherine OK, that's fine, but I don't want to set up a loan or an overdraft for the time being.

Gerhard No, no, that's OK. You can let me know whenever you need to do that. Moving on, I've just clicked here to order your debit card, so you should receive it in the post within ten working days.

Catherine Wonderful. Do I create my own PIN?

Gerhard No, we'll let you know what your PIN is. It will come in a separate letter from your debit card.
Now, what about online banking? Should we set that up now?

Catherine No, I think I want to get settled here first and then I will come in again and do that.

Gerhard OK, that's fine. Or, if you wish, you can go onto our website when you are ready and do it there. It's all clear and very easy to activate.

Catherine Good. Fine.

Gerhard Onto my next point: you are the sole account holder but if you wish, you can have a third party mandate.

Catherine Sorry, a third what?

Gerhard A third party mandate, or it is sometimes called power of attorney, means that you can designate a person who has access to your account and complete control over it, for example, if you are ill or seriously incapacitated for some reason. But, of course, there are a few restrictions to safeguard you, such as this person can't arrange an overdraft or close the account or give power of attorney to someone else.

Catherine Oh, I see. No, no, I don't think I need that, thank you.

Gerhard OK, fine. Now I just need to tick this box which says I have given you a copy of the bank's general terms and conditions – this is all part of the EU banking regulations. Nothing happens without Brussels these days!
And then I can get you to sign – which is the last step. I'll now print out the account details of the new account. I'll be back in just a moment.
Ah, here we are. Could you sign here, please?

B **Read or listen to the dialogue again and note down the steps to open a current account. Then compare your notes with a partner.**

6 Role-play

KMK

Ein/e Student/in aus Spanien hat einen Termin bei einer Bank. Der Bankberater / Die Bankberaterin kann kein Spanisch, jedoch sprechen sowohl der Bankberater / die Bankberaterin als auch der/die Spanier/in Englisch. Er/Sie kennt sich mit grundlegenden Dienstleistungen und Produkten einer Bank in Deutschland nicht aus, braucht also die Hilfe des Bankberaters / der Bankberaterin.

Spielen Sie mit einem Partner / einer Partnerin das Gespräch anhand der Informationen auf den Rollenkarten nach.

Partner/in A

Bankmitarbeiter/in
Zur Eröffnung eines Bankkontos benötigen Sie vom Kunden / von der Kundin Informationen

- zur Person, zum Wohnort und Einkommen

Sie beantworten Fragen

- zum Online Banking
- zu den Voraussetzungen zur Ausstellung einer Bank- und Kreditkarte
- zum Unterschied zwischen Dauerauftrag und Einzugsverfahren
- zu den Details bei einer Überziehung des Kontos

Fragen Sie den Studenten / die Studentin, ob er/sie jemandem Bankvollmacht erteilen möchte.
Fragen Sie, ob er/sie weitere Fragen hat.

Partner/in B

Student/in aus Spanien
Sie möchten:

- ein günstiges Angebot für ein Kontokorrentkonto
- die Möglichkeit zum Online Banking
- eine Bankkarte, eventuell auch Kreditkarte
- Informationen zu Überweisungen oder Bankeinzugsverfahren, da Sie die Miete für ein 1-Zimmer-Apartment und Kosten für Ihr Handy berücksichtigen müssen.

Überlegen Sie sich ggf. weitere Fragen und bedanken Sie sich.

GRAMMAR

Negative forms

1 Opening a new current account **doesn't require** a driving licence.
2 I **didn't know** the bank offered that service.
3 **Won't** my PIN and debit card **arrive** at the same time?
4 A standing order **isn't** the same as a direct debit.
5 The customer **needn't open** the account right away. He can do it later.
6 The adviser **mustn't open** an account without first photocopying the customer's passport.

- The verb *do* + *not* is used to make a negative sentence in the simple present (1) and the simple past (2).
- The verb *do* is not used with other tenses, e.g. the future (3), with verbs *be* (4) and *have got* and with modal verbs (5–6).
- The negative form *need not* (5) means 'It is not necessary to …' = *nicht müssen*; the negative form *must not* (6) means 'It is wrong to …' = *nicht dürfen.*

7 Practice

Complete these sentences with negative verb forms. Note: there may be more than one possible answer.

1 Shops in Germany … accept cheques nowadays.
2 Customers and employees … smoke in the branch.
3 Mr Brown … make any withdrawals last week.
4 Account holders who use the ATM … queue at the till.
5 In the eurozone people … use cheques these days to pay their bills.
6 If you pay the rent by standing order, you … miss a payment.
7 If you arrange a direct debit, you … remember to transfer the sum.
8 The bank … pay any interest on free-of-charge current accounts.

8 Practice

Complete the following sentences with 'must not', or 'need not'.

1 Students … pay fees for current accounts.
2 In Germany you can pay bills by credit transfer so you … write cheques.
3 If you have a debit or credit card with a PIN, you … queue at the till to make withdrawals. But don't forget, you … write your PIN on the card!
4 Customers who use online banking … pay fees for transferring money. They also … visit their branch so often.
5 If you have an overdraft facility, you … ask for permission to overdraw your account but you … exceed the agreed limit.

9 Paper versus paperless bank statements

The popularity of the internet has enabled bank customers to choose to have their monthly statements sent online or via regular mail. What's better? Here are some pros and cons.

Discuss the following points with a partner.

1 Do you agree with these pros and cons? Could you add any other points?
2 What are, for you, the advantages and disadvantages of receiving paperless statements?
3 Based on your experience at your bank, what is the customer preference for receiving statements?

Advantages of paper bank statements

» Many people continue to receive paper bank statements simply because that's how they've always done it.

» Some people are simply not used to doing their banking on a computer or do not even possess a computer.

» In case of a power outage, paper statements would have a clear advantage over digital statements.

Disadvantages of paper bank statements

» From an environmental point of view having paper bank statements is not good news. It might seem that the amount of paper used for a few statements is relatively small, but the overall impact of millions of statements printed every month for decades is considerable.

» Some people claim that paper statements are more likely to be tampered with or stolen if they are sent by post.

10 Understanding bank statements

Match the points 1–11 on this statement with the English equivalents in the box.

account holder • account number • cash deposit • credit note • current balance • interest rate on an overdraft • overdraft limit • previous balance • sort code • standing order • transfer

MUSTER

Postbank

Postbank Hamburg 22283 Hamburg
753/2401/0000001/30//60327-06.10/0,90EUR

Versandkennzeichen

Herr
Max Muster
Musterstraße 1
12345 Musterstadt

Postbank Hamburg
Postfach
22283 Hamburg

Postbank Direkt-Service:
Telefon: 0228 5500 5500
Erreichbarkeit: 7 x 24 Stunden
Telefax: 0228 5500 5515
E-Mail: direkt@postbank.de
www.postbank.de

02. Dezember 2013

Kontoauszug: Postbank Giro plus vom 04.11. bis 02.12.13
1 Kontoinhaber: Max Muster

Auszug	Seite	IBAN	BIC (SWIFT)	Alter Kontostand **2**	
6	1/2	DE05 2001 0020 0123 4567 89	PBNKDEFF	EUR	+ 704,00

Buchung	Wert	Vorgang/Buchungsinformation	Soll	Haben
04.11.	04.11.	Dauerauftrag **3** Max Muster Sparrate für Gewinn-Sparen Altersvorsorge Dauerauftragsnr. 0000000001 Max Muster	– 25,00	
06.11.	06.11.	Einzahlung **4** Bareinzahlung		+ 150,00
06.11.	06.11.	Überweisung Musterfirma	–35,00	
		Muster, Max		+ 100,00
22.11.	22.11.	Gutschrift **5** Max Muster Übertrag auf Postbank Girokonto Muster, Max		
		Rechnungsabschluss: Siehe unten stehenden Hinweis Abschlusssaldo per 30.11.13: Haben EUR 1.284,00		
02.12.	02.12.	Überweisung **6** Musterfirma Max Muster	– 35,00	
02.12.	02.12.	Dauerauftrag Max Muster Sparrate für Gewinn-Sparen Altersvorsorge Dauerauftragsnr. 0000000001 Max Muster	– 25,00	

Kontonummer **7**
123 456 789

BLZ **9**
200 100 20

Summe Zahlungseingänge
EUR + 700,00

Dispositionskredit **8**
EUR 6.100

Zinssatz für Dispositionskredit **10**
XX,XX % p.a.

Summe Zahlungsausgänge
EUR – 180,00

Zinssatz für geduldete Überziehung
XX,XX % p.a.

Anlage
1

Neuer Kontostand 11
EUR + 1.224,00

LANGUAGE

How to describe entries to accounts

When money is taken out of an account, the bank debits the account with the sum.
When money is paid into an account, the bank credits the sum to the account.
The passive is often used:
the account was / has been debited
the account is / will be credited

11 Working with words

A Complete the table.

Verb	Noun	Past participle
to withdraw	…[1]	…[2]
…[3]	deposit	…[4]
to debit	…[5]	…[6]
…[7]	credit	…[8]
…[9]	…[10]	overdrawn

B Now use words (in the correct form) from the table to complete the sentences.

1. You can … up to £300 per day using your debit card and PIN.
2. Current account holders can … cash using the bank's pre-printed credit slips.
3. Your statement shows your account was … by £251.22 for flights to London.
4. Some banks require you to make an initial … when you open a current account.
5. If you decide to use direct debit to pay your regular bills, you can specify the date on which your account will be … by the agreed amount.
6. I must warn you that to go into … can be an expensive business.
7. Some banks charge fees for … made at another bank's cash machine.
8. Her account is now … by £100 because she withdrew more than was in her account.

12 Registering for online banking

A You work at Horizons Bank and need to explain to Catherine how to register for online banking. You find the website on page 36 and read it before your meeting.

Now complete the sentences below.

1. A user ID should contain …
2. The bank will ring a customer to confirm …
3. If the bank can't reach a customer during the registration process, …
4. A person can start online banking as soon as …
5. The customer will need to provide more …
6. When an activation code is received, …
7. The tour of internet banking will inform you about …
8. If you need some assistance once you have logged in, …

B Compare this procedure with the one your bank uses.

NORTHERN STANDARD BANK

HOW TO ENROL

Get started with Online Banking in THREE simple steps

It will only take a few minutes to set up Online Banking for a convenient and secure way to manage your finances 24/7.

1.
Register online
The whole process should take no longer than 5 minutes to complete. Have your account details ready, enter your details and choose a user ID and password. Keep this information safe.

2.
We'll contact you
To confirm it's actually you enrolling for Online Banking, we'll call you on the number we have in our records. If we can't reach you by phone, we'll send you an activation code in the post instead.

3.
Log on
Enter the user ID and the password you selected during enrolment. Then you'll be asked you to set up some memorable information. You'll need this every time you log on.

And now to the details ...

LOG ON

Step 1
The first page of enrolment helps us identify you as the actual user. The personal details enable us to find you on our system. You'll need to have the information from of one of your NORTHERN STANDARD BANK accounts to hand.
The second page is where you select your log-on details. Choose a user ID which is 9-20 characters long and is something you can easily remember. You'll also need to select a password which has 6-12 characters. Make sure you avoid simple passwords like abc123.

Step 2
The next step is we'll call you to confirm that it's really you registering for Online Banking. You can choose which number we call you on as long as it's one we already have in our records for you. Clear instructions are given both on screen and when we call you on how to complete this part of enrolment. If we are not able to call you, we will send you an activation code instead to your home address within the next few days.

Step 3
Now enrolment is complete. If you've successfully completed our security call, you can log on immediately using your selected ID and password. You will then be asked to set up some memorable information, which you will always need to use when you log on in the future.
If you have to wait for an activation code, this should arrive in the post within the next few days. Once you get the code, log on using your chosen user ID and password, and then on the next screen you will be asked to enter this activation code.
After you log on successfully, you will be given a tour, and then you'll be able to enjoy all the benefits of Online Banking. If you need any further help, click on 'Customer Support' on the right-hand side when you're logged in where you'll find answers to frequently asked questions. There is also a 'Show Me How' help tool which can guide you through how to do various transactions.

13 Mediation

KMK

Ihre Bank diskutiert, wie andere Banken mit der Frage Kundenbindung umgehen. Sie haben den unten stehenden Text gefunden und möchten gerne bei Ihrer nächsten wöchentlichen Teambesprechung eine kleine Präsentation zu diesem Thema auf Grundlage des Textes halten. **Referieren Sie die Hauptpunkte, übersetzen Sie jedoch nicht Wort für Wort.**

BBC NEWS

11 September 2014 Last updated at 07:35 GMT

CURRENT ACCOUNT SWITCH GUARANTEE

Q&A: Switching bank accounts

A survey for Santander found that 20% of those questioned would rather go to the dentist than switch their bank accounts.

But in September 2013, the process of switching became a lot less painful.

That was when Britain's 50m current account holders were first able to move their bank account to another provider within seven days.

It followed a recommendation from the Independent Commission on Banking, which said there should be more competition in the market.

So how easy is it to switch? What can go wrong? And what guarantees do you have if your bank makes a mistake?

How common is switching?

Before the 7-day switching service started, around a million people switched bank accounts every year. In the first 11 months of the new system, 1.1m people switched – an increase of 2.2%.

Where do we bank at the moment?

The big four High Street banks have about a 75% share of the market, according to the Office of Fair Trading. Lloyds Banking Group (which includes TSB, Halifax and Bank of Scotland) is the largest bank in the UK, with 25.5 million accounts. Lloyds has around 28% of the personal account market, Barclays has about 14%, RBS (which includes Nat West) has 13%, and HSBC has 12%, according to John Gilbert Financial Research.

How can I switch?

You can contact your new bank, or choose a new one via www.simplerworld.co.uk. Once you have switched, payments in or out of your old account will be automatically re-directed for a period of 13 months, to cover once-a-year payments. So your employer, for example, will be notified, and payments will be automatically switched to your new account. No one whom you pay, or who pays you, will have to take any action.

So how long will switching take?

Once your new bank has acknowledged your application, the switching will take seven working days. Or the switch can happen on a date of your choosing.

Do I have to notify my old bank?

No, you only need notify the new bank. It will tell your old bank, and transfer all your direct debits and standing orders automatically. You will be given a new bank account number, and a new sort code.

What happens if I miss a payment as a result of the switch?

If anything goes wrong, and you miss a payment, your new bank will refund the charges, and make good any direct debits that did not go through.

Can I still switch if I am overdrawn?

This is down to your new bank. Depending on the size of your overdraft, they will choose whether to still accept you. They might increase (or decrease) the overdraft charges.

Which banks can I switch to?

Seventeen banks are participating in the switching scheme, involving 33 different brands. Lloyds is the largest bank taking part. The Reliance Bank, part of the Salvation Army, is the smallest. New entrants into the market include Metro and Marks and Spencer. Tesco entered the market early in 2014. Virgin is planning to offer a current account, but has not yet announced a date. Two building societies are taking part: Nationwide and the Cumberland .

14 Leseverstehen

Ihre Bank plant Veränderungen bezüglich der Konten für Kinder und Jugendliche. Ihr Chef bittet Sie, im Internet zu recherchieren, was andere Kreditinstitute anbieten. Sie finden zwei Angebote einer englischen Bank.

Beantworten Sie die nachstehenden Verständnisfragen in kurzen Stichworten auf Deutsch.

1

BANK UK gives your kids the right stepping stone towards a future of smart spending. Our STARTER ACCOUNT, a current or savings account, offers specialized features and benefits making it the perfect present for young people.

Anyone under 18 years of age can apply for our STARTER ACCOUNT.

Our account features are:

- first cheque book free
- free printouts of bank statements
- interesting welcome kit when opening account

We offer:

- a special ID card for your child. Along with the basic banking necessities, with the STARTER ACCOUNT, the child will get a specialized photographic membership card. This card gives access to great events and interesting offers thanks to our special partners. Your child will be offered discounts and vouchers in different areas of entertainment, as well as in toy and book stores.
- free insurance cover for parents provided by our special partners.

2

Our STUDENT ACCOUNT offers everything you need to help you make the most of your time at college or university. It helps you manage your money.

If you need to go overdrawn, we offer you a £20 overdraft limit. No overdraft fees apply if you overdraw your account by less than this amount.

Overdrafts that exceed this sum are available subject to application and approval and are repayable on demand. You will get a grace period if you go over your limit. This means that you have until 2.00 p.m. (GMT) to lodge enough money to avoid any overdraft fees that may be incurred that day.

You have the choice of transferring money from another personal account you have with us via mobile or internet banking, or you can pay the fee in cash in one of our branches.

On opening the account you will be provided with a welcome pack offering you discounts in different areas of entertainment, or in toy and book stores.

1 Welches der beiden Angebote richtet sich an die Kontoinhaber?
2 Wie viel kostet es, einen Kontoauszug beim *Starter Account* auszudrucken?
3 Warum ist das *Starter Account* ein perfektes Geschenk von Eltern an ihre Kinder?
4 Wodurch unterscheiden sich die beiden Angebote hinsichtlich:
(a) Alter? (b) Inhalt und Fokus? (je Angebot mind. 2 Antworten)
5 Was passiert beim *Student Account*, wenn man das Konto überzieht?
6 Was für unterschiedliche Sonderangebote bieten die beiden Konten?

INVESTOPEDIA

Wild Incentives For Opening A Bank Account

By Rachel Brown | May 13, 2012

Banks have always been keen to attract new customers and new business. Incentives have always been part of signing up to new bank accounts, with toasters being a common incentive to move banks. Some gifts have gone beyond household appliances. Here we look at some of the wilder incentives banks have offered their customers.

Gift Vouchers

Last year, HSBC offered customers who met certain specifications a $900 Saks Fifth Avenue gift card to tempt them to join the bank. While this seemed like a fantastic incentive, things got a little hairy when the taxman came a-calling.

According to the Desert News, HSBC Holdings mailed the IRS form 1099 to thousands of customers who accepted their incentive in the previous year. The forms list the income the banks reported to the government in the customers' names, reminding recipients they may be obliged to pay taxes on those sums. Perhaps this gift card did not seem such a lucrative gift once this tax reminder arrived.

Guns and Rifles

Michael Moore famously showed a bank giving away a gun as a wild incentive in the movie 'Bowling For Columbine'. A scene in the film depicts how Moore discovered a bank in Michigan that would give customers a free hunting rifle when they made a deposit of a certain size into a time deposit account. The film follows Moore as he goes to the bank, makes his deposit, fills out the forms and awaits the result of a background check before walking out of the bank carrying a brand new Weatherby hunting rifle.

Just before leaving the bank, Moore jokingly asks, 'Do you think it's a little dangerous handing out guns at a bank?'

The bank was North Country Financial Corp., and customers needed $869 in a 20-year certificate of deposit for the bank to hand over a Weatherby Inc. Mark V Synthetic rifle. If customers deposited more, they could have a choice of six Weatherby shotguns or a limited-edition rifle, reports the Chicago Sun-Times.

Mercedes Benz

Now customers can enjoy a brand new Mercedes Benz when they open an account at C1 bank. If they've got a million dollars to deposit that is. New customers should note that the car represents prepaid interest and the bank hopes the instant gratification of a spectacular Mercedes Benz will entice new clients to the bank. Consumers will get what amounts to a $61,294.00 car (including tax, delivery and registration) instead of five years of interest, worth around $60,000. Any customers who withdraw funds early will get the balance less the cost of the car. Just in case you're getting too excited, the bank offer is limited to only two cars per household.

Sports Tickets

Chase bank is offering customers two free front-row tickets to attend a New York City-based sports match, musical or concert. You need to deposit $100,000 to get the tickets for the prestige event. On average, the two free tickets have a value of around $400, which essentially translates into a 0.40% return.

The Bottom Line

In an era of low interest rates and austerity, banks are trying to entice us to deposit with them, especially if we are wealthy. The only question is, what will they come up with next?

http://www.investopedia.com/financial-edge/0512/wild-incentives-for-opening-a-bank-account.aspx

15 Discussion

1. How would you answer the last question in the text?
2. What do you think about such incentives? How far should a bank go in order to attract new customers?
3. If you opened a new account, what extras would you like the bank to offer you? Explain why.

UNIT 4

Payments

- Making SEPA transfers
- Explaining direct debits and standing orders
- Preventing debit card misuse

1 Warm-up

London buses go cashless

London's buses are no longer accepting cash. Transport for London (TfL) said dwindling numbers of passengers using money to pay for their journeys had prompted the change.
Research shows that 99% of customers use Oyster, prepaid tickets, contactless payment cards or free bus passes. TfL says the transition should be trouble-free ...

Oyster is a 'pay-as-you-go' travel card for the London transport system.

Read the text and answer these questions.

1 How can a bus go cashless?
2 Explain why you think Transport for London took this step.
3 As a bus passenger, would you welcome this change? Give your reasons.

CULTURE

Cheques in the UK and the USA

While German banks do not usually provide cheques, current account holders in the UK and the USA receive cheques (AE = checks) from their bank. They often write cheques for payment in shops and even send cheques by post to pay bills instead of paying by credit transfer.
62% of UK account holders used cheques in 2008. In 2013 it was 43%. Interestingly, 94% of the 16-24-year-olds do not write cheques today.

LANGUAGE

Filling in forms

Please	fill in	your name	on the top line / at the top.
Just	write	the payee's name	underneath / below / above / on the next line.
Now	put	the amount / sum	on the left / on the right.
	enter	the reason for payment	in this space (on the left / on the right) / in this box.
		the IBAN the account number the sort code	on the bottom line / at the bottom (of the page).

~~Please~~ fill ~~in~~ on the top line your custumer accaunt number

2 Online credit transfers

A new customer, Phil Hobbs from California, asks you about transferring money in Germany. He has heard about TANs but does not know how to use them. In the USA he paid bills by cheque.

Überweisung

Kontonummer Auftraggeber: custumer account number

Ausführungsdatum: exucantion date

Empfänger: Name, Vorname / Firma: ~~recipient~~ payee's name

☐ Neue Empfängerdaten speichern

Pleas

IBAN/Kontonummer (Empfänger): the IBAN

BIC/BLZ: sort code

bei Kreditinstitut
(Wird automatisch ausgefüllt)

Betrag: amount / sum €

Verwendungszweck: the reason for payment

Senden

A **Show Phil how to make a credit transfer online. Use this form or one from your bank. The expressions in the box above will be helpful.**

B **Explain how Phil can receive TANs from your bank and how to use them.**

C **Give Phil the information contained in this flyer.**

Die SEPA*-Überweisung – Die wichtigsten Merkmale

» Für inländische und grenzüberschreitende Euro-Überweisungen innerhalb der SEPA-Teilnehmerländer
» Sicherheit durch Verwendung von IBAN
» Europaweite Gutschrift innerhalb eines Arbeitstages nach Annahme
» Gutschrift des Betrages ohne Abzug
» Keine Begrenzung des Zahlungsbetrages

Mehr zum Thema SEPA finden Sie auf unserer Webseite.

*SEPA = Single Euro Payments Area

3 The EU, the euro and other currencies

You are taking part in an international banking seminar on payments within SEPA. A speaker hands out this map, but the names of some countries have been missed off.

Look at the map and do the following tasks.

1. Name the missing countries (1–8).
2. Say which EU countries have the euro as their currency.
3. List the EU countries that use a different currency and name the currency.

4 SEPA

At the seminar you are given this handout. A Czech participant who missed the workshop on SEPA asks you about it. Answer her questions below.

Since 2014 cashless payments within SEPA, the Single Euro Payments Area, have been standardized so that there are no differences for bank customers between national and cross-border payments denominated in euros.

To achieve this, the European Payments Council (EPC) evolved common standards in legal, technical and organizational matters (e.g. forms and bank codes), clearing and software solutions which all participating countries must meet. The member states at present comprise the countries of the European Union plus the other members of the European Economic Area, (Iceland, Norway and Liechtenstein), as well as Switzerland, Monaco and San Marino.

The EPC developed four systems: SEPA Credit Transfer (including SEPA Standing Order), SEPA Direct Debit Core for personal customers, SEPA Direct Debit B2B (= Business to Business) for corporate clients, and SEPA Cards Framework, which regulates the use of debit cards.

Over 500 million people live within SEPA, an economic area with some 20 million businesses and institutions.

1 What is the basic idea behind SEPA?
2 Do all the countries in SEPA have to be members of the EU?
3 Which means of payment are affected?

5 Direct debits and standing orders

VIDEO 3

You have been asked to present direct debits and standing orders as used in Germany.

building society payments • insurance premiums • loan instalments • membership fees • mortgage repayments • rent • savings/investment plans • season tickets • utility bills

A **Match the terms in the box above with these definitions.**

1 regular payments to savings accounts or funds
2 payments for electricity, gas, water, etc.
3 repayments of money borrowed from a bank
4 sums saved with a building society
5 regular payments for insurance
6 payments made by a tenant to the owner of a flat or house
7 repayments of a property loan
8 tickets for regularly using public transport, etc.
9 sums paid by club members

B To prepare your presentation you are going to watch the video "How to make payments using your bank account".

Make a copy of this chart to compare the direct debit and standing order systems and fill it in while you are watching.

	Direct debits	Standing orders
What sort of payments can be made? Give examples.	…	…
What happens when you set one up?	…	…
How does the system work?	…	…
How much does it cost?	…	…
Is there any risk?		

C **Present the direct debit and standing order systems to your fellow students, using the chart and expressions from A. Answer any questions you are asked.**

6 Standing orders

KMK

8

Mit der Einwilligung der Kunden/Kundinnen können Beratungsgespräche am Telefon zu Trainingszwecken aufgezeichnet werden.

Im Rahmen Ihrer Ausbildung hören Sie zwei Gespräche, die Callcenter-Mitarbeiterin Claudia Kölln mit englischsprachigen Kunden/Kundinnen führt.

Übertragen Sie diese Tabelle auf ein Blatt Papier. Während Sie zuhören, vervollständigen Sie sie auf Deutsch.

	1. Anruf	2. Anruf
Dauerauftrag: Einrichtung/Änderung/Löschung	…	…
Name des Auftraggebers / der Auftraggeberin:	…	…
Kontonummer des Auftraggebers / der Auftraggeberin:	…	…
Name des Empfängers / der Empfängerin:	…	…
IBAN des Empfängers / der Empfängerin:	…	…
Verwendungszweck:	…	…
Betrag:	…	…
Ausführung: monatlich/vierteljährlich/halbjährlich/jährlich	…	…
Erste Ausführung am:	…	…
Letzte Ausführung am:	…	…

7 Apologizing

8 **A Listen to the dialogues from exercise 6 again. Find out why Claudia apologized each time and note the expressions of apology she used.**

B Use your notes to apologize to customers in these situations.

1. A customer calls you on his mobile, but the reception is so bad that you cannot understand him.
2. Your computer has crashed and you have lost all the data that a customer has just given you over the phone.
3. A customer calls to complain about not receiving her statements, and you find that they have been sent to the wrong address.
4. You have to phone a customer at very short notice and postpone her appointment with a colleague who has suddenly been taken ill.
5. A customer wants to know whether his ex-wife, who also has an account with your bank, has got a credit card.
6. A customer wants to transfer money immediately, but all the systems are temporarily down for technical reasons.

8 Direct debits

9 Phil Hobbs from California comes into the bank again. Your colleague, Mia Lindner, is advising him. Phil has agreed that you may listen to their conversation.

A Listen and write down three aspects of direct debiting that Phil is worried about.

Phil … yes, I opened a current account here last month. Could I ask you about this letter I got yesterday?

Mia Of course, Mr Hobbs. Is it a letter from the bank?

Phil No, it's from a dance studio about a payment I have to make. You see, I gave my girlfriend a tango course for her birthday, and now they've sent me this. Here it is …

Mia Oh how nice! I'd love to tango, but my partner flatly refuses. … *(reading)* Ah yes, the dance studio wants you to pay the membership fees by direct debit. This is a SEPA direct debit mandate. It allows personal customers, like you, to pay by direct debit anywhere within SEPA, that's the Single Euro Payments Area.

Phil That all sounds very complicated. What is this mandate for?

Mia If you fill it in and sign it, you authorize the dance studio to claim the money from your account when the payments are due, and you allow us, your bank, to release the sum and debit your account every time. There are mandates for single or recurring payments.

Phil Hang on a minute. I'm not signing anything that lets other people take money out of my account whenever they feel like it!

Mia Please don't worry. That can't happen because the payee, that's the dance studio, has to fix a due date and give you advance notice when your account will be debited.

Phil But what if they take too much?

Mia You are allowed to limit the amount that can be debited from your account, and you can also restrict which payees may claim money.

Phil I don't feel happy about this at all. I like to stay in control of my money!

Mia I can understand that, but you will see the debits on your bank statement and you can revoke a direct debit within eight weeks, without giving a reason. If you didn't authorize the direct debit, you even have 13 months. You can easily check because every direct debit is shown on your statement with a credit identifier and a mandate reference.

Phil You've lost me now. What's a 'credit identifier' and a 'mandate whatsit'?

Mia A credit identifier is a number that shows who the creditor is. All credit identifiers in Germany are issued by the *Bundesbank*. The dance studio will give you a mandate reference so that you can identify the payment when you see it on your statement. Both can be a combination of up to 35 characters, though most are shorter.

Phil I just don't believe this! Look, why don't we forget the whole business and set up a standing order instead?

Mia Direct debiting actually gives you more protection than the standing order system does. And, of course, there are advantages for the dance studio because they can rely on getting payments punctually. That's probably why you had to agree to pay by direct debit when you signed up for the tango course …

Phil You mean, I've got no choice?

Mia It's not as bad as that! Well, Mr Hobbs, I'm afraid I have to attend a meeting now, but my colleague here can help you with the form if you like.

Phil That would be great, thanks.

B **Read the dialogue and complete the sentences below.**

1 If you fill in a direct debit mandate, you authorize …
2 The payee has to fix a due date and give you advance notice when …
3 You can limit the amount that can be debited from your account and restrict …
4 You can revoke a direct debit within …
5 A credit identifier is …
6 The payee will give you a mandate reference so that you can …

9 A direct debit mandate

Read the dialogue again and, with a partner who takes the role of Phil Hobbs, play the rest of the scene. Explain the form below and help Phil to fill it in. Mia has given you this useful vocabulary.

einziehen – to draw
anweisen – to order
einlösen – to release
Erstattung – refund
verlangen – to claim

Tanzstudio Toby Winter, Am Park 17, 50111 Köln

Gläubigeridentifikationsnummer: DE88 ZZZ0 5678 9012 34
Mandatsreferenz: 987543CB2

SEPA-Lastschriftmandat:
Ich ermächtige den Zahlungsempfänger Tanzstudio Toby Winter Zahlungsbeträge von meinem Konto mittels Lastschrift einzuziehen. Zugleich weise ich mein Kreditinstitut an, die von dem Tanzstudio Toby Winter auf mein Konto gezogenen Lastschriften einzulösen.
Hinweis: Ich kann innerhalb von acht Wochen, beginnend mit dem Belastungsdatum, die Erstattung des belasteten Betrages verlangen.

Zahlungsart: (bitte ankreuzen): Wiederkehrende Zahlungen ☐ Einmalige Zahlungen ☐

Name des/der Zahlungspflichtigen (Kontoinhaber/in): ____________________

Anschrift des/der Zahlungspflichtigen: ____________________

IBAN des/der Kontoinhabers/Kontoinhaberin: ____________________

____
Ort, Datum, Unterschrift des/der Zahlungspflichtigen

10 Role-play

KMK

Führen Sie mithilfe dieser Rollenkarten ein Beratungsgespräch am Telefon.

Partner/in A

Sie arbeiten im Servicecenter Ihrer Bank. Ihnen wird der Anruf einer englischsprechenden Person durchgestellt. Beginnen Sie das Gespräch.

- Melden Sie sich mit dem Namen Ihrer Bank und Ihrem Namen. Fragen Sie, ob Sie behilflich sein können.
- Begrüßen Sie die Person. Sagen Sie, dass es gar kein Problem ist, das Gespräch auf Englisch zu führen. Bitten Sie die Person, ihre Kontonummer und ihr Kennwort für Telefon-Banking zu nennen.
- Lassen Sie sich das Anliegen und das dazugehörige Problem erläutern.
- Erklären Sie, dass ein höherer Dispositionskredit nicht nötig ist. Schlagen Sie stattdessen das Einzugsverfahren als Problemlösung vor.
- Beschreiben Sie, wie das SEPA-Einzugsverfahren funktioniert.
- Sagen Sie, dass die Beträge jederzeit variieren können: Der Zahlungsempfänger / die Zahlungsempfängerin kann den jeweils fälligen Betrag einziehen, wenn er/sie den Zahlungspflichtigen / die Zahlungspflichtige im Voraus darüber informiert hat.
- Sie merken, dass Ihr/e Gesprächspartner/in erhöhten Beratungsbedarf hat. Bieten Sie einen Termin mit einem Kundenberater / einer Kundenberaterin in der Filiale an. Schlagen Sie einen Tag und eine Uhrzeit in der kommenden Woche vor.
- Verabschieden Sie sich.

Partner/in B

Sie sind Adam/Amy Bell aus Südafrika und leben seit zwei Jahren in Deutschland. Neben Ihrer Tätigkeit in einem Fitness-Studio möchten Sie privat als „Personal Trainer" arbeiten. Sie rufen das Servicecenter Ihrer Bank an.

- Stellen Sie sich vor. Entschuldigen Sie sich, dass Sie nicht so gut Deutsch sprechen, um Ihr Anliegen darstellen zu können und fragen Sie, ob es möglich wäre, das Gespräch auf Englisch zu führen.
- Nennen Sie die Nummer Ihres Girokontos (9743310) und Ihr Passwort für Telefon-Banking „Capetown".
- Beschreiben Sie Ihr Vorhaben, und äußern Sie Ihre Besorgnis: Weil Sie einen Trainingsraum mieten müssen, werden Sie in finanzielle Schwierigkeiten geraten, falls Ihre Privatkunden/-kundinnen nicht pünktlich zahlen. Bitten Sie deswegen um eine Erhöhung Ihres Dispositionskredits von 1000 € auf 5000 €.
- Lassen Sie sich erklären, wie das Einzugsverfahren funktioniert. Fragen Sie gegebenenfalls nach.
- Weisen Sie darauf hin, dass die Zahlungsbeträge Ihrer Kunden/Kundinnen jeweils nach der Zahl der gebuchten Stunden variieren werden.
- Sie sind verunsichert: Wie kommen Sie an Gläubigeridentifikationsnummern für Ihre Kunden/Kundinnen? Sie fühlen sich auch nicht in der Lage, ein Lastschriftmandat auf Deutsch zu formulieren.
- Stimmen Sie dem Ihnen angebotenen Beratungstermin zu.
- Bedanken und verabschieden Sie sich.

11 Debit cards

After receiving his first debit card, Phil Hobbs phoned to say he was worried about security, but you were unable to take his call.

Write Phil an email covering the following points. (The information in the leaflet below from a UK bank will help you.)

- Apologize for not being able to take his call.
- Inform him about the security features on his card.
- Tell him what precautions he should take when using his card.
- Close by offering help if he has any further questions.

PIN + CHIP = SECURITY

Did you know that we have introduced new technology that significantly improves the security of your debit card?

The gold chip on the face of your card stores encrypted data that is verified every time you use it.

Your PIN makes your card safer, too because, unlike a signature, your PIN cannot be forged.

When you use your debit card for withdrawing cash at an ATM or making a payment at a point of sale, you have three consecutive chances to enter your PIN correctly. After the third failed attempt, your PIN will be locked by the bank so that no one can access your account.

All we ask you to do is take a few simple precautions:

- Keep your card in a safe place so it cannot be lost or stolen.
- Keep your PIN and your card separate.
- Don't disclose your PIN to anyone else.
- Cover the key pad with your other hand when entering your PIN in case you are being watched.

If you notice that your card is missing or that your account has been debited with a sum you did not authorize, please phone our 24/7 emergency hotline immediately.

GRAMMAR

The passive

1 Your card stores encrypted data that **is verified** every time you use it.
2 Your PIN **will be locked** by the bank so that no one can access your account.
3 Your account **has been debited** with a sum you did not authorize.
4 Unlike a signature, your PIN **cannot be forged**.

- The passive is formed using a form of the verb *be* and the past participle. The passive can be used with all tenses of the verb *to be* (1–3) and modal verbs (4).
- The passive is often used in sentences in which the person or thing taking the action is not as important as the action itself.
- The word *by* is used if the agent is mentioned (2).
- The passive is often used with the verbs *to debit* (3) and *to credit*.

12 Practice

Put the underlined words into the passive, leaving out the words in brackets.

1 (You) <u>may use</u> your debit card at all ATMs within SEPA. *Your debit card may …*
2 (We) <u>will send</u> your PIN to you by separate post within a few days.
3 Whenever you pay by debit card, (the bank) <u>will debit</u> your account.
4 (The bank) usually <u>credits</u> the payee's account within two days.
5 If (you) <u>have lost</u> your card, please contact us at once.
6 Then (the bank) <u>can stop</u> payment on your card.
7 (We) <u>replace</u> lost or stolen cards immediately.
8 If you follow our security guidelines, (they) <u>will protect</u> you against card fraud.

13 If you lose your debit card, …

Summarize the main points of this article in German for your customers.

Imagine your train is pulling into the station. You have not got a ticket so you rush to the ticket machine, insert your debit card, grab the ticket when it pops out and jump on the train. As the doors close, you realize your card is missing! You must have dropped it or left it in the machine. After a moment's panic you relax: no problem, you think. You can phone your bank's emergency hotline and cancel the card.

Problem solved? Unfortunately not! It's true that the card can no longer be used with your PIN to make payments or withdraw cash at an ATM, but it can still be used with your signature to pay using the direct debit system. The thief can shop with your card if he forges your signature on the receipt you get in a shop. The forgery does not even have to be good: busy cashiers in shops rarely compare signatures and never have time to ask for proof of identity. The sum will simply be deducted from your account.

In Germany you can avoid this by arranging a KUNO* Card Stop as soon as you notice that your card is lost or has been stolen. To do this, you have to go to a police station and tell the police your account details and the serial number of your card. This is on the magnetic strip on your card but, as the number is not visible, you have to obtain it from your bank. This data is then entered into a central register, and payment on the stolen card is stopped. If later someone tries to pay with it, it will show up as stolen. But if you are not able to tell the police the serial number of your card, payment will be stopped on all the cards relating to your account and not just on this one.

There are, however, certain drawbacks with KUNO, the main one being that not all retail outlets take part in the KUNO system. The second drawback is that a KUNO Card Stop can only be put on card payments that you make by direct debit without your PIN, but not on ATM withdrawals and electronic cash payments with your PIN. It is therefore not an alternative to having your card cancelled by your bank, so you must inform your bank as well.

It is important to cancel a missing card as soon as possible. If you only notice the loss when strange debits start appearing on your bank statement, your entire account may have been cleared and you may be bombarded with demands for payment from people whose debits have been returned to them unpaid. Of course you can revoke every incorrect debit within a period of eight weeks, but you may be in for a lot of hassle in the meantime.

* KUNO = Kriminalitätsbekämpfung im unbaren Zahlungsverkehr unter Nutzung nicht-polizeilicher Organisationsstrukturen

14 Produktion

Nach dem Besuch mit einer Delegation deutscher Lehrer/Lehrerinnen in England erhält der Organisator der Fahrt, Herr Schröder, durch die Kollegin Jane Dean eine Rechnung der englischen Schule über Mittagessen in deren Kantine. Peter Schröder möchte das Geld überweisen, aber es fehlen noch einige Daten.

Peter Schröders Englischkenntnisse reichen nicht aus, um selbst einen Brief zu verfassen. Daher bittet er Sie, eine E-Mail an die Schule zu schreiben, um die fehlenden Daten zu erhalten. Er zeigt Ihnen folgende Rechnung.

Verfassen Sie eine E-Mail an das englische College.

Invoice

Business College Cramlington
5 High Street
Cramlington
NE22 3BN
Email: BCC@bcc.uk

Name:	Mr Peter Schröder	Invoice no.:	232
Address:	Business College Hamburg, Hochstraße 10	Date:	1 October 20..
City:	Hamburg, D-22283		

Quantity	Description	Unit Price	Total
22	lunch	£8.50	£187.00

15 Interaktion

Führen Sie in Partnerarbeit einen Dialog nach den folgenden Vorgaben.

Partner/in A: Bankmitarbeiter/in

- Sie begrüßen den Kunden / die Kundin am Schalter.
- Sie erkundigen sich genau nach den Bedürfnissen des Kunden / der Kundin.
- Sie beantworten alle Fragen und beraten eingehend zu den Themen:
  - das SEPA-Lastschriftverfahren und dessen Vorteile
  - den Gebrauch der EC-Karte
  - Vorgehen bei Kartenverlust
- Sie fragen, ob der Kunde / die Kundin weitere Wünsche hat.
- Verabschieden Sie sich.

Partner/in B: Kunde/Kundin

Sie sind Jack/Jill Scott aus Newcastle, GB. Sie werden ab sofort für ein Jahr als Fremdsprachenassistent/in an einem Bremer Gymnasium arbeiten. Vom Pädagogischen Austauschdienst erhalten Sie monatlich 956,- €. Vor einer Woche haben Sie ein Kontokorrentkonto eröffnet.

- Sie möchten wissen, wie Sie die Miete für Ihre 1-Zimmer Wohnung zahlen sollten. (Ihr Zimmer in einem Studentenwohnheim in England haben Sie per Dauerauftrag bezahlt.)
- Sie erkundigen sich nach weiteren Zahlungsmöglichkeiten für andere Zwecke (z. B. Handy, Einkaufen), stellen Fragen und lassen sich eingehend beraten.
- Sie bedanken sich für das Gespräch.

16 Mobile payments

While preparing for an international workshop on Innovations in Cashless Payment, you have come across the two graphs and the article below.

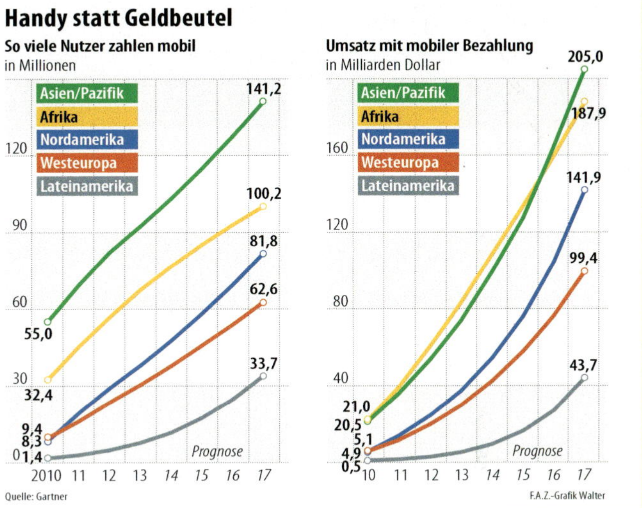

Quelle: Gartner · FAZ-Grafik Walter · FAZ vom 21. Juli 2014

A **Look at these two graphs. Note the main facts and comment on a development which may be surprising.**

B **Read this article. Using key words only, list the advantages and disadvantages of mobile payments for both users and providers.**

C **Using your notes, give a short presentation on mobile payments.**

The payment revolution

Fancy a bagel but got no cash on you? At a Frankfurt bakery customers can pay using their mobile phone and a PayPal app. When they log in, their photo appears on a screen at the cash desk. The cashier checks that it is the same person and the payment goes through – no cash, no signature, no PIN – and is free too, because the payee bears the charges.

Mobile payments are a huge issue and not just PayPal, a subsidiary of eBay, is keen to get a slice of the cake. Internet giants like Amazon, Facebook, Apple and Google want a share in this booming, highly lucrative market. Google has already developed the Google Wallet for mobile payments for its Google Play Store products. Accessible via the Android system integrated into most cell phones, it not only binds customers to Google but also reduces the company's bank charges.

German banks are in danger of missing the boat. Not so in the UK where the major high street banks have launched Paym (pronounced "pay em"), a system which allows account holders to transfer money by pressing a few buttons on their mobile. No need to bother with IBANs or bank codes, simply enter the payee's phone number, confirm his or her name, check the amount and press "send". UK banks estimate that by 2018 one billion payments will have been made using Paym, with 9 out of 10 people using mobile phones rather than visiting their bank, logging into their computer or carrying a wallet full of cards.

Mobile phone providers are active, too, with chips embedded in phones replacing debit cards. Vodafone has cooperated with Safaricom to produce M-Pesa, a mobile payment system widely used throughout Africa. In Europe, Vodafone and O_2 have developed Weve: more than just a payment system, Weve is a way for companies to geo-locate potential customers near shops and send them offers to tempt them inside. In a recent test Tesco sent text messages to a target group of young females who were within walking distance of its stores, offering a £5 discount voucher. Nearly 40,000 responded and used it to shop there.

Is this what customers want? Security is a big sticking point. What happens if your phone is stolen or infected by malicious software? What if a payment is made without your approval? Barclays says payments via Paym are protected by a password that only the user knows, but there is concern that consumers will face the burden of proof in the event of theft. In the light of data leaks in the USA, perhaps it all boils down to a question of trust: who do we want to handle our payments – our own bank or an internet company based in California?

UNIT 5

Credit cards

- Selling a credit card
- Explaining the different types of credit card
- Looking at the risks of credit cards

1 Warm-up

A **Do you have a credit card? If so, what do you use it for?**

B **Which credit cards does your bank sell? What do they cost?**

C **Look at the cartoons and do the tasks below.**

1. Describe the situation in both cartoons.
2. Explain the message of the first cartoon.
3. In the second cartoon, explain what the man's problem is.
4. Would a credit card prevent the customer's cheque from bouncing? Explain why/why not.

2 Prepaid credit cards

KMK

10

Übertragen Sie folgende Tabelle in Ihr Arbeitsheft und vervollständigen Sie sie. Hören Sie den Podcast über Prepaid-Kreditkarten.

Wo bekommt man die Karte?	…
Was kostet sie?	…
Wie wird die Karte freigeschaltet?	…
Wie kann Geld aufgeladen werden?	…
Bis zu welchem Höchstbetrag kann mit dieser Karte gezahlt werden?	…
Was geschieht, wenn Sie mehr Geld auf die Karte buchen wollen?	…
Benennen Sie die Vor- und Nachteile einer solchen Kreditkarte.	…

3 Selling a credit card

11

Julius Frank started a new job at a bank three months ago. Today he is advising Bob Hewitt, an Australian customer, about credit cards.

Read or listen to the dialogue and answer the questions below.

Julius Good morning, Mr Hewitt. Nice to see you again.

Bob Not exactly a good morning, is it? All this rain! Well, my wife and I are heading down under soon. Get a bit of sunshine, the weather there is much warmer than here in Germany, and visit our granddaughter in Sydney. Now, we're going to need some cash, and I assume we have to order Australian dollars or do you have any?

Julius No, you're right, we don't have any here in our branch, so we'll have to order them for you. How much would you like, Mr Hewitt?

Bob Hmm, good question. I think about A$5,000.

Julius OK, but that is quite a lot of cash, and there is obviously quite a security risk. Are you sure you want to have so much cash on you? Would you not like to consider taking a credit card? You could use that for any large expenditure, and actually, a credit card is nearly as good as cash.

Bob Well, I'm a bit of a "cash man" myself and don't have a credit card and have never needed one. And anyway, there is always the problem of losing it or having it stolen. And then I'd have no access to cash at all. So cash seems like a much better option to me.

Julius Ah, you needn't worry about that. In case of loss or theft, you just notify us, and we will stop payment on the card at once. Then you won't have to bear any of the costs if the card is misused.

Bob But then I'm stuck somewhere in the middle of Australia, with no card at all!

Julius No, no, don't worry, we would arrange to get a replacement card to you within 24 hours.

Bob So, how much would all this cost me?

Julius Well, we have three different credit cards: classic, silver and gold. I think the classic card suits your purposes fine. It costs 35 euros per year.

Bob And what do you mean by "classic"?

Julius This card gives you access to about 2 million cashpoints throughout the world, and there are over 30 million shops and stores where the card is accepted. I don't think you need either of the other cards because they're designed for the frequent traveller. They cost more, but they have additional services such as health insurance, baggage insurance, accident cover and so on.

Bob Oh no, I don't need all that. I've taken out some travel insurance for the trip for both of us, so that's all sorted. So, what other costs are involved apart from the annual fee?

Julius Well, when you are in Australia, or in any other country outside Germany, you will be charged a small percentage – it's 1.5% – on all purchases that you make. And if you use it to withdraw cash, you will pay a further 1.95% on the amount of cash withdrawn.

Bob Oh, that's quite hefty. So I am better off using my normal debit card for cash, right?

Julius Yes, exactly.

Bob What about security? You hear all sorts of stories about identity theft these days. You know, your card gets used, you know nothing about it and suddenly you end up with a lot of purchases on your card that you never made. Are these cards really safe?

Julius Yes, they are. The cards have the latest so-called EMV technology. That's the most advanced technology, and so you can rest assured that all your transactions are completely secure, and that when you use it, you will not be giving away any information about yourself, and you won't be opening any doors to hackers and allowing them to get into your account either.

Bob Good, that sounds reassuring. Now, if I use the card to buy something, can I decide when to repay what I owe?

Julius No, that only applies to the so-called revolving credit cards. And there you have to watch out because you can pay about 20% interest on your debt. That's serious money! This is not the case with the classic card. Here your current account will be debited automatically once a month: there are no interest charges, no extra costs. And we will send you a monthly statement showing what you have bought. You can also check your statement online at any time, of course.

Bob I see. Well, that all sounds fine. So, what's the next step?

Julius Well, you can either take this application form with you, fill it in and send it back to me, or we can do it together now.

Bob Let's keep things simple and do it now.

Julius Fine. So, here we are … now, would you like a partner card for your wife? There is no extra cost involved.

Bob Oh, yes, definitely.

Julius OK, fine, I'll just tick that box as well …

Bob But I still want some foreign currency, too! Err, I think I'll order A$1,000. That should be a good compromise between relying solely on my credit card or solely on cash.

Julius Yes, sure, I'll get that organized, too …

1. What are Mr Hewitt's plans at the beginning of the dialogue?
2. How have they changed by the end of the dialogue?
3. Compare the advantages of having a credit card rather than carrying cash.
4. Explain the terms of repayment with Mr Hewitt's classic card.

GRAMMAR

Comparative and superlative forms

1. The weather there is much **warmer than** here.
2. The cards have the **latest** so-called EMV technology.
3. That's the **most advanced** technology.
4. And a credit card is **as good as** cash.
5. Cash seems like a much **better** option to me.

- Adjectives with one syllable and some words of two syllables form comparisons with *-er/-est*. (1, 2)
- Most adjectives with two syllables and all words of three or more syllables make comparisons with *more/most*. (3)
- The comparative form + *than* is used in comparisons. (1)
- As … as is used to show if two things are equal. (4)
- Some adjectives have irregular comparative and superlative forms (*good – better – best; bad – worse – worst*). (5)

4 Practice

Complete these sentences using a comparative or superlative.

1. Banking has become a lot … (competitive) than it was ten years ago.
2. As banks offer a far … (wide) range of products nowadays, advice has become … (important) than ever before.
3. It is not as … (easy) as it used to be to find the … (suitable) product.
4. Carrying around lots of cash is … (risky) than paying by credit card.
5. It is difficult to decide which card is the … (good) for you, but you shouldn't go for the … (cheap) just to save money.
6. If you travel a lot, it is … (sensible) to have a credit card that includes travel insurance.
7. The … (bad) thing that can happen is that your credit card is stolen and you have to wait 24 hours for a replacement.
8. Even if you are … (old) than 65, it still makes sense to apply for a credit card.

5 A problem with a credit card

A little while later Julius Frank receives an email from Bob Hewitt. Your manager has asked you to answer Mr Hewitt's email. She has made some notes which you should cover in your reply.

An: julius.frank@thebankforyou.de
Betrifft: my latest credit card statement
Von: bob.hewitt@newwebsite.de Anlage(n):

Dear Mr Frank

A couple of months ago I was at your branch to apply for a credit card which I received a week or so later.

Yesterday I checked my credit card statement and I saw that there were purchases on that statement I never made. I am extremely concerned particularly since you assured me that credit cards are safe.

Please could you look into this for me?

I look forward to hearing from you.

Yours sincerely

Bob Hewitt

Read the notes and write the reply.

1. Ist die Kreditkarte unterschrieben, ordentlich aufbewahrt und die PIN keinem Dritten mitgeteilt worden?
2. Hat der Kunde das Servicecenter sofort nach Entdeckung des Missbrauchs informiert, die Karte sperren lassen und die Polizei benachrichtigt?
3. Wenn diese Voraussetzungen erfüllt wurden, haftet die Bank für Verfügungen bis zur Sperranzeige.

6 Mediation

KMK

Einige Zeit später kommt Mr Hewitt in Ihre Bank, ist jedoch in Eile. Er hat die unten abgebildete Werbung der Commerzbank gefunden. Er möchte die Hintergründe zu der beworbenen Karte wissen. Er bittet Sie, ihm die Informationen per E-Mail zu schicken.

Schreiben Sie eine E-Mail an Mr Hewitt, in der Sie (a) die Produktdetails und (b) die Vorteile der CashCards in englischer Sprache zusammenfassen.

COMMERZBANK

CashCard

Mehr finanzieller Spielraum für Sie.

Es kommen immer wieder günstige Gelegenheiten, die man direkt nutzen möchte – doch reicht Ihr finanzieller Spielraum auf dem Girokonto dann dafür auch aus?
Wenn nicht, dann nutzen Sie doch einfach die Karte für alle Gelegenheiten: die CashCard[1]. Denn mit ihr erweitern Sie Ihren finanziellen Spielraum – schnell und unkompliziert. Sie bietet Ihnen in Form eines Rahmenkredits die Möglichkeit, alle günstigen Gelegenheiten zu nutzen, und Sie genießen die Freiheit, immer spontan „Ja" sagen zu können.
Sichern Sie sich Ihre CashCard jetzt einfach kostenlos!

Die Karte für alle Gelegenheiten

Produktdetails

- **Verfügungsrahmen:** von 1.500 bis 20.000 Euro.[2]
- **Zeitlich unbefristet:** Den Verfügungsrahmen können Sie jederzeit in Anspruch nehmen, unbefristet und ohne Bearbeitungsentgelt.
- **Jederzeit verfügbar:** Ihre neue CashCard ist eine Maestro Karte, mit der Sie direkt zahlen und Geld am Automaten abheben können – an den Geldautomaten der CashGroup[3] selbstverständlich kostenfrei.
- **Flexible Rückzahlung:** Die Rückzahlung beträgt monatlich lediglich 3 % der höchsten Inanspruchnahme, mindestens jedoch 18 Euro pro Monat. Sondertilgungen sind jederzeit und ohne Zusatzkosten möglich – komplett oder in Teilen.

Ihre Vorteile

- **Günstig:** Die CashCard selbst ist grundsätzlich kostenlos, denn es fällt keine Kartengebühr an. Sie zahlen nur Zinsen für den Betrag, den Sie tatsächlich in Anspruch nehmen.
- **Sicherheit:** Auf Wunsch mit Versicherungspaket, das u. a. für den Fall von Arbeitslosigkeit absichern kann. Darüber hinaus sind z. B. Ihre Einkäufe mit der CashCard gegen Raub, Einbruch-Diebstahl oder Beschädigung geschützt. Bei Bestellungen im Internet kann der Internetschutzbrief die Zahlung des Einkaufspreises übernehmen, wenn ein bestellter Gegenstand gar nicht oder der falsche Gegenstand geliefert wird. Details dazu finden Sie in den Versicherungsbedingungen, die Sie bei Ihrem Berater erhalten.
- **Mehr Spielraum:** Mit der CashCard haben Sie mehr finanziellen Spielraum – für günstige Gelegenheiten und unerwarteten Finanzbedarf.

Bei weiteren Fragen stehen wir Ihnen gerne zur Verfügung:
Um Wartezeiten zu vermeiden, vereinbaren Sie bitte einen Termin.

Jeden Tag 24h für Sie da:
069 98 66 09 66

Terminvereinbarung:
www.commerzbanking.de/termin

E-Mail:
www.commerzbanking.de/email

1 Vertragspartner ist die Commerz Finanz GmbH.
2 Abhängig von Ihren persönlichen Vorstellungen und Möglichkeiten.
3 Zur CashGroup gehören Commerzbank, Deutsche Bank, HypoVereinsbank, Postbank sowie deren Tochterunternehmen.
Stand: Juli 2013

0000/00/00 VB000000 PC-PK M

7 Role-play

KMK

Führen Sie mithilfe der Rollenkarten ein Beratungsgespräch.

Bankmitarbeiter/in: Sie beraten den Kunden / die Kundin über die neue Kreditkarte.

Kunde/Kundin: Sie sind ein/e englischsprachige/r Kunde/Kundin und haben von einer neuen Kreditkarte gehört, an der Sie sehr interessiert sind. Deswegen haben Sie einen Termin bei Ihrer Bank vereinbart, den Sie heute wahrnehmen.

Bankmitarbeiter/in

Begrüßen Sie den Kunden / die Kundin, stellen Sie sich vor und fragen Sie nach dem Anliegen.

Kunde/Kundin

Erwidern Sie die Begrüßung und stellen Sie sich vor. Sagen Sie, dass Sie über Weihnachten nach Australien fahren möchten. Sie haben von der neuen MasterCardFlexKredit gehört und möchten mehr darüber erfahren.

Sie stellen die Flexibilität der MasterCard-FlexKredit vor, mit der eine flexible Ratenzahlung der monatlichen Abrechnung von 2 % bis 50 % möglich ist. Der Mindestbetrag liegt jedoch bei 50,00 € monatlich.

Fragen Sie, ob Sie auch jederzeit eine Komplettrückzahlung zum nächsten Abrechnungstag vornehmen können.

Sagen Sie, dass dies möglich ist und dann auch keine Zinsen auf den noch ausstehenden Betrag erhoben werden.

Bedauern Sie, dass Sie leider nicht jedes Mal in die Bankfiliale kommen können, um eine Änderung der Ratenzahlung vorzunehmen.

Antworten Sie, dass Änderungen der Ratenzahlungen jederzeit telefonisch oder im Internet unter www.spare.de im Spare-Onlinebanking unter der Rubrik Service/Aufträge möglich sind.

Fragen Sie, ob Sie Kündigungsfristen für eine Beendigung des FlexKredites einhalten müssen.

Verneinen Sie diese Frage, denn der FlexKredit kann jeweils zum nächsten Abrechnungstag per Telefon, im Internet oder in der Filiale beendet werden. Voraussetzung dafür ist natürlich eine 100%ige Rückzahlung.

Äußern Sie die Vermutung, dass für diese Leistung Gebühren zu zahlen sind. Fragen Sie, wie hoch diese Gebühren sein mögen.

Versichern Sie, dass für diese Leistungen keine Gebühren anfallen. Man muss lediglich die jährliche Kreditkartengebühr von 40 € zahlen.

Sie haben auch von sehr sicher geltenden Reiseschecks gehört und möchten welche mitnehmen.

Bedauern Sie, dem Kunden / der Kundin sagen zu müssen, dass Sie keine Reiseschecks verkaufen. Weisen Sie noch auf zwei Vorteile der Kreditkarte hin.

Beantragen Sie eine Kreditkarte und verabschieden Sie sich.

Bedanken Sie sich für den Auftrag und verabschieden Sie sich.

CULTURE

Revolving credit cards

The US standard credit card allows you to have a balance up to a certain agreed credit limit. This means that this amount of credit is always available to you. Your credit card issuer gives you the credit limit (also called the overdraft facility), based on various factors such as your creditworthiness, your credit history, your ability to repay, your income and the type of credit card itself.

Some of the credit is used up when you make a purchase, but as soon as you have paid off the amount for that purchase (i.e. paid the balance), you have access to your maximum line of credit again. If you only pay part of the balance, then the unpaid amount is subtracted from your total credit limit.

However, this type of credit card has a minimum payment that must be made by a certain due date every month to avoid late-payment penalties. Interest on the remaining debt is always high (it can be as much as 25%).

If you carry your balance (= your debt) over from one month to the next, banks call this "revolving your debt".

8 Explaining a revolving credit card

An English-speaking customer comes into your bank and asks you to explain this flyer that your bank has recently sent him.

A **Read the bank's advertisement and explain the flyer to him.**

B **With a partner, list what you think are the main advantages and disadvantages of a revolving credit card.**

Unser neues Angebot für Sie!

» Mit der extra für Sie eingerichteten Teilzahlungsfunktion können Sie Ihre Kreditrechnung in mehreren Teilbeträgen begleichen. Der monatliche Betrag liegt ganz bei Ihnen.

» Dadurch bieten wir Ihnen einen finanziellen Spielraum, den Sie nach Ihren Wünschen gestalten. Sie entscheiden, ob 5 %, 10 %, 25 % oder 50 % des Rechnungsbetrages im Monat angemessen sind (mindestens 30 Euro). Natürlich können Sie jederzeit die Höhe Ihrer Rückzahlung ändern, Sonderzahlungen vornehmen oder den gesamten Betrag mit einer Zahlung begleichen.

» Für den von Ihnen in Anspruch genommenen Kredit berechnen wir Zinsen. Der aktuelle Zinssatz beträgt zurzeit lediglich 15,68 % p.a.

» Sie erhalten selbstverständlich monatlich von uns eine Kontoübersicht mit allen Details Ihrer Teilzahlungsfunktion. Bei uns sind Sie immer umfassend informiert.

9 Working with words

1 The bank can *receive/decline/accept* a charge if it's over the limit.
2 A *billing/invoicing/adding* cycle shows a customer's ongoing charges within a certain time frame.
3 My bank *issues/insures/gets* Mastercard, not VISA.
4 Charges are *asked/applied/offered* when a customer pays a bill late.
5 Standard German credit cards are *debited/tied/charged* to a customer's bank account.
6 The amounts charged to a standard German credit card are *added/debited/declined* once a month.
7 It is usual for *creditworthy/standard/applied* customers to receive premium cards with extra benefits.
8 Your *balance/debt/overdraft facility* is based on your creditworthiness.

10 Holly's story

'I'm from California and I studied there, too. I finished college two years ago. What I enjoyed most was that I was able to walk away with a degree in economics and modern languages … what I regret most is getting a credit card, racking it up and getting another credit card and doing the same thing. And it's not as if I went over the top and bought lots of luxury stuff – I went out with friends, went on vacations, did some shopping, yes, true, I bought a few nice clothes but I only wanted to keep up with everyone else – that's normal, isn't it? And I thought, these few debts, no problem, I can deal with that later when I have a job.

So when I graduated I had just over $8,000 of high-interest debt. Today, I have quite a good job in an office but paying off that debt is a real killer: it's taking 20% of my take-home salary. On top of that I've got to pay for the rent on my small flat, health insurance, smart office clothes, groceries, tax, gas …

There is very little left for ME! I have learnt the hard way that if you live like a professional in college, you live like a student when you get out.'

A Explain these expressions.

1 racking it up
2 went over the top
3 stuff
4 to keep up with everyone
5 deal with that
6 a real killer

B Explain Holly's last sentence.

C Nearly 83% of American college students have at least one credit card and 21% graduate with $7,000 debt. Do you think German students face the same problem? Why/Why not? Give reasons.

D Imagine you have a credit card debt of €10,000 and every month you just make the minimum required payment of €142. Assuming the interest rate on the outstanding balance is 17%, when will you have paid off your debt and how much interest will you have paid altogether?

11 Preventing credit card debt

Your department head is concerned about the increasing problem of credit card debt with customers at your bank. She has found this article on the internet.

Ten top tips to avoid credit card debt

1. Borrowing on a credit card can give you a bit of extra flexibility – but try and pay back the debt in full each month.
2. Have an emergency fund. Use it instead of borrowing on a second or third credit card. And once you've used it, top it up again before you put more expenditure on your card.
3. Avoid balance transfers. If you transfer your debt to another card, you must have a very good reason for doing this, such as a much better interest rate. Otherwise, don't do it. It is the first step on the slippery slope.
4. Weigh up introductory offers on new cards. Don't be tricked. Banks often tempt you with offers that only last for a few months – the most common is to pay 0% interest on things you buy or balance transfers. Make sure you pay off the card before your introductory period ends.
5. Read the small print and check the fees. Make sure you know what you'll be charged for late payments, exceeding your credit limit, and returned payments. There are often all sorts of "nasties" built in there.
6. Don't use credit to "afford" things you can't afford. Do you really need what you are about to buy? Do a reality check: ask yourself "Can I afford my current lifestyle?"
7. Have a plan to pay off your credit card debt. Remember the old saying: "Failing to plan is planning to fail".
8. Never lend your credit card to anyone, not even to your best friend. Even if he or she promises to repay you, it is your door the bank will be knocking on when you default.
9. Don't go for cash advances on your credit card. These can be very expensive.
10. Make a budget and stick to it.

A Read the article and explain the following expressions.

1 an emergency fund (tip 2)
2 to top it up (tip 2)
3 the slippery slope (tip 3)
4 to weigh up (tip 4)
5 returned payments (tip 5)
6 all sorts of "nasties" (tip 5)
7 to "afford" things (tip 6)
8 reality check (tip 6)
9 to knock on someone's door (tip 8)
10 to default (tip 8)

B With a partner, discuss whether you both agree with the ten tips. Are there any others you would give?

C Prepare an English brochure for your bank using your tips and/or the ones in the article above.

12 Contactless credit cards

A customer who wants to travel to Britain in the summer brings this screenshot to your branch and asks you for advice regarding contactless payments.

A **With a partner, collect the relevant information you need from the flyer and, using your own words, prepare a dialogue between you and the customer.**

B **Present the dialogue in class.**

How to use Easypaycard contactless

Look out for this symbol – it's everywhere …

Do you want to make a quick and easy payment? Then this is your symbol. And there are thousands of such symbols in thousands of shops around Britain. Now you can go shopping with no cash and no PINs …

How do I pay contactless?

All you have to do is hold your card in front of the card reader. The card is read, a green light confirms the payment and off you go! No messing about looking for notes, finding coins, keying in PINs – that's history, this is the future.

But is it safe?

We use the most advanced technology to protect you and your card. If you lose the card or it gets stolen, we give you 100% protection against fraud. You just contact us and we'll do the rest. It's safer than cash!

How much can I spend?

Contactless is for small payments, so you can use the card for anything up to £20. And, of course, as often as you like!

How can I keep track of my purchases?

We will mark all your statements with a contactless symbol – so you can always keep an eye on what you have bought. Easy!

Interested?

Then just get in touch with us today on www.easypaycard.co.uk – your new card is waiting for you!

13 Mediation

Ein Kunde auf Reise durch Großbritannien kommt zu Ihnen in die Bank. Er hat beim Einkaufen das unten abgebildete Werbematerial überreicht bekommen und möchte von Ihnen wissen, um was genau es sich bei diesem Angebot handelt.

Übertragen Sie für den Kunden die wesentlichen Inhalte der folgenden Werbung ins Deutsche und erklären Sie die Vor- und Nachteile.

Balance transfer with a Creditbuy credit card

Are you paying too much interest?

Do you want to save money?

How about paying no interest for 36 months?

If your answer to any of these questions is **YES**, you should read on ...

With a Creditbuy credit card ...

- ✔ you pay 0% interest on all balance transfers for the first 36 months
- ✔ you can transfer your balances from all your credit cards to us
- ✔ there is a small, one-off balance transfer fee of 2.95%
- ✔ you earn points whenever you use your card

Representative example	Interest rate on purchases	Assumed credit limit
18.75% APR (variable)	18.75% (variable)	£1,500

Balance transfer explained

This simply means that you can transfer your balance or debt from one credit card to another.

The benefits explained

- ✔ If you are paying high interest rates on your current credit card, you can save money by transferring the debt to us.
- ✔ If you pay off your debt within the 36-month period, you pay 0% interest.
- ✔ If you are paying 0% interest, you will be able to pay off your existing debt much more quickly.
- ✔ If you have several credit cards and transfer all the debts to us, you will gain a much better overview of your financial situation.

Balance transfer in action

Let's take an example: you have a debt of £1,000 on your current credit card and you are paying 17.95% interest.

- ✔ You transfer this debt to your Creditbuy credit card and your payments on your old credit card stop immediately because that card is now debt-free. We debit your new card with the transfer charge of £29.50 (2.95%).
- ✔ Future repayments you make on your Creditbuy credit card all go towards paying off your debt because you are now paying zero interest.
- ✔ You will be able to clear the balance much more quickly and you have 36 months to do so.

Credit card market faces inquiry into aggressive marketing

Financial Conduct Authority to study fairness and transparency of £150bn-a-year market affecting 30m UK cardholders.

The City regulator is to investigate whether credit cards are being marketed too aggressively, amid concerns that plastic payment is allowing consumers to run up debts they cannot afford.

At £150bn a year, the UK credit card market is the largest in Europe, with 30 million people holding cards with total debts of £60bn.

The Financial Conduct Authority (FCA) said it would launch an investigation into the market when it took over regulation of the sector in April.

On Tuesday it revealed the full scope of its inquiry. It will look at the complexity of credit cards, the fairness and transparency of their terms and conditions, and whether consumers can easily switch between different credit card providers.

The regulator will also inquire into whether the cards are marketed "in a way that works against the best interests of consumers".

In April, its research showed that many consumers tried to resist the lure of credit cards "but were eventually worn down by continual marketing", especially when companies sent them targeted mailing shots pre-approving them for cards.

The market study will look at all issues around unaffordable lending and whether consumers are borrowing too much on their cards and making repayments too slowly.

The FCA has previously flagged up its concern that consumers may be getting "payday loans with plastic" in the form of cards with low credit limits and high interest rates.

"The credit card market is well established and hugely important for UK consumers, who hold around 70 % of all credit cards in Europe," said Christopher Woolard, FCA director of policy, risk and research. "We want to make sure that the market works well for all consumers and that cardholders get a fair deal."

The FCA will officially begin the in-depth market study in January with the results expected to be published at the end of 2015.

Mike O'Connor, chief executive of the Step Change debt charity, welcomed the announcement. "Too many people are using credit as a safety net when all too often it is a trap which leads to problem debt. Credit card debt is one of the most common debt problems we see. Many people are struggling with multiple debts, high balances and interest rates."

Around half a million people contact Step Change each year for advice about their debts. On average, they have £9,047 of credit card debt and 10% have five or more credit cards. "People will always need to borrow to cope with the ups and downs of income and the costs they face, but we need to ensure that the credit market is operating in the best interest of consumers and with good levels of protection, especially for vulnerable people," said O'Connor.

The UK Cards Association, which represents the industry, said it would study the FCA's observation carefully. "The industry has a long-standing commitment to responsible lending and transparency and over the last five years has introduced many changes including on credit limits and repricing of debt, improved transparency, and forbearance for those who find themselves missing repayments," said Richard Koch, head of policy at the trade body.

14 Checking you have understood the text

A **Outline the main aims of the inquiry.**

B **Explain why, in the end, many consumers decide to have a credit card after all.**

15 Discussion and group work

In a small group, discuss whether consumers in Germany should have greater access to the flexible kind of credit card that is readily available in Britain.

UNIT 6

Savings and investments

- Selling savings products
- Giving investment advice
- Talking about stock markets

1 Warm-up

Here are some more quotes from Warren Buffett.

> Risk comes from not knowing what you are doing.

> I try to buy stock in businesses that are so wonderful that an idiot can run them. Because sooner or later one will.

> Price is what you pay. Value is what you get.

> Rule No. 1: Never lose money. Rule No. 2: Never forget Rule No. 1.

A **What can we learn from each of these quotes?**

B **How would you sum up Warren Buffett's investment strategy?**

CULTURE

Saving in Germany and in the UK

While German building societies offer only building society policies, UK building societies compete with banks and sell the same products: current and savings accounts, overdrafts and loans, investments, etc. Many British people use a building society for everyday saving. The UK government encourages people to save in the form of Isas = Individual Savings Accounts. Savings in an Isa (pronounced "eye-sa") are tax free.

In Germany the state encourages savers with the *Arbeitgeber-Sparzulage* for *vermögenswirksame Leistungen*. The *Arbeitgeber-Sparzulage* can be explained as a state subsidy that employers make towards certain asset-building savings or investments (= *vermögenswirksame Leistungen*) of their employees, such as building society policies, life assurance policies, savings plans or investments in funds.

2 Savings accounts

VIDEO 4

Some of your bank's customers have savings accounts in the UK.

Watch the video "How to choose a savings account" to see if British savings accounts are different from the ones your bank offers.

A The expressions on the left below are used in the video. Link them with one with a similar meaning on the right.

1	to give notice	**a**	sums saved in a savings account
2	rainy day money	**b**	to lock money away
3	deposits	**c**	to get at your money
4	to access your money	**d**	a fixed rate
5	a set rate	**e**	money saved for future spending
6	to tie money up	**f**	to inform the bank in advance

How would you say them in German?

B Say why customers need help when choosing a savings account.

C Now watch the video again and take notes using this chart.

Type of account	What is it for?	Advantages	Disadvantages
An Easy Access Account	*money you want to get at any time*	…	…
A Regular Saver	…	…	…
A Fixed-Rate Account / Bond	…	…	…
A Notice Account	…		

D What are these four savings products called in German? Point out any differences between the UK ones and those offered by your bank.

E Towards the end of the video the speaker gives some advice. Explain the points he makes. Which of them would you tell a customer at your bank?

3 Saving in Britain

KMK

Sie haben den folgenden Artikel gefunden und möchten nun seinen Inhalt für einen Beitrag zum Thema „Sparverhalten in Europa“ in der hauseigenen Zeitschrift Ihrer Bank verwenden.

Fassen Sie dafür auf Deutsch die wesentlichen Punkte zusammen.

Women open more savings accounts but men deposit more cash

Women open more savings accounts than men – but the value of men's savings is far greater, according to a new research note by Halifax.

Last month, women opened the majority of savings products, opening 57% of all new Fixed Term accounts, 53% of Instant Access accounts and 55% of tax-free Isas.

However, despite opening fewer accounts, men tended to open their accounts with larger balances. The average balance for variable rate products opened by men was £8,936, compared to £7,664 for women – a difference of 17%. For fixed rate accounts, though, male customers had an opening balance of £7,516, only 1% higher than that of female savers (£7,426).

Cash saving is not the only area of financial planning in which women fail to equal their male counterparts. A survey of 1,600 adults by Prudential found that women are less likely to save for their retirement than men. Four in ten women say that they do not have a pension, compared to three in ten men.

They also save less in pensions, with women who belong to defined contribution schemes contributing only £90 a month, compared with men's £170, while women with private pensions pay in around £185 a month compared with the £330 contributed by men.

But the savings inequality may simply be due to earnings inequalities, as women continue to earn less than men on average. The Office of National Statistics' 2011 Annual Survey of Hours and Earnings (ASHE) showed that median gross annual earnings for men were £28,400, whereas for full-time women they were £22,900 – a difference of 24%.

www.telegraph.co.uk

4 Working with words

Choose one of these pairs of words to complete the sentences.

safe / save
1 It is important to … a part of your salary every month.
2 Your money will be … if you … it in a bank account.
3 Customers can … tax on their interest income.

raise / rise
4 The European Central Bank is expected to … interest rates soon.
5 If interest rates …, saving becomes more attractive.
6 Employees will want their employers to … their salaries if prices … any higher.

advice / advise
7 We can … you how to invest your money.
8 If you follow our …, you will receive a guaranteed interest income.

economic / economical
9 The … climate is not as good as it was ten years ago.
10 It is not … to keep large sums in a current account.

LANGUAGE

Giving advice

Three useful verbs for giving advice are *advise, recommend* and *suggest.*
Use *advise* and *recommend* with a gerund (*-ing* form) or with an object + infinitive:

I'd	advise	investing in a fund.
	recommend	you to invest in a fund.

Use *suggest* with a gerund:
I'd suggest investing in a fund.

You can also say:
You would be well advised to invest in a fund.
In your case, it would be advisable to invest in a fund.

5 Role-play: selling savings products

KMK

Working with a partner, use these role cards to play the role of the adviser and the customer in the bank. If you are the adviser, use expressions from the box above.

Bankmitarbeiter/in: Sie haben einen Gesprächstermin mit einem englischsprachigen Kunden, Sam Sheppard, um für ihn eine geeignete Sparanlage zu finden. Der Kunde hat bereits ein Girokonto bei Ihrem Institut.

Kunde: Sie sind Sam Sheppard, 25, aus Bristol, England, wo Sie Informatik studiert haben. Vor Kurzem haben Sie eine Arbeitsstelle bei SAP in Deutschland angetreten. Sie haben jetzt einen Termin bei Ihrem Kreditinstitut.

Bankmitarbeiter/in

- Begrüßen Sie den Kunden und stellen Sie sich vor.
- Informieren Sie sich nach etwas „Small talk" über das Anliegen des Kunden.
- Erkundigen Sie sich, wie viel und für wie lange gespart werden soll, ob regelmäßig oder nicht und mit welchem Ziel.
- Bieten Sie zwei geeignete Sparprodukte Ihres Instituts an. Weisen Sie auf deren Vorteile hin.
- Beantworten Sie alle Fragen zu den Produkten.
- Erklären Sie, warum Ihr Gesprächspartner von der Arbeitgeber-Sparzulage für vermögenswirksame Leistungen profitieren würde. Beantworten Sie Fragen diesbezüglich.
- Überreichen Sie zwei Prospekte zu den von Ihnen vorgestellten Sparprodukten.
- Vereinbaren Sie einen weiteren Gesprächstermin und verabschieden Sie sich.

Kunde

- Stellen Sie sich vor.
- Sagen Sie, dass Sie vorhaben, für mindestens fünf Jahre in Deutschland zu arbeiten, und für diese Zeit geeignete Sparmöglichkeiten suchen.
- Beantworten Sie alle Fragen: Sie möchten monatlich sparen, zurzeit 200 €, später mehr, mit dem Ziel, sich jedes Jahr eine Fernreise leisten zu können. Außerdem haben Sie Ihr Auto für 10.000 € verkauft und möchten diese Summe als „Notgroschen" bereithalten.
- Stellen Sie Fragen zu den zwei Sparprodukten, die Ihnen angeboten werden: z.B. Risiko, Verfügbarkeit des Geldes, Zinssätze.
- Fragen Sie, ob es in Deutschland eine Sparförderung wie „Isas" gibt.
- Lassen Sie sich die Arbeitgeber-Sparzulage erklären. Fragen Sie, welche Zahlungen als vermögenswirksame Leistungen gelten.
- Bitten Sie um Bedenkzeit, bevor Sie eine Entscheidung treffen.
- Stimmen Sie einem weiteren Gesprächstermin zu. Verabschieden Sie sich.

6 Shares

Shortly after your meeting with Sam Sheppard, you receive this email with the following article as an attachment.

From: s.sheppard@mailissimo.co.uk
Subject: Apple shares

Morning!

Have come across this article online. Am thinking of putting my €10,000 into Apple shares. Sounds like a great investment! Would appreciate your advice asap.

Best

Sam Sheppard

von meinem iPhone gesendet

PDF

10/30/2014

Apple Inc. Stocks Hit New Highs

Increasing demand for Apple products on the Chinese market led analysts to raise the price target for Apple stocks from $115 to $125 yesterday. As a result, Apple leapt sharply in trading on NASDAQ, closing at a record high of $111.25. After opening today at $111.81, Apple stocks fluctuated slightly at first but are now trading at $113.07 for a gain of 1.64%. If that rise holds, Apple looks set to reach another all-time high today.

Analysts described the outlook for Apple in China as very positive. China is the source of over 15% of Apple's revenue, where the iPhone is the preferred cell phone with the highest retention rate. Figures indicate that the Chinese actually like the larger 6 Plus phone, which means higher earnings for Apple.

With Christmas round the corner, what could go wrong? Apple's current high comes amid predictions that sales of the latest iPad in the first quarter of next year may fall far below expectations.

A In a small group, discuss these questions and note your group's ideas.

1. What positive and what negative information about Apple shares (AE: stocks) can be found in the article?
2. What general information does a first-time investor like Sam need about the risks of buying shares?
3. Why do you think investors should be particularly careful when investing in US companies?

B Write an email to Sam with your findings.
Important: DO NOT tell him what to do! Give him all the facts to make his own decision. Suggest an appointment with your colleague, Lisa Meinke, an adviser in the securities department.

7 Funds

12

Sam Sheppard's next appointment is with investment adviser Lisa Meinke in the securities department. You are present at the meeting.

A Lisa mentions seven advantages of a fund. Listen and note at least four.

Lisa Good morning, Mr Sheppard. Pleased to meet you, I'm Lisa Meinke.
Sam Morning. Pleased to meet you too.
Lisa Do take a seat. You've already met my colleague …
Sam Yes, I have. Nice to see you again.
Lisa I understand from what you told me on the phone that you're planning to invest regularly on a medium to long-term basis now.
Sam That's right. My contract with SAP has been changed into a permanent one with promotion and a rise in salary as well, so it looks like I'll be staying here for a while.
Lisa Congratulations!
Sam Thanks, and I'd like to thank your colleague for stopping me from making an investment in shares that could have been quite a disaster!
Lisa Well, shares are not necessarily a bad investment. In fact, over the years, shares have yielded far higher returns than bonds or real estate …
Sam That may be, but how can I know which shares to buy and when to sell them?
Lisa Well, have you considered investing in a fund instead?
Sam I've heard of funds but I don't know what they do. Will a fund buy shares for me?
Lisa Basically yes, but you won't hold the actual shares. The fund managers pool your capital with that of other investors, so you hold a number of units that represent your part of the cake, so to speak. That has a lot of advantages for you …
Sam You mean the managers will do the work for me?
Lisa Exactly. They have specialist knowledge, experience and access to information that you don't have. They take the decisions and trade on your behalf.
Sam And is this service included in the price?
Lisa I'm afraid not. There is usually an initial charge of between two and five per cent, plus a management fee of one to two per cent a year.
Sam What about the money the fund makes? Will it be paid out?
Lisa With most funds the profits are automatically reinvested in new units, so your investment grows and you don't have to bother about it.
Sam Hmm. Do I have to invest regularly or can I pay in lump sums if I like?
Lisa You can pay money in whenever you like, but funds are ideal for investing on a regular basis. The more you save, the more units you'll have.
Sam I see. But I suppose these units go up and down in price like shares do?
Lisa Yes, but the fluctuations aren't so great because of the different investments in the fund. A fund aims to spread the risk over a large number of securities but to obtain a good yield at the same time. If you wanted to do that on your own, you'd need a huge amount of capital to build up such a diversified portfolio.
Sam Will €250 a month be enough then?
Lisa Certainly. You can invest in funds with as little as €50 a month. Of course, if you need the money at any time, you can return your units to the fund, though I'd advise you to see a fund as a longer-term investment.
Sam Sounds good, but the only problem is, I'm not particularly keen on shares any more.
Lisa There's a wide range of funds to choose from. Some invest in bonds, in real estate, in a particular sector, like energy, or in a region, like the emerging markets. Or you can invest in a fund of funds to spread the risk even further. I've printed out a selection of funds which have good prospects for growth …

B **Listen again or read the dialogue and find the other advantages of a fund.**

C **Find expressions in the dialogue which mean the following:**

1 Erträge
2 Agio
3 Verwaltungsgebühr
4 Schwankungen
5 breit gestreutes Depot
6 Schwellenländer
7 Dachfonds
8 Wachstumsaussichten

GRAMMAR

Adjectives and adverbs

1 You're planning to invest **regularly** on a medium to long-term basis now.
2 The profits are **automatically** reinvested in new units.
3 I'm not **particularly** keen on shares any more.
4 Funds are ideal for investing on a **regular** basis.
5 That sounds **good**.

- Adverbs describe verbs (1, 2) or adjectives (3).
- Adjectives describe nouns (4) or pronouns.
- The verbs *be, look, sound* (5) and *seem* are followed by an adjective.
- Adverbs are formed by adding *-ly* (1, 3) or *-ally* (2), but there are exceptions:

Many customers speak good English.	They speak English **well**.
Jane is a hard worker.	She works **hard**. (hardly = *kaum*)
I was late for work.	I arrived **late**. (lately = *neulich*)
My colleague is friendly.	She behaves **in a friendly way**.

8 Practice

A **Use adjectives or adverbs in these sentences.**

1 Many people cannot … (easy) understand financial news.
2 A fund is … (ideal) for investing small sums … (regular).
3 Most funds pay profits … (annual) and reinvest them … (automatic).
4 Technology shares performed … (good), but the forecast is … (poor).
5 The new CEO speaks … (fluent) Spanish, and his Russian seems … (excellent) too.
6 In emerging markets share prices can rise … (fast) but fall just as … (rapid).
7 Units of new energy funds have risen … (steep) in price because of the … (strong) demand for eco-friendly investments.
8 The company's sales figures were announced too … (late) for the European markets, but Wall Street reacted … (immediate), and the shares plunged … (dramatic).

B **Rewrite the following sentences using adverbs instead of adjectives.**

Example: It is hard to make the correct decision. (to decide)
It is hard to decide correctly.

1 The company had a good performance in the first quarter. (to perform)
2 Energy prices saw a sharp rise. (to rise)
3 The was a drastic fall in the demand for cars. (to fall)
4 There will be an abrupt decline in the yields on bonds. (to decline)
5 Growth in the automobile sector is slow. (to grow)
6 That fund of funds has very active managers. (to be managed)

9 Selling a fund

After talking to Lisa Meinke, Sam Sheppard is interested in investing in a fund. Lisa is going on maternity leave, so she asks you and a colleague to advise Sam at his next appointment.

A **With a partner, choose a fund on offer at one of your banks. Divide up the following aspects so that you have equal parts to present. Then prepare the presentation. Use expressions from the box below.**

- the type of assets in the fund
- the aim of the fund
- the fund's past performance
- the opportunities the fund offers
- the risks involved
- the costs

B **Present the fund to your fellow students. Answer any questions they may have.**

LANGUAGE

Describing trends

Verbs to describe a rise / an upturn: climb – increase – leap* – jump* – rise – soar*
Verbs to describe a fall / a downturn: decline – decrease – drop – slump – plunge*
* Use these verbs if the rise or fall is dramatic.

Adverbs to describe trends more precisely:

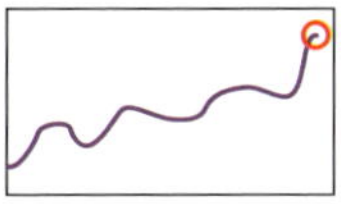
all-time high

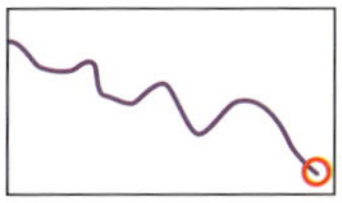
record low

rise/fall	gradually slightly steadily
rise/fall	abruptly rapidly sharply

If prices frequently rise and fall:	be volatile – fluctuate – vary
If prices fall and then rise again:	rally – rebound – recover
If prices do not change:	remain constant/stable/unchanged

10 Talking about the markets

A **Complete these sentences about stock market fluctuations with a suitable verb in the correct tense. Use the box above.**

1. The gold price … ↓ for the last quarter.
2. Yesterday the DAX … ↑ by 101 points within an hour.
3. Technology share prices … ∿ since the markets opened this morning.
4. When the latest sales figures were announced, Siemens shares … ↓.
5. It is expected that bonds … ∿ in the coming months.
6. The Nikkei … ↑ over the past weeks.
7. Commodity prices … → at the moment.
8. Analysts predict that BASF shares … ↗ soon, following their recent fall.

B **Write the sentences above adding an adverb to each one to describe the developments more exactly.**

11 Share volatility

A **Was Sam Sheppard well advised not to buy Apple shares? Answer this question by going online to see how Apple shares have performed since the end of 2014. Use expressions from the last box to describe their performance.**

B **Print out the chart of shares of the German company SAP for the same period. Describe their performance. Compare it with that of the Apple shares.**

12 Tax on investment earnings

Sam Sheppard wants to find out about tax on investment earnings (= *Abgeltungssteuer*). Your colleague, Hans Meister, does not speak English and asks you for help.

Mediate in the discussion between Hans Meister and Sam Sheppard.

Sam Sheppard	You	Hans Meister
How much is the tax-free allowance for savers in Germany?	… 1	Momentan 801 Euro pro Person, wenn Sie einen Freistellungsauftrag bei uns stellen*.
And if I earn more than 801 euros?	… 2	
	… 3	Auf Einkünfte aus Geldanlagen, die diesen Betrag übersteigen, müssen Sie Abgeltungssteuer zahlen.
What sorts of investment are affected?	… 4	
	… 5	Das sind alle Gewinne aus Aktien, Fonds, Zertifikaten, Dividenden und Zinsen.
Even the interest on my savings account?	… 6	
	… 7	Ja, Zinsen aller Art werden besteuert, z.B. aus Sparbüchern, Termingeldern, Anleihen oder Bausparverträgen.
But what about my private pension plan?	… 8	
	… 9	Formen der Altersvorsorge wie Gold, selbstbewohnte Immobilien und Lebensversicherungen unterliegen nicht der Abgeltungssteuer.
How much is this investment tax?	… 10	
	… 11	25 % plus Solidaritätszuschlag und Kirchensteuer, also insgesamt rund 28 %. Sie wird direkt von der Bank abgezogen und an das Finanzamt weitergereicht.
Thank you.	… 12	

Abgeltungssteuer: Stand 2015

* *einen Freistellungsantrag stellen* = to make an application for tax exemption

13 Bonds

Both national and local governments and companies issue bonds to raise capital.

A This table shows an issue of German government bonds. Use it to give a customer the figures for the points listed below.

Zins	Laufzeit	Zinstermin	05.12. 18:55	05.12. Rendite
1,5	Bund v. 13/23	15.05.	107,61	0,5566

Frankfurter Allgemeine Zeitung, 6. Dezember 2014

- the coupon
- the current price
- the issue date
- the maturity date
- the term
- the yield

B Explain why the yield on the bonds in the table is lower than the coupon.

C The customer is also interested in these corporate bonds issued by the insurance group Talanx. Compare them with the government bonds shown above. Explain any differences.

Zins	Laufzeit	Zinstermin	05.15. 18:55	05.15. Rendite
3,125	Talanx 13/23	13.02	113,35	1,3871

Frankfurter Allgemeine Zeitung, 6. Dezember 2014

D Shares in Talanx are traded on the stock exchange. Using Talanx as an example, point out the advantages and disadvantages of investing in a company's bonds rather than in its shares.

14 Working with words

Form nouns from the words in this box. Then use the nouns to complete the text.

consult • decide • fluctuate • grow • intend • invest • mature • provide • recommend • retire • select • solve • suggest • yield

As state pensions in future will be lower than they are today, it is important for young people to make …[1] for the future, even if …[2] seems a long way off. There is, however, such a huge …[3] of securities on the market that it is hard for the inexperienced …[4] to make the right …[5] on which ones to buy. The best …[6] to this problem is to make an appointment for a …[7] in the securities department at the bank.

Before an adviser can make a suitable …[8], it is important to find out what the customer's …[9] is. Some customers are willing to tolerate a high degree of risk in order to obtain the greatest possible …[10]; in this case the adviser may suggest a share fund with good prospects for …[11] in the long term. Other customers are more cautious; in their case a bond fund containing bonds with different coupons and …[12] dates would be less volatile with less …[13] in its prices. An alternative …[14] could be a fund of funds which would combine the advantages of both investment strategies.

15 Mediation

Ihr Kunde Sam Sheppard hat Sie gebeten, ihn über neue Anlagemöglichkeiten in Apple auf dem Laufenden zu halten. Sie sind auf den folgenden Zeitungsartikel gestoßen.

Schreiben Sie Sam eine Mail, in der Sie die Hauptaussagen des Textes auf Englisch kurz wiedergeben.

iBonds

Erstmals hat in der vergangenen Woche der amerikanische Technologiekonzern Apple Unternehmensanleihen in Euro aufgelegt. Die Zinsen, die Apple dafür zahlen muss, sind ungewöhnlich niedrig. Die Anleihen mit einer Laufzeit von acht Jahren werden jährlich mit einem Prozent verzinst, die zwölfjährigen mit 1,6%. Nach Angaben des Finanzdaten-Anbieters Dealogic waren das die niedrigsten Zinsen, die jemals ein amerikanisches Unternehmen für Euro-Anleihen mit diesen Laufzeiten gezahlt hat. Wie ist das zu erklären?

Offenbar nutzt Apple vor allem das niedrige Zinsniveau in Europa aus. In Amerika, wo im kommenden Jahr eine Erhöhung der Leitzinsen durch die Notenbank Fed erwartet wird, sind die Zinsen am Kapitalmarkt bereits gestiegen. In Europa dagegen, wo Mario Draghi, der Präsident der Europäischen Zentralbank, die Leitzinsen noch lange Zeit niedrig lassen will, verharrt das Zinsniveau am Kapitalmarkt auf niedrigem Level. Kein Wunder, dass Apple es so attraktiv findet, zumindest einen Teil seiner Schulden in Euro aufzunehmen.

Bemerkenswert dabei ist: Der Hersteller von Smartphones und Tabletcomputern verfügt eigentlich über außergewöhnlich große Geldreserven. Sie sollen rund 155 Milliarden Dollar umfassen. Die Erlöse aus den Anleihen verwendet Apple unter anderem für Dividenden und Aktienrückkaufprogramme. Offenbar ist es für das Unternehmen angesichts des niedrigen Zinsniveaus günstiger, neue Schulden aufzunehmen, als bestehende Ersparnisse aufzulösen. [...]

Frankfurter Allgemeine Sonntagszeitung, 2. November 2014

16 Produktion

Your bank wants to sell more savings products to customers who have large cash deposits.

Write a short letter in English, to be personalized for individual customers, containing these points.

- Describe this chart.
- Explain what it means for the customer.
- Say how the bank can help.
- Offer an appointment with an adviser.

Sparbuch
Angenommener Zinsatz 0,14 Prozent

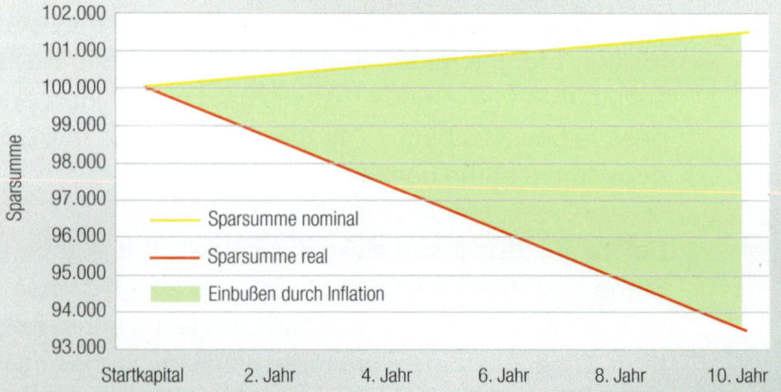

Fallbeispiel: 100.000 € Startkapital, Anlagezeitraum 10 Jahre, Inflationsrate 0,9 Prozent
Quelle: www.manager-magazin.de

Worse than nothing

MANY German savers already see the paltry interest they earn on the savings they stash in banks – typically even lower than the country's minuscule rate of inflation – as an affront. So the news that Deutsche Skatbank, in the eastern state of Thuringia, plans to apply a negative rate of interest to some deposits, was greeted with consternation.

The penalty will only apply to balances of over €500,000 ($625,000) in instant-access accounts, of which there cannot be very many. It is not, technically, the first time that German banks have applied negative rates: a few banks require businesses to pay to have their money looked after. Some government bonds have traded with negative yields. But this is the first time personal accounts have received such treatment. Presumably the bank hopes to nudge savers into other longer-term, less liquid or higher-return investments, which it can make some money by selling.

German savers are a strange lot; they shun stocks, bonds and houses, instead parking over €2 trillion in ordinary savings accounts. In other words, they are cautious to a fault. Some think that banks are simply flogging high-commission products; others that speculating in stock and property markets is a form of shameful gambling.

The European Central Bank has been hoping to encourage banks to lend by charging them a negative interest rate on the excess deposits they stash with it. But Germans are sceptical that ultra-loose monetary policy can spur lending and thus economic activity without deeper fiscal and structural reform. They accuse the ECB of postponing an inevitable reckoning for past mistakes with its interest-rate policy. Relations between the ECB and the Bundesbank, Germany's traditionally hawkish central bank, are in the dumps.

The ECB's intention, however, is not so different from Deutsche Skatbank's: to encourage savers to switch to riskier assets, spurring productive investment. It does not seem to be working. Germans have responded to low rates by saving less. But private investment has plunged in recent years, mirroring the German state's own underinvestment. Lack of investment is increasingly recognised even by Germans as a national problem. It is a hard one for the thrifty to shirk.

The Economist, November 8, 2014

17 Reading for gist

Read the article without looking up any vocabulary and decide if these statements are true or false. Correct the false ones.

1. German savers are satisfied with the interest they receive on their savings.
2. Germans tend to mistrust their bank when advised how to invest their money.
3. Sometimes it is possible to be too cautious when saving and investing money.
4. The ECB and the Bundesbank agree that charging negative interest on bank deposits will encourage lending.
5. The ECB policy of charging negative interest is leading to more investment in Germany.

18 Discussion

Read the article again and discuss this question.

"Does the writer approve of the Germans' attitude towards saving and investing?"

UNIT 7

Personal borrowing

- Talking about loans and overdrafts
- Arranging a personal loan
- Assessing creditworthiness

1 Warm-up

Overnight queues for a new phone

A **Is there any item that you would queue for overnight to buy? If so, what?**

B **Would you borrow money to buy something? If so, what would you buy and how would you borrow the money?**

C **What should you consider before borrowing money from a bank?**

D **How can banks protect themselves against 'bad borrowers'?**

CULTURE

Credit reference agencies in the UK and the USA

Dealing in credit data is big business in the UK and the USA where there is no single equivalent of the German SCHUFA. Credit reference agencies (UK) and credit bureaux or consumer reporting agencies (USA) are commercially run. Alongside the main ones like Experian and Equinox, there are dozens of smaller agencies, and all are in competition.

Banks, credit card issuers and companies that offer goods or services on credit use these agencies to protect themselves against bad debts. They buy information relating to the creditworthiness of individuals from the agencies, and also supply data to them. The information is stored in each individual's credit record and used for credit-scoring which may determine whether an application for credit is approved, and what level of interest is charged.

Consumer organizations such as the Citizens Advice Bureau recommend borrowers check their credit records once a year.

2 A personal loan

Your bank is planning a brochure on loans for its English-speaking customers. The flyer below from a UK bank is a good example of the kind of text required.

A personal loan – borrowing made simple

Isn't it time to buy that new car? Carry out those home improvements? Have the holiday of a lifetime?
Or would you like to consolidate some debts and repay in fixed instalments you can afford?

Whatever the purpose, a personal loan could be the answer!

- Borrow any round sum from £5,000 to £20,000. The loan amount will be paid directly into your current account as soon as your application has been approved.
- Choose a repayment loan with a set instalment every month that is tailored to suit you. (Alternatively, take an interest-only loan with two payments per month: one for the interest on the loan, the other for an endowment insurance that repays the loan at the end of the term.)
- Take advantage of our competitive interest rates. The APR* is fixed for the full term, so you will know right from the start how much you will have to pay. (There may be extra fees for borrowers asked to provide security for loans of £15,000 and over.)
- Enjoy peace of mind with our loan protection plan. For a small extra premium, your repayments will be covered by loan insurance if you cannot work as a result of accident or illness, if you become unemployed through no fault of your own or if you pass away.

If you are aged 18 or over and seeking to borrow, call in at any of our branches, fill in the loan application form at the back of this brochure or visit our website.

* annual percentage rate of interest

A Find expressions in the text which mean the following.

1. Privatkredit
2. Zweck
3. Annuitätsdarlehen
4. eine feste Rate
5. endfälliges Darlehen
6. Kapitalversicherung
7. Laufzeit
8. effektiver Jahreszins
9. Kreditnehmer/in
10. Sicherheiten
11. Versicherungsbeitrag
12. Kreditantrag

B How would you say the following in German?

1. carry out those home improvements (line 1)
2. consolidate some debts (line 3)
3. your application has been approved (line 7)
4. tailored to suit you (lines 8–9)
5. enjoy peace of mind (line 15)
6. through no fault of your own (line 17)
7. pass away (line 18)

C Write the text for a flyer to advertise a personal loan on offer at your bank. Include all the loan terms.

3 Loan or overdraft?

13 Lukas Meier opened a current account for Bianca Bower from Australia six months ago. When she phoned to say that she needs a larger overdraft, Lukas asked her to come into the branch.

A **What do you think Lukas wants to find out during their conversation? Note your ideas.**

B **Listen to the dialogue and see whether your ideas for A were correct.**

Bianca G'day. Nice to see you again.
Lukas Hi, nice to see you too, Ms Bower. How are you finding life in Germany?
Bianca Great, thanks. My job's fantastic, and I've joined a water-sports club and made masses of friends.
Lukas I remember, didn't you tell me you were junior Australian champion in kayaking?
Bianca Yes, and that's sort of why I'm here today.
Lukas Well, what can we do for you?
Bianca When I left home, I had to leave my kayak behind. It would have cost a fortune if I'd shipped it over to Europe, so I need to buy a new one. The overdraft limit on my account is 1,000 euros, but that's not going to be enough. I'm going to need about five thousand to get a really good boat, a roof rack for the car and some camping equipment as well. We're going to Sweden to train there this summer.
Lukas Sounds great. Can you give me your account number, please?
Bianca Sure. It's 34776901.
Lukas Thanks. Let me just get your file up on the screen … ah yes, here we are. Well, we could extend your overdraft facility, but have you thought about applying for a personal loan instead?
Bianca A loan? Why? Wouldn't that be very complicated?
Lukas Not at all. You just have to fill in an application form. The full loan amount will be paid into your account after your application has been approved.
Bianca Wouldn't that take a long time?
Lukas It's not something we decide here in the branch. All loan applications have to be credit-scored to assess the applicant's creditworthiness, but that doesn't take long.
Bianca I see, but wouldn't a loan be more expensive for me than an overdraft?
Lukas No, in fact it would work out cheaper for you. You see, the APR for loans is much lower than the rate we charge for overdrafts.
Bianca Err … AP what?
Lukas Sorry, APR stands for "annual percentage rate of interest". It's the true interest rate that you pay because it includes the debit interest rate plus the arrangement fee or other costs for setting up the loan as well.
Bianca Yes, but if I have an overdraft, I won't have to pay an arrangement fee, will I?
Lukas That's true, but with an overdraft the debit interest rate can vary. If you took out a loan, you'd have a set interest rate for a fixed term.
Bianca Yes, but I still think I'd be a lot more flexible if I had an overdraft because I could repay it whenever I liked.
Lukas Well, our loans are flexible too. If you tell us your average monthly expenditure, we can arrange a repayment plan with fixed monthly instalments that suit you best, so you'll know right from the start how much you have to pay.
Bianca Can I pay more than the instalments? Sometimes I get a bonus at work. Could I use that to repay the loan as well?
Lukas That depends on the type of loan. Some loans allow lump sum repayments.

Bianca And don't banks want to have security for loans? I haven't got anything I could offer you, except my car and that's not worth much.

Lukas Larger loans generally have to be secured, for example if you needed money to buy a property, we would ask you to give a guarantee or have it registered in the so-called Land Register. With small loans we usually ask the borrower to take out loan insurance instead. If you can't repay the loan for any reason, the insurance pays it for you.

Bianca Would I have to pay extra for that?

Lukas Just a small premium, but why not talk everything over with one of our advisers, Ms Fischer or Mr Novak? They'd be glad to tell you more about the loans we offer. Would you like me to see if either of them is free now?

Bianca Sure, why not?

Lukas Great. One moment, please. I'll be right back.

C **Listen to the dialogue again or read it and find differences between loans and overdrafts. Make a table like the one below to compare the two. Add ideas of your own.**

Personal Loans		Overdrafts	
1	The borrower has to pay an arrangement fee.	**1**	There is no …
2	The interest rate is …	**2**	…

GRAMMAR

If-sentences

1. If I **have** an overdraft, I **won't have to** pay an arrangement fee.
2. If you **took out** a loan, you **would have** a set interest rate for a fixed term.
3. **I'd be** a lot more flexible if I **had** an overdraft.
4. It **would have cost** a fortune if **I'd shipped** it over here.
5. If you **can't repay** the loan for any reason, the insurance **pays** it for you.

- There are three main types of *if*-sentence. Note the tenses used.

if-clause	main clause
simple present	*will* + infinitive (1)
simple past	*would* + infinitive (2, 3)
past perfect	*would* + *have* + past participle (4)

- If you start an *if*-sentence with the *if*-clause, you need a comma. (1, 2, 5)
- In general statements that are always true, both clauses are in the present tense. (5)

4 Practice

A **Make meaningful sentences using this table.**

If you	have had take took	a loan, an overdraft,	you	will won't would wouldn't	have to pay an arrangement fee. have a fixed APR. borrow for an agreed term. repay it in set instalments. need loan insurance. have to sign an agreement.

B Put the verbs in brackets into the correct tenses.

1. If you … (need) money, we would increase your overdraft facility.
2. Your overdraft will cost you more if the interest rate … (rise).
3. If you borrow for a longer term, your instalments … (be) lower.
4. A loan protection plan … (cover) your loan if you were unable to repay it.
5. If interest rates fall, borrowing generally … (become) cheaper.
6. If I … (have) a loan, the interest rate would have been fixed.
7. I … (pay) less if I had taken out a loan instead of overdrawing my account.
8. If we arranged a loan, the instalments … (be fixed) for the full term and so you … (know) exactly how much the loan … (cost) you.

5 Role-play: arranging a personal loan

KMK

Führen Sie in Partnerarbeit einen Dialog nach den folgenden Vorgaben.

Partner/in A: Sie sind Marie Fischer / Jan Novak und arbeiten in der Kreditabteilung Ihrer Bank, wo Sie Bianca Bower beraten werden.

Partnerin B: Sie sind Bianca Bower, 29, aus Australien. In der Kreditabteilung Ihrer Bank möchten Sie sich über einen Privatkredit informieren.

Partner/in A

- Begrüßen Sie Ms Bower und stellen Sie sich vor.
- Machen Sie etwas „Small Talk".
- Erkundigen Sie sich nach dem gewünschten Kreditbetrag und dem Kreditzweck.
- Sagen Sie, dass ein Privatdarlehen günstiger als ein Dispositionskredit ist, da es einen festen Zinssatz hat.
- Informieren Sie die Kundin, dass der Sollzinssatz 4,49 % p.a. beträgt. Der effektive Zinssatz ist 4,56 % p.a. Es gibt keine Bearbeitungsgebühren. Erkundigen Sie sich nach der gewünschten Laufzeit.
- Bitten Sie um etwas Geduld, während Sie das PC-Programm aufrufen. Sie geben die Daten ein, um die Rate zu ermitteln. Bei einer Laufzeit von 36 Monaten und einem Nettodarlehensbetrag von 5.000 € beträgt die monatliche Rate 148,72 €.
- Informieren Sie die Kundin, dass Sondertilgung und Ratenaussetzung möglich sind.
- Weisen Sie die Kundin darauf hin, dass das Darlehen nur nach Abschluss einer Restschuldenversicherung bewilligt werden kann.
- Erklären Sie, dass die Versicherung einen Schutz im Falle von Arbeitslosigkeit, Arbeitsunfähigkeit oder Tod bietet.
- Überreichen Sie sowohl Ihre Karte als auch eine Broschüre und verabschieden Sie sich.

Partnerin B

- Entschuldigen Sie sich, dass Sie noch nicht in der Lage sind, das Gespräch auf Deutsch zu führen.
- Sagen Sie, dass Sie bei der australischen Botschaft arbeiten. Sie möchten für circa fünf Jahre hier bleiben, dann werden Sie an den nächsten Dienstposten versetzt werden.
- Sie brauchen 5.000 € für ein neues Kajak. Am Schalter hat man Ihnen zu einem Privatdarlehen geraten.
- Fragen Sie nach den Kosten eines Darlehens. Stellen Sie sicher, dass es keine versteckten Kosten gibt.
- Erklären Sie, dass Sie den Betrag innerhalb von drei Jahren zurückzahlen möchten. Dies hängt jedoch von der Höhe der monatlichen Raten ab.
- Erkundigen Sie sich, ob Sie an die Ratenzahlung gebunden sind.
- Fragen Sie, ob Sie den Kreditantrag gleich ausfüllen können.
- Zeigen Sie sich irritiert, dass eine Versicherung nötig ist. Schließlich verdienen Sie mehr als genug, um die Raten zahlen zu können!
- Sagen Sie, dass Ihre Arbeitsstelle sicher ist. Leider müssen Sie jetzt zu einem dringenden Termin. Sie möchten alles nochmal überschlafen.
- Bedanken und verabschieden Sie sich.

LANGUAGE

Talking about sums of money

When adding up sums of money, you can say:

Your joint income Your average expenditure	comes to amounts to totals	3,000 euros.

If you cannot give an exact figure, you can say:

My expenditure	is	roughly approximately about	1,000 euros.
My income	averages 2,000 euros a month. is 2,000 a month on average.		

Note:
die Höhe der Raten = the amount of the instalments
ein Darlehen über 5.000 € = a loan of five thousand euros / a five thousand-euro loan

When saying long numbers, the word "and" follows the word "hundred": 1,257,364 = one million, two hundred *and* fifty-seven thousand, three hundred *and* sixty-four.

6 Assessing creditworthiness

KMK

14

Marie Fischer, Beraterin in der Kreditabteilung Ihrer Bank, hat zwei Termine mit Kunden vereinbart. Alle Kunden haben zugestimmt, dass Sie während des Gesprächs anwesend sein dürfen. Frau Fischer hat Sie gebeten, zu jedem Gespräch Notizen zu machen.

Fertigen Sie eine Kopie der folgenden Tabelle an. Während Sie zuhören, füllen Sie sie auf Deutsch aus.

	Liz und Mike Jones	Colin und Evelyn Wells
Kreditzweck	...	...
Gewünschter Kreditbetrag	...	...
Einnahmen/Ausgaben		
Nettoeinkommen (Gehalt/Rente/Pension)	...	...
Einkünfte aus selbstständiger Tätigkeit	...	...
Sonstige regelmäßige Einkünfte	...	...
Miete / Belastungen Eigentum	...	...
Lebenshaltungskosten	...	...
Versicherungsbeiträge	...	...
Sparverträge	...	...
Bestehende Kredite / Ratenzahlungen	...	...
Unterhaltszahlungen	...	...
Sonstige regelmäßige Verpflichtungen	...	...

7 Working with words

A Match each of the German terms from the table in exercise 6 with one of the expressions below.

1 Expenditure
2 Rent
3 Insurance premiums
4 Maintenance payments / Alimony
5 Other sources of regular income
6 Living expenses
7 Loan instalments
8 Other regular commitments

B Choose the correct term for each sentence.

1 Why do you need a (*credit / loan*)?
2 How much would you like to (*borrow / lend*) for the car?
3 The interest (*is / are*) included in the monthly instalments.
4 The interest rate is (*varying / variable*).
5 For (*large / high*) loans customers will be asked to provide security.
6 For loans under 10,000 euros no security (*is / are*) necessary.
7 The bank has to estimate the customer's (*disposable / free disposable*) income.
8 Your application for a loan has been (*accepted / approved*).
9 The bank will grant you a loan (*of / over*) 10,000 euros.
10 You can dispose (*of / over*) the sum immediately.

8 Writing a letter of confirmation

Marie Fischer has asked you to write to one of the customers from exercise 6 to confirm the bank's offer of a loan.

A Before you write the letter, do these tasks.

1 Look at your chart from exercise 6 and choose whether to write to Liz and Mike Jones or Colin and Evelyn Wells.
2 Work out the most suitable loan amount, term and repayment method for this couple.
3 Find out your bank's current conditions for the amount and term you have chosen.
4 Decide whether the bank will ask for loan insurance or security for this loan.

B Write the letter offering a personal loan. State all the terms and ask the couple to come to the branch to complete the formalities. The model letter on page 124 will be of help.

CULTURE

Borrowing in Germany and in the USA

While Germans are still largely a nation of savers with restricted opening hours for shops, in the USA there is a culture of spending: Americans are told that the economy demands increased consumer spending, so it is their duty to shop. Germany has a tradition of promoting savings schemes for its citizens, whereas US government policies have long encouraged Americans to borrow to buy homes and products which, in many cases, they cannot afford. Why save, when it is so easy to borrow? Over-large mortgages and credit card debts are the result. Roll-over loans (in which the repayment date is postponed but the interest rate is doubled) and payday loans lead many into financial disaster.

9 Generation debt

While preparing to attend an international seminar on lending, you have come across this article on the web.

theguardian.com/money/2014/oct/16

Young people with debt more likely to get payday loan than go to bank

by Lisa Bachelor

Young people under the age of 25 are more likely to turn to payday loan companies such as Wonga to make ends meet than approach their bank, building societies or a credit card company, according to Citizens Advice.

It analysed 30,000 of the most serious debt problems it sees in its bureaux and found that while 10% of these were suffered by 17-14-year-olds, payday loans accounted for 62% of the credit used by this age group. Only 8% of the 3,000 youngsters were in debt because of mainstream credit such as overdrafts, bank loans or credit cards.

Over a third of those who were suffering severe debt problems were not "Neets" – Not in Education, Employment or Training – said Citizens Advice, but were in work.

"Generation Y is fast becoming generation credit," said Citizens Advice Chief Executive, Gillian Guy. "It is a big concern that so many young adults are turning to some of the most expensive types of loan to get by. Taking out a payday loan in your late teens or early twenties can have significant and damaging consequences in later life."

Less well-known types of high-interest credit, such as guarantor and logbook loans, are also contributing to the severe debt problem suffered by the youngest borrowers. Guarantor loans are those in which another individual is listed as being liable for repayment if the borrower cannot make payments, while logbook loans use people's cars as security.

Separate research from the Financial Conduct Authority found that around 40,000 consumers took out logbook loans in 2013, typically borrowing £1,000 a time, although lenders offer sums up to £50,000. Citizens Advice said it expected the number of logbook loans to rise by 61% this year.

A **Summarize the main points in the article in English for your fellow participants at the seminar.**

B **Working in a group, suggest reasons for this development and possible solutions. Point out how banks can help.**

10 Hörverstehen

15 Als Auszubildende/r der XY Bank absolvieren Sie ein Praktikum bei einer schottischen Bank. Sie helfen zurzeit am Schalter aus und dürfen auch Kundengesprächen beiwohnen. Eines Morgens betritt Rebecca Derek die Bank und bittet den Abteilungsleiter Stewart Ferguson um ein Beratungsgespräch.

Hören Sie dem Gespräch aufmerksam zu und machen Sie folgende Aufgaben. Sie hören den Text zwei Mal.

Fertigen Sie mithilfe der folgenden Fragen eine Gesprächsnotiz in kurzen Stichworten auf Deutsch an.

1 Welches Anliegen hat Rebecca?
2 Warum bittet sie um das Beratungsgespräch?
3 Welche Erfahrungen kann Rebecca vorweisen?
4 Was muss Rebecca tun, um die Bank davon zu überzeugen, ihr ein Darlehen zu gewähren?
5 Welche wesentlichen Voraussetzungen für ein Darlehen nennt Stewart?

11 Mediation

Jaraminda Pavel hat einen Kredit bei ihrer Bank beantragt, um sich eine Eigentumswohnung kaufen zu können. Sie hat folgendes Schreiben von der Kreditabteilung erhalten, kann es aber nicht verstehen.

Schreiben Sie Frau Pavel eine E-Mail und informieren Sie sie über die wichtigsten Punkte dieses Briefes.

Aktenzeichen: 567703201 10.11.2015

Sehr geehrte Frau Pavel,
wir freuen uns, Ihnen mitzuteilen, dass wir am 10.11.2015 für Sie die Vollauszahlung Ihres Darlehens vorgenommen haben.
Wir machen Sie darauf aufmerksam, dass für Ihr Darlehen die folgenden Leistungen am **01.12.2015** fällig werden:

1,700% Sollzinsen aus EUR 130.000,00 vom 11.11.2015 bis 30.11.2015

Gesamtbetrag **EUR 121,09**

Sofern sich keine Veränderung ergibt, werden ab dem 30.12.2015 die weiteren Leistungen jeweils am letzten Kalendertag eines jeden Monats in folgender Höhe fällig:

Gesamtbetrag **EUR 671,67**

Aufgrund des uns vorliegenden SEPA-Lastschriftmandats 401-0400-000000546282 werden wir die zu zahlenden Beträge zum Fälligkeitstermin unter Angabe der Gläubiger-ID DE3822000000050669 einziehen. Fällt der Zahlungstermin auf ein Wochenende oder einen Feiertag, so erfolgt die Belastung am darauffolgenden Bankarbeitstag.
Für alle Fragen steht Ihnen Ihr/e persönliche/r Berater/in in Ihrer Filiale selbstverständlich zur Verfügung.
Wir freuen uns, dass wir Ihnen bei der Realisierung Ihrer Immobilienfinanzierung behilflich sein konnten.

12 Security for loans

You are on a work placement in a London bank. Your English colleague, Mark Webber, wants your opinion on how the bank should secure three separate loans.

A Mark has emailed you this information about security with the important terms underlined. Translate them.

Securing Loans
When the bank secures a loan, it is vital that the collateral[1] given should cover the cost of the loan for the full term of borrowing. It is equally important that it should be easy for the bank to store and dispose of, should the borrower default[2]. Types of security that fulfil these criteria are guarantees[3], whereby another person or an institution acts as guarantor and repays the loan if the borrower fails to do so. Assignments[4] are also suitable, e.g. if the rights to insurance policies or savings are assigned to the bank. An assignment by bill of sale[5] allows the borrower to use the item, perhaps a car or machine, while the bank is the owner. If a house or land is pledged, the customer can take out a mortgage[6] on the property, or the bank can register a land charge[7]. UK banks work with mortgages, while land charges are commonly used in Germany. A pledge[8] of valuable articles, on the other hand, can involve risks and other problems for the bank, especially in the case of jewellery, fine art or antiques.

B These are Mark's notes on the three loan applications. Work out the advantages/disadvantages of the different types of security he has suggested. Decide which would be suitable in each case.

Sophie Wilding

- runs an art gallery in Chelsea
- wants to install a security system after a break-in
- needs a loan of £20,000

Security: a pledge of a painting valued at £50,000 OR an assignment of her life assurance policy worth £45,000 OR a guarantee from her father, a retired doctor?

Marianne Gerster

- owns an apartment in Berlin worth €700,000
- wants to buy a cottage in Cornwall, valued at £470,000
- has applied for a loan of €300,000

Security: a mortgage on the cottage OR a registered land charge on her German home?

Dave and Cherry Bower

- have a veterinary practice in Ealing
- want to spend £50,000 on an outdoor swimming pool
- need a loan of £35,000

Security: an assignment by bill of sale of their Range Rover SUV, worth £75,000, OR an assignment of their British government bonds, currently valued at £50,000?

C Choose one of the three cases, write notes and present your findings at a meeting.

UNIT 8

Business banking

- Dealing with business and corporate clients
- Writing a credit reference
- Understanding liquidity problems

1 Warm-up

A **Why do banks sponsor events?**

B **Does your bank sponsor or run any events? If so, give examples and say what sort of customers such events aim to attract.**

2 Business clients and corporate clients

16

Money Matters interviewed Kate Westwood, communications manager for an international bank in Abu Dhabi, United Arab Emirates.

A **Say what you think a communications manager in a bank is responsible for.**

B **Listen to the dialogue and note three topics which Kate talks about.**

MM So how long have you been in Abu Dhabi, Kate?

Kate I've been working here since 2012, and I've been communications manager for the last two years. I love living in a place where so many different cultures meet.

MM It must be exciting, and thanks for offering to talk to us about business banking. I suppose there's a big difference between personal banking and business banking?

Kate Oh yes. In personal banking, products are standardized and rates are fixed by the bank, but in business and corporate banking the products are more complex, more tailored to suit the client's needs. There is room for …[1] of terms, fees and interest rates, and, especially with corporate clients, the relationship is very important.

MM You said "business and corporate banking". Aren't business clients and corporate clients the same?

Kate No, they aren't. Business clients are small or medium-sized companies, while corporate clients are much bigger companies with a larger …[2]. Of course we try to meet the needs of both, but corporate clients usually require specialized products.

MM I see. What products does the bank offer its corporate clients?

Kate Lots of our clients trade globally, so we offer accounts in all major currencies and documentary credits for import-export business. We also provide treasury services.

MM I'm sorry, what exactly are treasury services?

Kate That means buying and selling foreign currencies for corporate clients and transferring money as well – for example, if a company had to pay a bill in yen in six months' time, we'd help them to do that.

MM And I suppose lending is important too?

Kate Absolutely. Our lending services range from overdrafts and loans for our business clients to what we call "structured finance" for corporate clients. That includes …[3] when several banks join together to lend huge sums of money, as well as financing for ships and trucks. And of course we also arrange and finance takeovers and mergers.

MM Those are very complex bank products. How do you market them?

Kate In business banking we market our products directly, usually by advertising, but in corporate banking we don't do that. Instead we focus on improving our relationship with our existing corporate clients and acquiring new ones. We use …[4]. For example, last year we sponsored the Abu Dhabi Formula One Grand Prix and gave our clients free tickets with access to our VIP area.

MM Does the bank organize its own events, too?

Kate Yes, we also run so-called …[5]. We have already held several regattas and have often invited clients to golf days. They get lunch, free gifts and maybe their photo in the local press. But there are, of course, more serious events too, like …[6] on topics our clients are interested in.

MM Are lots of your clients Arabs?

Kate Some yes, but not all. Most are …[7] from all over the world who have come to do business in the Gulf region. And they all speak English of course!

C **Fill in the gaps in the dialogue with the words from the box below. Listen to the interview again and check your answers.**

corporate hospitality • customized events • expats • negotiation • round-table discussions • syndicated loans • turnover

D **Decide whether each statement below is true or false. Correct the false ones.**

1. Terms in business banking are more flexible than in personal banking.
2. Business clients have a larger turnover than corporate clients.
3. Syndicated loans are granted by more than one bank.
4. Treasury services include dealing in foreign currencies.
5. Corporate banking products are not marketed directly.
6. The Abu Dhabi Formula One Grand Prix is a customized event.
7. A round-table discussion takes place between a client and an adviser in the bank.
8. Expats are native speakers of English.

E **Explain the difference between personal customers, business clients and corporate clients. Say how the bank treats each type of customer.**

GRAMMAR

The present perfect (continuous) and the simple past tense

1. We **have** already **held** several regattas and **have** often **invited** clients to golf days.
2. How long **have** you **been working** in this department?
3. Last year we **sponsored** the Formula One Grand Prix and **gave** our clients free tickets.

- The present perfect tense is used to say that something has happened before the moment of speaking. The emphasis is on the result of the action (1).
- The present perfect continuous is used when an action began in the past and has continued up to the moment of speaking. The emphasis is on how long the event has continued. (2)
- The present perfect is also used when no particular time is mentioned but when there is a connection to the present, especially with words like *already*, *just*, *often*, *ever, never, already, recently, so far* and *(not) yet.* (1)
- The simple past is used when the action was completed at a named or known time in the past. (3)
- State verbs like *believe*, *know*, etc. refer to states and not activities. They have no continuous form.

Note: For the German word 'seit', *since* and *for* are used: *since* = from a point in time, *for* = over a period of time. In questions, the expression *how long* is used for the German 'seit wann' (2).

3 Practice

A **Put the verbs in brackets into the present perfect / present perfect continuous and use 'since' or 'for' to fill the gaps in these sentences.**

1. The company … (have) an account with our bank … nine years.
2. They … (always repay) their loans punctually.
3. Their current account … (never be) overdrawn.
4. Their turnover … (increase) steadily … 2011.
5. We … (grant) the company a line of credit.
6. Our firm … (sell) goods in the Gulf region … many years and we hope this continues.

B **Write three questions beginning 'how long' which you might ask a new business customer.**

4 Practice

Answer these questions using the present perfect or the simple past.

1 Have you ever been to the Gulf region? Yes, I … (work) there in 2014.
2 Have you met Mr Rashid yet? Yes, we … (already meet) him.
3 Has the company started trading yet? Yes, they … (begin) trading two years ago.
4 Have they already opened an account? Oh, yes, they … (open) one on 1 July.
5 Have you seen the company's turnover? Yes, I … (see) the figures last month.
6 Have we worked with them before? Yes, we … (often do) business with them.
7 Have the clients been invited to the event? Yes, the invitations … (go out) yesterday.
8 Has anyone arranged the catering? No, nobody … (organize) it yet.

5 A status enquiry

One of your bank's clients, WohnArt GmbH, a furniture-making business, has recently set up business in Dubai. You are working in the corporate business department when this letter arrives.

A Read the letter and say why the Dubai bank has approached your bank.

Jumeirah Bank, 1 Capitol Building, Dubai, UAE

Ref.: 3528990/154

3 November 20..

STRICTLY CONFIDENTIAL

Dear Sirs

Re: Credit reference for WohnArt

The above-mentioned company has made an application to open a credit line with one of our bank's clients, Deira Timber Trading Co., and has asked us to contact you for a credit reference. Enclosed please find a copy of their credit application in which your institution is named. We are thereby authorized to request you to provide us with a credit reference.

We would be grateful if you could supply the following information:

1. How long has WohnArt been a client with your bank?
2. Does the company have any overdrafts or loans with you? If so, please provide details regarding the outstanding sums, the collateral and the repayment so far.
3. Has the company repaid past loans punctually?
4. Do the company's current annual turnover and balance sheet show them to be creditworthy for a credit line of USD 100,000?

Please be assured that this information will be treated in the strictest confidence.
We thank you for your cooperation.

Yours faithfully

Enclosure: Credit Application

B With a partner, work out what information would have a positive/negative influence on WohnArt's credit status. Note your findings.

6 A credit reference

You have been asked to reply to Jumeirah Bank.

Write a letter containing either a positive or a negative credit reference for WohnArt as follows. There is a model letter on page 124.

- Make the subject of your letter clear.
- Say that your bank is pleased to offer assistance.
- Answer the four points in the Dubai bank's letter, using your notes from exercise 5.
- Say you have enclosed a copy of WohnArt's latest balance sheet.
- Ask for all the information to be treated in strict confidence.

7 A balance sheet

WohnArt's balance sheet could look like this. The figures have been omitted.

A Give the German equivalent of each item on the balance sheet.

Balance Sheet WohnArt GmbH
as of December 31, 20..

ASSETS	LIABILITIES
Fixed Assets	**Owners' Capital**
Buildings and land	Retained profits
Machinery	
Vehicles	**Long-term Liabilities**
Tools and equipment	Loans and mortgages
Current Assets	**Current Liabilities**
Stock	Overdrafts
Accounts receivable	Accounts payable
Cash at bank	Interest payable on loans
	Provision for taxes
Total Assets	**Total Liabilities**

B Find items on the balance sheet above that have the following meaning.

1. the credit balance of the company's bank accounts
2. the value of the company's trucks, cars, vans, etc.
3. the value of all raw materials, work-in-progress and finished products
4. all the amounts owed to the company by its debtors, e.g. its customers
5. the sums owed by the company to its creditors, e.g. its suppliers
6. profits kept from previous years for reinvestment in the company
7. the total value of the company's possessions and all sums owed by its debtors
8. the total value of the company's capital, and long-term and short-term debts

CULTURE

Dealing with Middle-Eastern Clients

Here are some helpful rules to follow:

- Be patient: your client may arrive late or not at all if family business calls.
- Avoid touching and making eye contact with women. Ask them nothing personal.
- Always accept hospitality: eat and drink everything you are offered.
- In small talk, ask after the client's family but never mention his wife or daughter.
- Stay cool. If you are energetic, you may be seen as disorganized and incompetent.
- Do not feel you have to talk: silence is not embarrassing.
- Let your client choose when to talk business. Then come to the point at once.
- Do a presentation "upside-down": start with the product you want to sell.

8 Liquidity problems

You are taking part in an international seminar on the subject of banking for small businesses.

Work in a group and do these tasks.

1 What situations can lead to a liquidity problem? List as many as you can think of. Use vocabulary from the last exercise.

2 Say what advantages a business overdraft (AE: business line of credit) can offer a small business as regards (a) saving money, (b) protecting creditworthiness.

This brochure from the US bank Wells Fargo will give you some ideas.

To build a successful business, it takes hard work, creativity and, above all, capital.

Quick access to cash. It's an essential tool of the small business owner. It helps you seize opportunities when they arise. And get what you need when you need it.

That's what the BusinessLine® Line of Credit is all about. With a credit line of up to $100,000, it puts you in charge of your finances. You can access the amount you need, repay it over time at favorable rates and then reuse your credit as often as you like.

Grow Your Business and Manage Your Finances with a BusinessLine® Line of Credit

It's a fundamental fact of business. Having money on hand can help you earn more and save more in the long run. You can invest in your business when the time is right and keep your enterprise running smoothly regardless of the marketplace's ups and downs.

- **CONSOLIDATE DEBT** with a lower interest rate.
- **MAINTAIN CASH FLOW** during fluctuations in the business cycle.
- **SAVE MONEY** by buying in bulk or making special purchases.
- **KEEP YOUR GOOD CREDIT REPUTATION** by paying receivables promptly.
- **EXPAND WHEN THE TIME IS RIGHT** – with new offices, equipment, employees or product lines.
- **ACCESS CASH** when important opportunities arise.

9 Role-play: discussing a business overdraft

KMK

Führen Sie mithilfe der Rollenkarten ein Beratungsgespräch.

Partner/in A

Sie beraten Geschäftskunden in der Kreditabteilung Ihrer Bank. Ihre Kollegin, Frau Hof, ist vor kurzem in den Ruhestand gegangen, und Sie haben ihren Kundenstamm übernommen. Heute haben Sie einen Termin mit Mr/Mrs Jennings. Sie beginnen das Gespräch.

- Sie begrüßen den Kunden / die Kundin und stellen sich vor. Bieten Sie Ihre Hilfe an.
- Erklären Sie, warum Frau Hof nicht anwesend ist. Versuchen Sie den Kunden / die Kundin kennenzulernen. Benutzen Sie auch Small Talk.
- Erkundigen Sie sich genau nach dem Grund des Besuchs.
- Informieren Sie sich über die gegenwärtige finanzielle Lage des Geschäfts.
- Fragen Sie nach einer Vollmacht des Geschäftspartners. Lassen Sie sich die Bilanzen der letzten drei Jahren in Kopie geben.
- Erläutern Sie die Gründe, warum ein Dispositionskredit vorteilhafter wäre als ein Darlehen: Verbesserter Cash Flow durch die ständige Verfügbarkeit der vereinbarten Summe sowie Flexibilität bei der Rückzahlung.
- Machen Sie sehr deutlich, dass ein Kredit nur nach eingehender Prüfung der finanziellen Lage des Geschäfts möglich wäre. Vereinbaren Sie deshalb einen weiteren Termin in der kommenden Woche.

Partner/in B

Sie sind John/Joanna Jennings aus England. Seit fünf Jahren leben Sie in Deutschland, wo Sie mit einem Partner ein kleines Fischrestaurant betreiben. Wegen eines drohenden Liquiditätsproblems haben Sie einen Beratungstermin bei Ihrer Bank.

- Sie sind leicht irritiert, da Frau Hof, die Bankberaterin, die Sie bisher auf Englisch betreut hat, nicht anwesend ist.
- Beantworten Sie alle Fragen zu Ihrer Person und Ihrem Geschäft.
- Stellen Sie das Problem dar: Wegen des heißen Sommers ist Ihr Umsatz leicht zurückgegangen. Gleichzeitig sind die Preise für Fisch gestiegen. Jetzt ist Ihr Geschäftspartner, der auch Ihr Koch im Restaurant ist, erkrankt und muss für zwei Monate ersetzt werden.
- Bisher konnten Sie allen Verbindlichkeiten (Lieferanten, Miete, Personalkosten usw.) nachkommen. Um ein Liquiditätsproblem zu vermeiden, bitten Sie um ein Darlehen zur Überbrückung der nächsten drei Monate. Im Winter erwarten Sie mehr Umsatz. Sie haben vor kurzem einen preiswerten Mittagstisch eingeführt, der erfolgversprechend läuft.
- Eine Vollmacht Ihres Geschäftspartners liegt vor. Sie haben die Bilanzen der letzten drei Jahre mitgebracht.
- Fragen Sie, ob Sie gleich einen Dispositionskredit beantragen können.
- Stimmen Sie einem weiteren Termin in der kommenden Woche zu.

10 Comparing business overdrafts and loans

Complete these sentences to compare these two forms of business lending.

1. With a business loan the amount can be used once, while with an overdraft …
2. A business loan has to be used for a specific purpose, while an overdraft …
3. The interest rate of a business loan is normally fixed, while …
4. A business loan is usually repayable in set instalments, while …
5. Business loans run for a fixed term, while …
6. Business loans are often used for financing fixed assets, while …

11 A business loan

A colleague shows you this brochure about loans from the UK bank Northern Standard. He has highlighted some parts he does not understand.

Northern Standard – Your Partner in Business

**Is your business growing? Are you seeking to expand?
That's where we can help!**

A Northern Standard Business Loan makes borrowing so simple, allowing you to concentrate on your business.
At Northern Standard our aim is to reward growing businesses with fairer lending terms. **1**

Here's how your business can profit:

- **Take out a loan of up to £250,000 with no arrangement fees charged.**
- **Rely on a fixed rate that supports your cash flow.** **2**
- **Borrow for a term of between one and ten years.**
- **Enjoy flexibility in repaying your loan with no early repayment charges.** **3**
- **Be free to take 'repayment holidays' from making capital payments without penalty. Interest will be charged during repayment breaks which may increase your payments afterwards.** **4**

Let's start working together now!

Phone our Business Manager any time
from 8.00 am – 8.00 pm
Mondays – Saturdays.
- Use our free Business Banking app.
- Visit us at www.northernstandard.co.uk

Please note: security may be required. Any property, which may include your home, may be repossessed if you fail to make the agreed repayments of a loan that has been secured on it. **5**

A Choose one of these pairs of sentences which is closest in meaning to each part your colleague has marked.

1 a The lending terms are designed to help businesses to grow.
b Growing businesses will get more favourable lending terms than others.

2 a Fixed instalments ensure that the same amount is repaid every month.
b A fixed interest rate allows a business to budget better.

3 a Lump-sum repayments can be made at no extra cost.
b This loan can only be repaid in the agreed instalments.

4 a Interest is charged if repayments are late due to public holidays.
b It is possible to miss an instalment but this will incur costs.

5 a The borrower can lose his/her home if the loan is not repaid.
b The borrower will get his/her property back if the loan is repaid.

B Point out three differences between this loan and the business line of credit in exercise 8.

LANGUAGE

How to link sentences

If two sentences are connected in meaning, it is sometimes better to link them to make one longer sentence using a clause. The connecting element may be a time, a place, a reason, a condition, a concession, a result or a purpose.

If it is a time, use 'after', 'before', 'since', 'when' or 'while',
e.g. Before he could set up the business, he had to apply for a loan.
If it is a place, use 'where',
e.g. The goods are made in China, where production costs are lower.
If it is a reason, use 'as', 'because' or 'since',
e.g. As the company has a cash flow problem, we cannot approve the loan.
If it is a condition, use 'if' or 'unless',
e.g. Unless the economy improves, sales will go on falling.
If it is a concession, use 'although' or 'though',
e.g. They decided to invest in new machinery though sales were poor.
If it is a result, use 'so … that' or 'such a … that',
e.g. The new product was such a success that profits rose by 25%.
If it is a purpose, use 'so that',
e.g. They bought land so that they could build new premises.

12 Working with words

A Use words from the box above to fill these gaps.

1 The new managing director joined the company … he was a trainee.
2 The Gulf region is an area … many expats work.
3 The bank will grant an overdraft … the company can solve its liquidity problems.
4 … earnings have increased, the company's shares have risen in value.
5 The firm has … a large turnover … it will need new premises soon.
6 … they can provide suitable security, the bank will not offer them a loan.
7 Last year's losses were … great … the company went bankrupt.
8 … they have made a profit, they have decided not to pay a dividend this year.

B Using a word from the box, link each pair of sentences to form one sentence. Note: there may be more than one correct answer.

1 The company has recently set up business in Dubai.
In Dubai they expect to find new customers.
2 The demand for the goods has risen.
The company does not yet need to increase its production capacity.
3 The sales staff have to improve their English.
They can communicate better with overseas clients.
4 Two years ago the company's profits fell drastically.
They lost their main customer.
5 The profits continue to grow.
The company will pay the workers a bonus.
6 In 2012 Ms Church took over as managing director.
She immediately introduced a policy of cutting costs.
7 Profits last quarter were much higher than expected.
The company's shares rose by 15%.

CULTURE

Types of Company in the UK and USA

In the UK and USA a business / an enterprise is any commercial organization that produces, buys, sells or supplies goods or services. A person who owns a business is an entrepreneur.
A person who owns and runs a business alone is a sole trader. The term single trader (proprietor) is also used.
The head of any type of British company is the Managing Director; the head of any type of US corporation is the Chief Executive Officer (CEO), although this title is increasingly used in UK companies, too.

The main types of company (AE: corporation) with their abbreviations are:

- Ltd (e.g. Smith & Sons Ltd) means a privately-owned company in the UK. The minimum capital requirement is £1. Ltd = Limited, which means that the shareholders liability is limited. This kind of company is similar to the GmbH in Germany, but here the minimum capital requirement is €25,000.
- plc (e.g. Proctor & Gamble plc) means a joint stock company in the UK. It is a public limited company whose shares are registered on the stock exchange, similar to a German AG. The minimum capital requirement is £50,000.
- LLP (e.g. Granger and Jones LLP) means that the company is a limited liability partnership in the UK. Such partnerships are often used by professional companies such as law firms.
- Inc. (e.g. IBM Inc.) means that the company is an incorporated company in the USA. There are various types largely according to tax arrangements.

13 Raising capital

KMK

17

Im Rahmen eines Praktikums bei einer britischen Bank hören Sie ein Gespräch zwischen Claire Hardy, Teilinhaberin einer GmbH, die einen Wäsche-Service für Hotels anbietet, und ihrem Bankberater Jeremy Clark. Ms Hardy hat um das Gespräch gebeten, weil ihre Firma expandieren möchte.

Kopieren Sie die folgende Tabelle und notieren Sie die Vor- und Nachteile der drei Finanzierungsmethoden vom Standpunkt der Kundin.

Finanzierungsmethode	Vorteile	Nachteile
Finanzierung aus Eigenkapital	…	…
Bankdarlehen	…	…
Aktienemission	…	…

14 Leseverstehen

Die Leiterin der Corporate Banking Abteilung Ihrer Bank wird an einer Konferenz in London teilnehmen, bei der auch der Geschäftsführer vom Rexam plc, Graham Chipchase, anwesend sein wird. Sie sind vor kurzem auf folgenden Zeitungsartikel gestoßen.

Notieren Sie auf Deutsch acht Fakten, die für Ihre Vorgesetzte nützlich sein könnten.

I wanted to be a fighter pilot but I ended up as the King of Cans

by John Collingridge

Graham Chipchase's heart sank as the RAF recruiting officer told him the news. His vision was fine but his eyes were set at the wrong angle in his head: becoming a fighter pilot would put too much strain on his eye muscles. He could fly passenger jets, the officer suggested, but Chipchase "did not want to fly buses round the world". The 17-year-old left Biggin Hill airport devastated, his dream in tatters.

His parents sat him down and told him to do something he enjoyed. The grammar school boy from Sunbury, southwest London, took a degree in the only subject that interested him, chemistry. A spell as an accountant followed, but after five years with Coopers and Lybrand he realized that he enjoyed working inside companies more than auditing their accounts. Chipchase rose through the ranks at the industrial gases group BOC and aircraft-wing maker GKN, before a headhunter offered him the position of finance director of a company he knew nothing about.

He has now spent 11 years at Rexam, expanding it and latterly knocking it into shape. The FTSE 100 manufacturing giant, which most consumers have never heard of, is one of the world's two top suppliers of drinks cans to big names such as Coca-Cola, Carlsberg, Pepsi and Red Bull.

Rexam was struggling when Chipchase was asked to step up to chief executive officer in January 2010. Canned drinks consumption had slumped in the recession and retailers were slashing stock to preserve cash. Five months earlier Rexam had begged shareholders for £351m to protect its debt rating as it struggled with hefty borrowings. [...]

Rexam had overstretched itself, opening too many production lines in Europe just as shoppers were spending less on canned drinks. Its plastics business, which made packaging for water, cosmetics and medicine, had suffered as make-up sales slumped and shoppers switched from bottled water to tap.

The 51-year-old in a white shirt and black trousers, sits impassively on a leather sofa as he recalls how he dealt with the 2008 slump – the biggest challenge of his career. "Our core markets changed overnight. You could see it happening through the sales line. I had to make some tough decisions. We took out 10% of our capacity, several thousand people." [...]

Chipchase is steadily driving Rexam, which grew out of the Bowater paper-making conglomerate, into the emerging markets. The opportunities posed by the growing middle classes are vast. Americans consume one can of fizzy drink per head per day; the average person in India drinks one can a year. Rexam is opening a second can plant in India and has bought land for a third. Coca-Cola and Pepsi are pouring billions into factories there. "India will develop like no other market you have seen," was the sage advice of one Rexam customer. [...]

Downtime

Chipchase relaxes by playing golf and is a member of a club on the south coast. His mother supported Tottenham Hotspur and his father supported Chelsea but he is a Manchester United fan. A self-confessed motorhead, Chipchase attends a couple of Formula One races every year. He is also a plane spotter, and collects aircraft tail numbers. Wine is another interest – he has a cellar with a few thousand bottles. "For drinking, not investment," he says.

The Sunday Times, 31 August 2014

15 An Initial Public Offering (IPO)

On 1 October 2014 the German online retailer Zalando went public.

A Before the IPO, Zalando published these statistics. On the basis of the figures, would you have advised personal customers of your bank to subscribe to the shares?

Give reasons.

B The first report below appeared before the IPO, the second one was published after the shares had been launched.

Say whether Zalando met the market's expectations.

C **In a group discuss the question "What makes for a successful IPO?"**

Zalando Worth $6.8 Billion after Pricing IPO at over $27 a Share

Zalando, Europe's largest online-only fashion retailer, priced shares on Monday at $27.28 in its initial public offering, valuing itself at almost $6.8 billion. At that price, the Berlin company raised $668 million in the largest German tech IPO since the 2000 listing of Deutsche Telekom. According to its prospectus, Zalando expects to start trading on the Frankfurt Stock Exchange on Wednesday, October 1st.

After experiencing strong demand from institutional investors, Zalando priced its shares at the higher end of the book-building range of $22.86 to $28.54 per share. The company sold at least 24.5 million shares to underwriters, who also have the option to purchase a further 3.7 million shares in an over-allotment agreement. If this option is exercised in full, Zalando could raise up to $768 million.

Zalando Surge Fizzles Kick-off to Busy German IPO Week

Zalando shares gave up all their earlier gains on the online retailer's debut today, providing a meager opening to the biggest week in German technology stock sales in a decade.

At the close of trading in Frankfurt the shares were unchanged at €21.50 ($27.28) after rising as much as 14%. That left the Berlin-based company with a market value of €5.3 billion ($6.7 billion). Zalando's performance contrasts with the 38% first-day gain in shares of Alibaba. The Chinese online retailer had the biggest initial public offering last month. After pricing the shares near the top end of the range, Zalando's day was more similar to that of Facebook. That stock lost half its value in the following months.

UNIT 9

Global banking

- Describing terms of payment in foreign trade
- Arranging a documentary credit
- Understanding Incoterms

1 Warm-up

Look at these photos and answer the following questions.

1. What is the connection between these photos?
2. Globalization has both positive and negative effects. What are they?
3. How have banks been affected by globalization?

2 Working with charts

The charts below compare volumes of trade in the developed countries and in emerging market economies.

A What are emerging market economies? Give examples.

B Look at the charts and choose the correct terms in the statements below.

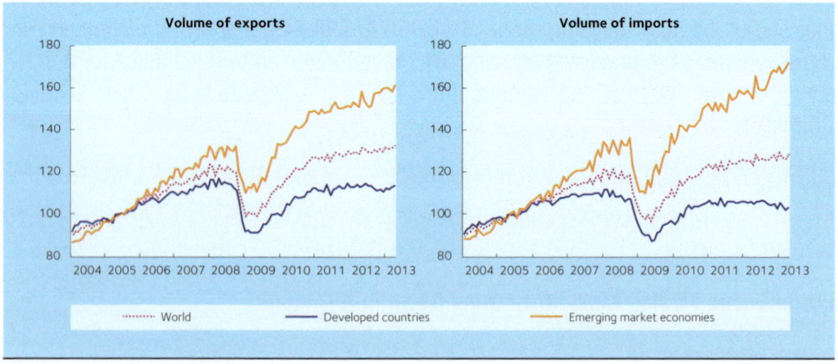

World Trade By Volume, January 2004-April 2013, Trade and Development Report 2013, United Nations. Reprinted with the permission of the United Nations.

1. The volume of world trade as a whole (*rose / fell*) at the end of 2008.
2. After 2009, the emerging market economies saw a dramatic (*decline / growth*) in their volume of exports.
3. The volume of imports is (*decreasing / increasing*) faster in the emerging market economies than in the developed countries.
4. In 2013 the developed countries had a trade (*deficit / surplus*) while the emerging market economies had a trade (*deficit / surplus*).

3 Chairing a discussion

A Work with a partner and answer these questions. Write down your ideas.

1. What caused the volume of world trade to fall at the end of 2008?
2. Why is the volume of exports growing faster in the emerging market economies than in the developed countries?
3. What reasons lie behind the emerging market economies' trade deficit?

B Discuss your findings in a small group. For each of the three questions in A, choose one person to chair the discussion and another to write down the group's conclusions. Use expressions from the Language box below.

C Every group member should get a copy of the group's conclusions and put them together in a short written report.

LANGUAGE

How to clarify and summarize information

To make sure you have understood someone correctly, you can say:

If I understand you correctly, …
So what you're saying is, …
In other words, you think that ...
Let me just check I've got this right, you mean …
Could you give an example of that?
Could you be more specific?

To summarize what someone has said, you can say:

To sum up, we can say that …
To recap, then, we can see that …
So the key points are …
So the overall picture shows us that …
If I may / Let me just go through the main points again, …

4 Terms of payment

A new colleague from the USA has never worked in the foreign trade department before. Help your colleague by doing these tasks.

A Choose one of the definitions below to explain each of these terms of payment. There is one term that you do not need. Which is it?

- documents against acceptance (D/A)
- documents against payment (D/P)
- payment in advance
- payment on open account
- 30 days after sight
- a documentary credit (D/C) or letter of credit (L/C)

1. The exporter dispatches the shipment after receiving payment.
2. The exporter dispatches the shipment, sends the invoice and waits for payment.
3. The importer's bank releases the documents when the importer has paid the invoice.
4. The importer's bank guarantees to make payment against presentation of the documents.
5. The importer's bank releases the documents when the importer has accepted a bill of exchange (B/E).

B **Copy this chart and fill it in to show your colleague where the advantages and disadvantages/risks of each of the terms of payment lie.**

Terms of payment	For the seller		For the buyer	
	Advantages	Disadvan-tages/risks	Advantages	Disadvan-tages/risks
Payment on open account				
Payment in advance				
D/P				
D/A				
A documentary credit				

5 Payment: foreign trade

18

You are on an internship at a UK bank. Harry Oldham, the owner of a small business that makes industrial glue, has received an enquiry from a company in Malaysia. As he has never exported before, Mr Oldham has made an appointment with Jim Asbury, an adviser in the foreign trade department. Mr Oldham has agreed that you may listen in on the consultation.

A **Prepare for the consultation by listing the points that you think Harry Oldham will ask about.**

B **Listen to the consultation and check if you were right.**

C **Read the dialogue and find the five terms of payment mentioned in it. Decide which one Harry Oldham prefers.**

Jim What can I do for you, Mr Oldham?

Harry I need a bit of advice on exporting. This company in Kuala Lumpur saw our website, asked for a sample of our products and is now enquiring about placing a large order with us.

Jim Oh! Congratulations! Is this your first export transaction?

Harry Yes, going global at last! And I don't know much about the Far East, so I thought I'd better ask you about arranging the payment.

Jim Of course. You can hardly allow payment on open account, can you?

Harry You mean, ship the goods, send an invoice and then wait for them to transfer the money? Goodness, no! I can't take a risk like that.

Jim And I doubt the buyer will agree to payment in advance …

Harry They pay the bill first and I only send off the shipment when the money's in my account? That'd be nice, but I can't see them agreeing to it!

Jim That's why it would be safer for you to arrange collection of documents …

Harry Hang on a minute. You've lost me there. What documents?

Jim I'm sorry, the shipping documents – that's the bill of lading, the commercial invoice, the certificate of insurance, the certificate of origin and the packing list. They will need the bill of lading to collect the goods.

Harry I see. I suppose my freight forwarder will deal with all those?

Jim Yes. Collection of documents works in two different ways. If you agree on documents against payment, the buyers will have to pay your invoice before they can get the documents from their bank.

Harry But what if they want to pay later? We let some of our customers in this country pay 30 days after sight.

Jim That would be the second way. If you agree on documents against acceptance, the buyers will have to accept a bill of exchange in order to get the documents from their bank.

Harry Hmm. I'm not so sure I'd trust a bank that I don't know to get it right.

Jim I'd recommend asking the buyers to apply for a documentary credit.

Harry I've heard of a letter of credit. Are documentary credits the same?

Jim Yes, they are. With a documentary credit a bank guarantees to make the payment when the documents are presented to them. It's the safest of all the terms of payment.

Harry D'you know, exporting might be a lot less risky than I thought! Can you tell me how a documentary credit works?

GRAMMAR

Gerunds

1 **Exporting** might be a lot less risky than I thought.
2 I'd recommend **asking** the buyers to apply for a documentary credit.
3 I thought I'd ask you about **arranging** the payment.

- The gerund is formed with the *-ing* form of the verb. (1–3)
- Gerunds can be used as the subject of a sentence (1) or as the object after certain verbs (2). Here are some common ones:
  avoid – consider – dislike – enjoy – finish – hate* – imagine – involve – like* – love* – (not) mind – recommend – risk – suggest
- Verbs used after prepositions must be in the form of the gerund. (3)
- These expressions are followed by a gerund:
  advice on – consist of – (dis)advantage of – information about – look forward to – means of – method of – possibility of – reason for – service of – specialize in – way of

* The verbs *hate*, *like* and *love* can also be followed by an infinitive.

6 Practice

A Replace the words in italics with an expression with a gerund.

Example: Mr Oldham needs information on *how to export goods safely.*
Mr Oldham needs information on exporting goods safely.

1 Mr Oldham is worried about the risk *that he may lose money.*
2 He hopes to find a way *how he can avoid this.*
3 Jim Asbury gives him advice on *how to secure the payment.*
4 They discuss the reasons *why he should ask for a documentary credit.*
5 A D/C offers the possibility *that he can get the payment guaranteed by a bank.*
6 The importer's bank will charge for the service *when they issue a letter of credit.*

B Complete these sentences using gerunds.

1 My bank specializes in …
2 Working in a bank, I particularly enjoy …
3 Of all the departments I have worked in, I recommend …
4 At the moment, my daily work mainly consists of …
5 In future I look forward to …

7 A documentary credit

A The points (1–10) on the chart show how a documentary credit works. Use them to put the sentences (a–j) below into the correct order.

- **a** The seller's bank credits the sum to the seller's account.
- **b** The buyer's bank issues an *irrevocable* documentary credit and notifies the seller's bank.
- **c** The buyer asks his bank to open a documentary credit *in favour* of the seller.
- **d** The buyer's bank transfers the money to the seller's bank.
- **e** The seller gives the shipping documents to his bank.
- **f** The seller *ships* the goods.
- **g** The buyer pays or accepts a bill of exchange and the documents are *released* against payment or acceptance.
- **h** The seller's bank either *advises or confirms* the D/C and informs the seller.
- **i** The buyer's bank *presents* the documents to the buyer for payment or for acceptance of a B/E.
- **j** The seller's bank checks that the documents *conform* with the D/C and *forwards* them to the buyer's bank.

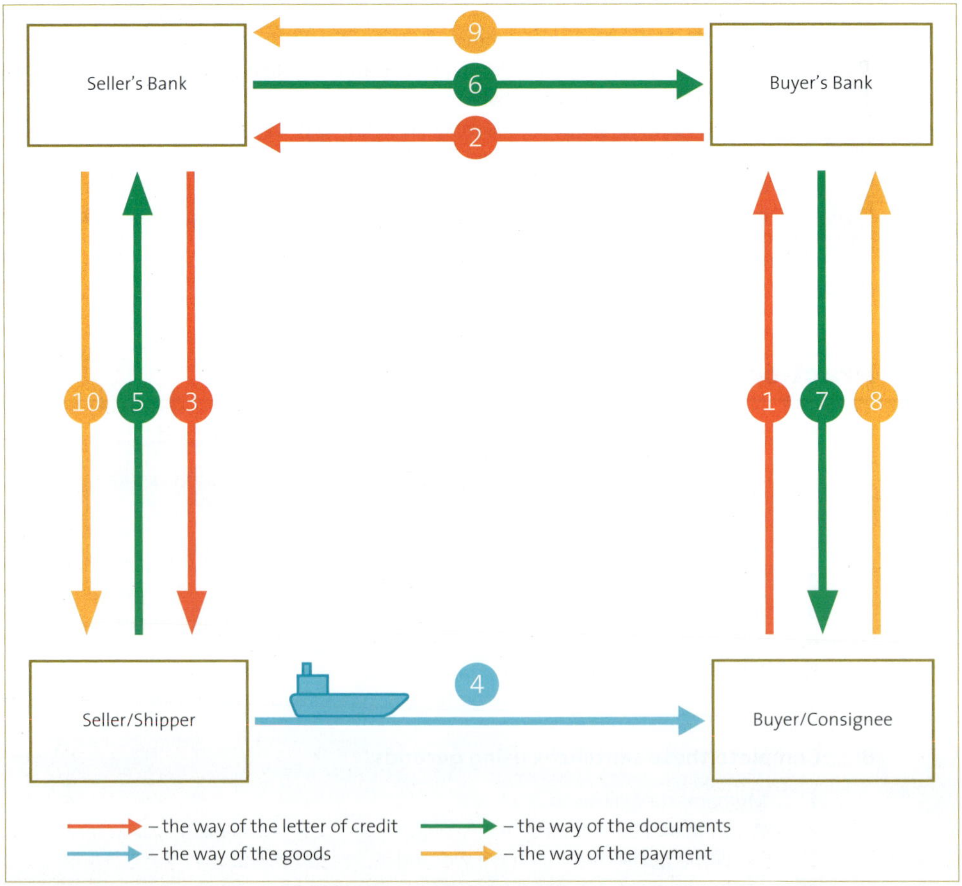

B How would you say the expressions in *italics* in sentences (a–j) above in German?

CULTURE

Dealing with Far-Eastern customers

There are many ethnic groups and cultures in the Far East, but here are some basic points.

- Be careful: if you have offended someone, they may say nothing or even keep smiling.
- Avoid direct confrontation. Look for other ways to resolve differences of opinion.
- Read between the lines. Many Asians communicate indirectly or implicitly, e.g. a Japanese person who says "That would be difficult" means "That is impossible".
- Always ask after the client's family in small talk.
- Never say the word "no" in China. Use expressions like "That is not correct" or "I see things differently".
- Avoid the numbers 13, 4 and any number ending in a 4 (these numbers are considered unlucky). In China, the number 8 brings good luck, especially if it is at the end of a long number.

8 Using a D/C

KMK

19

Jim Asbury erklärt Harry Oldham, wie ein Warenakkreditiv funktioniert.

A Hören Sie sich diesen Teil der Beratung an und machen Sie Notizen.

B Nach der Beratung stellt Ihnen Jim die folgenden Fragen. Verwenden Sie Ihre Notizen, um sie zu beantworten.

1. Wer beantragt das Warenakkreditiv?
2. Was ist der Unterschied zwischen einem avisierten und einem bestätigten Warenakkreditiv?
3. Wann kann der Importeur seine Frachtpapiere erhalten?
4. Wer übernimmt die Kosten eines Akkreditivs?

9 Working with words

Jim Asbury has drawn this diagram to show how Harry Oldham's goods will be shipped to Malaysia.

Match the numbers 1–8 on the diagram with the terms a–h below.

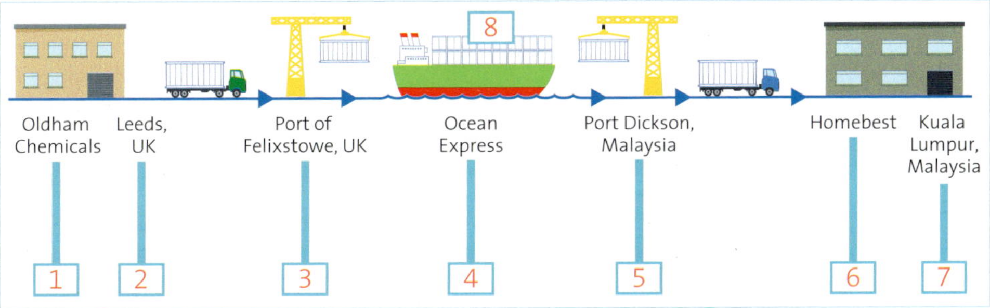

a buyer / consignee / importer
b place of delivery / place of destination
c place of dispatch / place of loading
d port of discharge / port of destination
e port of loading / port of shipment
f seller / shipper / exporter
g ship / vessel
h consignment / shipment

10 A D/C application form

The documentary credit application form that Jim Asbury uses is like the one on page 122.

Look these terms highlighted there in yellow and translate them into German.

1 Irrevocable
2 Sight Payment
3 Transferable
4 Beneficiary
5 Date of DC expiry
6 Partial shipment
7 Transshipment
8 Drafts
9 Issuing bank
10 Ultimate Buyer
11 Place of final destination
12 Issuance charges
13 Acceptance commission
14 Confirmation

11 Role-play: advising on a letter of credit

KMK

Führen Sie mithilfe der Rollenkarten ein Beratungsgespräch.

Bankberater/in

Sie arbeiten in der Auslandsabteilung Ihrer Bank. Sie haben einen Termin mit Simon/Simone Foster.

- Begrüßen Sie den Kunden / die Kundin. Stellen Sie sich vor.
- Fragen Sie, wie Sie dem Kunden / der Kundin behilflich sein können.
- Erklären Sie, dass ein Akkreditiv vor allem am Anfang einer Geschäftsbeziehung und bei hohen Rechnungsbeträgen häufig verwendet wird.
- Sagen Sie, dass die Akkreditiv ausstellende Bank dem Begünstigten die Zahlung garantiert. Er kann die Lieferung verschiffen und sicher sein, dass sie bezahlt wird.
- Erklären Sie, dass der Zahlungspflichtige das Akkreditiv bei seiner Bank beantragen muss. Die Bank prüft seine Bonität, erteilt das Akkreditiv und informiert die Bank des Zahlungsempfängers, die das Akkreditiv avisiert oder bestätigt.
- Sagen Sie, dass der Antragsteller die Kosten des Akkreditivs trägt. Weisen Sie darauf hin, dass es zu den Aufgaben der Bank gehört, die Dokumente noch vor der Zahlung zu prüfen. Insofern ist auch der Antragssteller durch das Akkreditiv geschützt.
- Nennen Sie das Konnossement, die Handelsrechnung, das Versicherungszertifikat, die Packliste und das Ursprungszertifikat. Sagen Sie, dass die Dokumente von der Art der Waren abhängen.
- Überreichen Sie ein Antragsformular und Ihre Karte mit Ihrer Telefonnummer, falls es weitere Fragen geben sollte.
- Verabschieden Sie sich.

Kunde/Kundin

Sie sind Simon/Simone Foster aus den USA. Sie haben ein junges, florierendes Geschäft für vegane Lebensmittel in Berlin. Ein Großhändler in Jakarta, Indonesien, hat Ihnen ein gutes Angebot für Soja-Produkte unterbreitet, verlangt jedoch ein Akkreditiv. Sie haben ein Akkreditiv noch nie benutzt und wenden sich an Ihre Bank.

- Stellen Sie sich vor.
- Erklären Sie den Grund Ihres Besuches: Sie können nicht verstehen, dass der Exporteur ein Akkreditiv verlangt. Ihre bisherigen Geschäftspartner haben an Ihrer Bonität nie gezweifelt!
- Sie verstehen immer noch nicht den Grund, warum der Exporteur ein Akkreditiv von Ihnen verlangt!
- Fragen Sie, warum die Bank des Exporteurs diese Aufgabe nicht übernehmen kann.
- Sie möchten wissen, wer die Kosten eines Akkreditivs trägt.
- Erkundigen Sie sich, um welche Dokumente es sich handelt.
- Bitten Sie um ein Akkreditivantragsformular. Sie werden es in Ruhe lesen.
- Bedanken und verabschieden Sie sich.

12 Bills of lading

Jim Asbury has given you this text about bills of lading that passed through his department.

A Read the text and decide whether the statements below are true or false or contain information that is not in the text. Correct the false ones.

What is a Bill of lading?

A bill of lading is a receipt signed at the place or port of loading by the carrier, the agent of the transport company or the captain of the vessel. It has to state the names of the shipper and the consignee, the places or ports of loading and destination, the terms of transportation and a description of the goods, their weight and the packing. The bill of lading confirms that the consignment has been received for shipment either on board (a Shipped on Board B/L) or at the place of loading (a Received for Shipment B/L). If the issuer is satisfied that the consignment appears to be in good condition, the B/L is clean; any visible damage, for example to the packing, must be noted on the B/L, which is then unclean.

Bills of lading are usually issued in full sets – that means there are two or three signed originals which are identical. The shipper sends them separately to the consignee in case one gets lost. As the bill of lading is a title document, the consignee (or the consignee's forwarding agent) needs it to take possession of the shipment when it arrives at the port or place of discharge. It also gives the consignee the right to re-route the consignment during transportation. Bills of lading can be negotiable, which means that the consignee may even sell the goods during transportation, simply by endorsing the B/L and transferring the rights to another person, but there are also non-negotiable bills.

There are various types of bill of lading, and the one required depends on where the goods are shipped and the mode of transport used. An Inland B/L covers the transport of the goods as far as the port of loading, but if the goods are shipped overseas, an Ocean B/L is required. So, some export transactions require both. Often more than one mode of transport is necessary: in this case a Through B/L covers multi-modal transport. An Air waybill is a type of bill of lading that is used for transportation by air and can cover both domestic and international flights. The terms of the contract of sale or the letter of credit specify which type of bill is used.

1. The shipper makes out and signs the bill of lading.
2. A bill of lading need not state the value of the shipment.
3. A bill of lading shows that a consignment has been loaded onto a ship.
4. A clean bill of lading means that the goods are not damaged in any way.
5. The holder of a bill of lading can take possession of the goods.
6. Importers often pledge bills of lading as security for short-term loans.
7. Only the original consignee named on the bill can receive the shipment.
8. Two bills of lading may be necessary to cover both land and sea transport.

B Look at the bill of lading on page 123 and with a partner ask and answer questions about it.

13 The Incoterms

Read about the Incoterms on pages 125–127. Choose one Incoterm, say what costs and risks it involves for the seller and buyer, and ask the class which Incoterm it is. The student who names it correctly takes over and asks the next question.

14 Mediation

Ein britischer Kollege, der auf einem Londoner Seminar zum Thema „Global Money Movement" referieren soll, hat Sie um Material gebeten. Bei Ihrer Recherche sind Sie auf den folgenden Zeitungsartikel gestoßen.

Fassen Sie auf Englisch die wesentlichen Aussagen des Textes zusammen.

Hawala

Geld außerhalb SEPA zu überweisen kann oft zu einer teuren Angelegenheit werden. Bankgebühren und der Wechsel in die jeweilige Währung verursachen Kosten. Noch schwieriger ist es, wenn Geld in Länder ohne Netz von zuverlässig funktionierenden Banken überwiesen werden soll (wie Afghanistan oder Bangladesch) oder wenn der Zahlungsempfänger kein Bankkonto besitzt. Um diese Problematik zu umgehen, wird vor allem in muslimischen Ländern ein Zahlungssystem namens Hawala benutzt. Hawala bedeutet auf Arabisch „Wechsel" oder „Überweisung". Der deutsche Begriff „Avalkredit" ist eine Ableitung daraus.

Hawala wird auch in nicht-muslimischen Ländern praktiziert. Ein Arbeiter pakistanischer Herkunft, der in Duisburg lebt, möchte zum Beispiel einen Teil seines Lohnes seinem Vater im Osten Pakistans zukommen lassen. In Duisburg betritt er ein Café und übergibt dem Betreiber, einem sogenannten Hawaldar, eine Eurosumme in bar. Beide haben vorher ein Buchstaben- oder Zahlencode für die Transaktion vereinbart. Innerhalb von Stunden kann der Zahlungsempfänger in Pakistan seinen Friseur besuchen, der – ebenfalls in seiner Rolle als Hawaldar – ihm die Summe in Rupien abzüglich einer kleinen Provision aushändigt. Das System ist schnell, billig, bequem und zuverlässig. Die beteiligten Hawaldar rechnen später über andere Transaktionen, Waren, Dienstleistungen oder Gold miteinander ab. Das System basiert auf Vertrauen: Ein Hawaldar-Betrüger würde seine Ehre und seinen Platz in den finanziellen und religiösen Kreisen der Gesellschaft verlieren.

Diese Vertraulichkeit ist der Grund, warum Hawala-Überweisungen in Deutschland nicht zulässig sind. Es gibt keine Belege für die geleisteten Zahlungen. Per Gesetz müssen Zahldienste jedoch von der Finanzaufsicht Bafin genehmigt und kontrolliert werden. Im Falle von Hawala ist das nicht möglich. Hawala-Überweisungen bleiben geheim und anonym.

Ein Nachteil ist auch, dass Hawala-Überweisungen dadurch das ideale Geld-Transfersystem für

Kriminelle und den internationalen Terrorismus ist. Für Terrornetze gibt es immerhin nur zwei Möglichkeiten, sich zu finanzieren: Entweder wird Bargeld direkt in einem Koffer ins Ausland transportiert. Das ist jedoch riskant und die Summe kann schnell aufgebraucht sein. Oder sie nutzen Hawala. Es hinterlässt keine Spuren und ermöglicht Terroristen, unbegrenzte Summen zu bewegen. Aus dem Bericht des US-Senats zum 11. September 2001 geht hervor, das Al-Qaida regelmäßig Hawala benutzt. Die Attentäter des Anschlags auf das Büro „Charlie Hebdo" 2015 in Paris gaben zu, Geld von einer Al-Qaida Zelle in Jemen erhalten zu haben.

Hawala wird auch zur Geldwäsche verwendet, sowohl von lateinamerikanischen Drogenkartellen als auch von albanischen Drogenhändlern. Die enormen Summen für den Kauf illegaler Waffen und Kriegsmaterialien werden ebenfalls auf diesem Wege bewegt. Hawala wird in Ländern genutzt, in denen Korruption herrscht und zwischen Milizenführern, Regierungsbeamten, Polizisten und Terroristen kaum zu unterscheiden ist. Nach einer Schätzung der Weltbank läuft 65% des Geldes, das ins südliche Afrika fließt, über Hawala. Durch Hawala werden täglich Milliarden Dollar um die Welt bewegt, häufig über Dubai als Drehpunkt zwischen Ost und West.

Was können westliche Regierungen dagegen unternehmen? Es müssen legale, billige und sichere Wege gefunden werden, um Geld ins Ausland zu überweisen. Kriminelle und Terroristen würden zwar weiterhin Hawala verwenden, aber für einen Teil der Nutzer gäbe es zumindest eine Alternative. Effizienter aber ungleich schwieriger wäre es, die Quellen des Geldes zu kontrollieren: den illegalen Drogen- und Waffenhandel und den internationalen Terrorismus.

15 Islamic finance

You are taking part in an international conference for young employees from different European banks. The subject is Islamic banking.

A **Use information from this article to summarize the main aspects and the importance of Islamic banking.**

B **In a small group, discuss changes German banks could make to attract more Muslim customers. Consider**

- their bank branches and branch network
- the staff and staff training
- the range of banking products
- communication and marketing

C **Present your results as a group. Ask the other students for their feedback.**

Islamic Banking

What has The Shard, one of London's most spectacular buildings, got to do with Islamic finance?

Half-owned by the Emir of Qatar, The Shard was built using Sharia-compliant finance. This is just one example of the booming market for banking products that conform to Islamic law: in Britain, Islamic banking is growing 50% faster than traditional UK banking business, and worldwide 1.5 billion euros are invested yearly under the principles of Islamic law, the Sharia.

The basis of all Islamic banking, the Sharia, stipulates that money is simply a means of exchange and has no intrinsic value. As a matter of faith, a Muslim may not benefit by earning interest when lending money to – or receiving money from – anyone else. This prohibition of interest, called *riba*, means that Islamic banks do not offer loans, overdrafts, mortgages or savings plans; nor do they trade in bonds, debentures or any funds which contain such investments. Holding shares can be permitted, but not if the company produces or trades in certain goods, for example alcohol, pork or weapons. The prohibition both of gambling and speculation further rules out trading in derivatives such as options, futures and swaps

How can a bank function without its two main sources of income: loans and investment products? According to Islamic law, money must be used productively with investor and bank sharing both the risk and the profit from any financial success. This means that trading lies at the heart of Islamic banking. Instead of granting a customer a loan to buy a house, for example, an Islamic bank buys the house itself, then resells it to the customer at a higher price, payable in instalments, a system called *murabahah*. Islamic banks also sell *sukuk*, Sharia-compliant bonds that pay a rent to the holder instead of interest. These bonds are backed by physical assets, such as property, so that the issuer can guarantee to repay the nominal value of the bond at maturity.

Since the 2008 financial crisis, the issue of Islamic bonds has increased six-fold and demand is growing. Studies have shown that 15% of the approximately four million Muslims living in Germany are interested in Sharia-compliant banking with the tendency rising, particularly in North-Rhine Westphalia where over 1.5 million Muslims live. An Islamic banking project in Düsseldorf has even reported that 20% of its customers are non-Muslims who support the principles of Islamic finance.

Islamic finance is a sector that European banks cannot afford to ignore.

UNIT 10

Applying for a job

- Writing a CV
- Writing a covering letter
- Attending an interview

1 Warm-up

An opinion poll was carried out among trainee bank advisers to find out what skills they thought were important for getting a job in a bank in an English-speaking country.

A **Read what some of the trainees said, then work in groups and rank the skills in order of importance.**

B **When you have decided, look at File 1 on page 119 and compare your ranking with the trainees.**

I think your chances depend on how well you fill in the application form. If you don't do that first step correctly, then you will never be considered for an interview.

Being able to handle the interview is the most important thing. You should be able to respond to the interview questions and to give positive replies even if you're asked difficult questions. Try to be positive and confident.

Understanding the job advertisement is the most important thing. You need a clear idea of what the job is and what the employer is looking for.

Writing a good covering letter is crucial. It should complement your CV and highlight why you're the right person for the job.

I believe that writing a good CV is the most important skill you need. A good CV shows a prospective employer at a glance whether your educational and professional experience matches the needs of the bank.

2 A job advertisement

Elisabeth Frey has been working in the branch office of a German bank for the last three years. Now that she has finished her training, she is interested in working abroad. She has found the advertisement below on the internet.

A Study the advertisement and do these tasks. In some cases, the information for your answer can be found in different parts of the text.

1. Name the job and describe the duties the applicant would have.
2. State where the prospective employee would work.
3. Say how much he/she would earn to begin with.
4. Point out the benefits the successful applicant can expect.
5. Describe the qualifications, personal characteristics and professional skills required for the job.
6. Explain how someone should apply and what will happen next.

Banking sector **Job title: Banking Customer Service Adviser** Add to job shortlist

Job Type: Permanent
Starting salary: £18,000 per annum
Location: Edinburgh
Reference: AQ16582

We are a leading international bank that is looking to recruit a Customer Service Adviser for one of our branches in Edinburgh.

Responsibilities include

- setting up and maintaining customers' accounts.
- processing cheques, handling cash and dealing with payments and withdrawals.
- using a computerized system to update account details.
- contacting customers to inform them of our latest products.
- exchanging foreign currencies.
- general administration tasks.

We are looking for

- excellent communication and people skills.
- the ability to work as part of a team.
- strong personal drive, the ability to think on your feet.
- a willingness to learn and a pro-active approach to your own personal development.
- reliability and discretion, especially in dealing with confidential information.
- good computer skills.

What we offer

- starting salary of £18,000 rising incrementally after initial training to £26,000 per annum.
- in-house training and development scheme, learning on the job from experienced staff.
- opportunities for promotion.

Entry requirements

- a recognized banking qualification or a degree
- two years' experience in a bank

We are looking for commitment to providing excellent customer service, so any experience in this area will be useful. It will also help you if you have experience in handling cash.

As a Banking Customer Service Adviser, you are a customer's first point of contact, so if you enjoy talking to a wide range of people and you are interested in finance, this job could be perfect for you.

The position, which is permanent, offers a superb opportunity for a hard-working, enthusiastic person.

Complete online application form

Successful applicants will be asked to send their CV together with a covering letter.

Initial interviews by telephone.

B **Find the English equivalents of these German words in the advertisement.**

1	Engagement	**5**	vertraulich
2	jdn einstellen	**6**	anfänglich
3	Bereitschaft	**7**	schrittweise
4	Verlässlichkeit	**8**	pro Jahr

3 Understanding job advertisements

A **Work with a partner. You are each going to read a job advertisement and answer your partner's questions.**

Partner A: Look at File 2 on page 119
Partner B: Look at File 6 on page 121

Read your job advertisement. Then take turns to ask and answer questions on:

- the position
- where the job is
- the salary
- what the requirements are
- how to apply
- what happens if the application is successful

B **Discuss the advertisements with another pair. Say which position interests you most and why. Explain why you are (not) qualified for the position.**

GRAMMAR

Relative pronouns

1 The colleague **who/that** wrote the advertisement has a temporary position.
2 She works for a firm **which/that** recruits personnel for banks.
3 The bank, **whose** offices are located in London, is one of the biggest in the UK.
4 This is the candidate (**who/that**) I interviewed last week.

- Relative pronouns introduce relative clauses.
- A relative clause which contains information necessary to understand the sentence is called a defining relative clause (1, 2); non defining relative clauses give extra information and are separated by commas (3).
- The relative pronoun can be left out in a relative clause if it is the object of that clause. (4)

4 Practice

Complete the sentences using a suitable relative pronoun where necessary.

1 The bank is looking for someone … has already done a period of training.
2 Always print out a copy of an application form … you have completed online.
3 The trainee … application has just arrived looks ideal for the position.
4 The CV … I received this morning is very interesting.
5 This is the position … I've applied for.
6 It is a bank … deals exclusively with private clients.

5 Continuing the application process

KMK

Elisabeth möchte sich auf die Stelle als Kundenberaterin in Edinburgh bewerben. Da ihr Lebenslauf und Anschreiben auf Englisch verfasst sein müssen, schaut sie sich auf der Webseite *Your Money Matters* nach Tipps um. Sie versteht vieles nicht und bittet ihre Freundin Lucy um Hilfe.

Lesen Sie die folgenden Fragen und beantworten Sie sie auf Deutsch.

1 Wie sieht das Format eines britischen Lebenslaufs aus?
2 Welche Kontaktdaten muss ich angeben?
3 Welche Reihenfolge meiner Berufstätigkeit, Schulbesuche usw. ist angebracht? Chronologisch? Oder das Aktuellste zuerst?
4 Was schreibe ich unter „allgemeine Kenntnisse"?
5 Wie gebe ich Referenzen an?

www.yourmoneymatters.com/bankingCVs

Your Money Matters

Your CV is a summary of your abilities, work experience, education and qualifications. There is no set format for a British CV, but you should keep it short, using headings to guide the reader. Make sure your CV is honest and factual.

TIPS

1 Give your name and address, telephone number(s) (home/mobile) and email address.

2 This should be a short message that catches the attention of the reader and summarizes your skills and experience relevant to the job which you are applying for.

Use note form and write in the third person throughout. This helps to keep your CV focused and direct, for example: *Motivated Banking Customer Service Adviser with experience in German branch office.*

3 As a general rule, CVs should be in reverse chronological order, listing the most recent position first. For each position held you should provide the dates of the start and end of employment, the employer's name and address, the job title, the main duties and responsibilities and achievements.

4 Give a brief description of qualifications (school, academic and/or professional). Give the names of schools or colleges in reverse chronological order.

5 Write about skills gained throughout your education and work experience, such as languages, IT skills or a full, clean driving licence. These skills are of interest to any employer. You should also describe your character using words like *good maths skills, team-orientated, flexible, energetic,* etc.

6 Writing about your hobbies and interests could help to create a more rounded picture of your personality and provide something more personal to discuss at an interview. Be careful about what you write – a dangerous sport or *socializing with friends* may not be what an employer wants to hear!

7 Due to data protection laws, candidates should not provide referees' names, addresses or any other contact details on CVs, but should state that details are available on request. Always ask your referees' permission before you give someone their contact details.

6 Preparing your CV

Elisabeth has prepared her CV using the tips from the website. You are going to use this to prepare your CV.

A First, look at Elisabeth's details. What differences can you find between her CV and a German CV?

Elisabeth Frey
Am Kattenkamp 236, 33611 Bielefeld, Germany
Mobile: (+49) 176 3946772
Email: lisa.frey@gmx.com

Personal statement
Highly-motivated, team-orientated, trained banking professional with experience in German branch office. Seeking experience on the British market using language skills.

Work experience
Since March 20.. Bank Trainee, Sparkasse, Olderdissen
General banking duties, dealing with customers at service desk, assisting with matters relating to customers' accounts, explaining banking products, contacting customers on the phone

Education
August 20..– July 20.. ABC Vocational College, Bielefeld, 3 years, part-time vocational school
August 20..– June 20.. Bielefeld Gymnasium
Abitur (Final exams similar to A levels)
Main subjects: Economics, English, German

Skills
Excellent IT-Skills (MS Office); data-base management
Good at working under pressure, friendly, flexible
Native language, German; fluent English (oral and written)

Hobbies and interests
Travelling, foreign languages

References
Names of referees available on request.

B Now use the tips from the website in exercise 5 to prepare your own CV. Copy the layout of Elisabeth's CV and use any words and phrases from it which are appropriate.

7 A covering letter

A covering letter is a formal letter with a standard structure. Don't always use the same letter but write a covering letter tailor-made for each job you apply for.

Read Elisabeth's covering letter and say which parts (1–5) go with which explanations from the box. There is one explanation too many. Which is it?

asking the employer to invite applicant for an interview • referring to details on CV • referring to the position • saying why the applicant is applying for the position • explaining typical customer problems • stating why the applicant is the best person for the job

Elisabeth Frey
Am Kattenkamp 236
33611 Bielefeld, Germany
Mobile: (+49) 176 3946772
Email: lisa.frey@gmx.com

The Edinburgh Bank
Attn. Mr Ian McKenzie (HR Department)
42-44 Princes Street
EDINBURGH
EH2 4EQ
Great Britain

20 April 20..

Dear Mr McKenzie

Banking Customer Service Adviser

1 With reference to your advertisement Ref. No. AQ16582 on the internet, I would like to apply for the above post.

2 I am very interested in the job you are offering as I feel sure it will give me the opportunity to develop both on a personal level and on a career basis. I am particularly keen to work in an English-speaking country where I can apply my knowledge of English on a daily basis.

3 As you can see from the enclosed CV, I am currently employed in a German bank, learning on the job, as a Trainee Bank Assistant. My tasks include all general banking duties, dealing with customers at the service desk, sorting out customer difficulties relating to day-to-day banking issues, updating the customer database, explaining banking products and contacting customers on the phone.

By the end of this summer, I will have completed my three-year, part-time Banking Trainee course at the ABC Vocational College in Bielefeld.

4 Through the experience I have gained in my present position, I believe I can add value to any bank in the United Kingdom. My language abilities will also make me an asset to any team I join. My English is excellent as I studied English for eight years up to A level. English also makes up part of my training at vocational college. My native language is German.

5 My CV is enclosed. I am available for an interview at short notice.

I would appreciate it if you could consider my application and hope that you will grant me an interview.

I look forward to hearing from you soon.

Yours sincerely
Elisabeth Frey
Encl.

LANGUAGE

How to write a covering letter

Remember:
- Your covering letter should be only one page long.
- Avoid too many sentences that begin with "I".
- After the "Dear XX" all letters and emails then start with a capital letter.
- If you start a letter / an email with a personal name (Dear Anne, Dear Ms Green), finish it with "Yours sincerely".
- If you begin a letter / an email with a no personal name (Dear Sir or Madam), you always finish it with "Yours faithfully".

---

1 Opening phrases
- With reference to / Re: your advertisement on/in … (website, newspaper, magazine, etc.) of … (date).
- I see that you are looking for a/an … (name of job).

2 Education/training; present employment
- I attended … (name of school/college) for … (length of time).
- I studied … (subjects) at vocational school in … (name of town/city) from … (date) to … (date).
- At present, / In my current role, I am working for … (employer) as a/an … (name of job). My responsibilities are …
- I will / expect to complete my period of training on … (date).

3 Why you want the job and reasons for seeking new position
- I am very interested in working abroad.
- It is time for me to seek a new and more challenging position.
- Having worked with … for … years, I now feel it is time to gain further experience.

4 What you can offer the employer
- My skill set matches your requirements perfectly.
- Self-motivation and good time management are part of my skill set. It is precisely these skills that I would like to use in your bank and further develop …
- As an open and communicative person, I will be able to use my solid, interpersonal skills within your …

5 Closing paragraph
- Enclosed / Attached (for online applications) is my CV / résumé (AE) / list of qualifications and experience.
- As regards my availability, I can start work immediately / as of next month / in … (month).
- I am available for interview at any time / from …
- I look forward to hearing from you in the near future / at your earliest convenience.

8 Writing your covering letter

KMK

Lesen Sie die Stellenanzeige aus Übung 2 und die Anzeigen auf S. 119 und 121 erneut. Schreiben Sie eine Bewerbung für die Stelle, die Sie am meisten interessiert.

Decken Sie folgende Punkte in Ihr Anschreiben ab:
- worauf Sie sich bewerben
- wo Sie die Anzeige gefunden haben
- was Sie motiviert
- warum Sie sich besonders gut für die Position eignen
- Ihre Bereitschaft, zu einem Vorstellungsgespräch zu kommen

9 Handling telephone interviews

KMK

Elisabeth wurde informiert, dass sie nächste Woche ein Telefoninterview führen wird. Sie sucht im Internet nach Tipps.

A Lesen Sie die Tipps und machen Sie sich auf Deutsch Notizen. Benutzen Sie diese Notizen, um die Tipps mit einer deutschen Kollegin aus der Personalabteilung zu besprechen. Sie möchten wissen, ob sich deutsche und englische Bewerbungsgespräche unterscheiden.

www.moneymatters.com/phoneinterviews

Your telephone interview

One short phone call is all it takes to get you to the next level in your job application process – or not. By asking just a few questions, an interviewer can quickly decide if you are a likely candidate for the job.

Don't let your interviewer think that this phone call is not as meaningful to you as if it were a face-to-face interview.

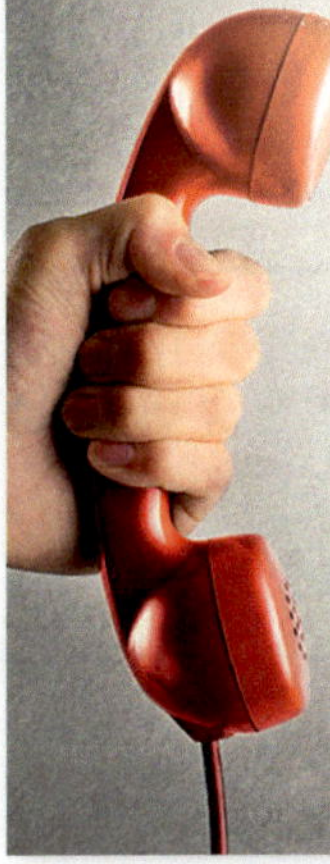

Be prepared!

Have these things ready beside your phone:

- a copy of the job description
- a copy of your letter of application, your CV and your references
- a notebook and a couple of pens so that you can take notes during the interview
- a list of questions you want to ask the interviewer
- a list of your strengths

Sell yourself!

A good story is much more interesting than a bullet-point list of job skills so, before the interview, write down all your success stories and practise telling them in a concise form. These can be academic achievements or work stories related to the position you're applying for.

Remember, if you don't make a good impression on the phone, you won't be invited to the face-to-face interview. As the saying goes: you only get one chance to make a first impression!

B Work with a partner and read the questions the interviewer asked Elisabeth. Reading between the lines, decide together what the interviewer wanted to find out by asking these questions. Choose from the list of suggestions (a–f).

1 Do you have a few minutes to talk to me so that I can get a better idea of what it is you're expecting from the position?
2 What led you to apply for the position?
3 You're currently working in a German bank. Why do you want to leave?
4 What would you like to be doing five years from now?
5 I think we've covered everything, but is there anything you'd like to ask me?
6 We'll be interviewing candidates in Edinburgh next week. Would you be interested in coming in and talking to us?

a If we were to hire you, would we be making an investment in the future of the bank?
b Have you done any research on our bank?
c Why do you think you're the right person for the job?
d What kind of person are you? Should we go further with your application?
e Are you still interested in the job?
f Why do you want to change your employer?

10 Preparing for a face-to-face interview

KMK

20 Ian McKenzie, the HR (Human Resources) manager of The Edinburgh Bank, invites Elisabeth to a face-to-face interview. In order to prepare herself, Elisabeth listens to a podcast in which an expert gives tips about face-to-face job interviews.

Read the introduction to the podcast and copy the "Five stages of an interview" into your notebook. After that, listen and make notes.

www.yourmoneymatters.com/interviews

Five stages of an interview

In today's podcast, our business coach, Pat Klein, is going to give us some advice about how to prepare for a face-to-face job interview.

Stage 1: Greetings and introductions	Stage 4: Questions from the candidate
Stage 2: Small talk	Stage 5: Further arrangements and the end of the interview
Stage 3: The main part of the interview	

11 Practising the main part of an interview

In exercise 8, you applied for one of the three positions which have been advertised in this unit. In this exercise, you are going to develop questions for an interview for that position with a partner and then role-play the interview.

A **Work with a partner who applied for a different job to the one you chose.**

Develop questions an interviewer might ask during an interview for each of your jobs.

Compare your questions with the list of common interview questions (and how to answer them) in File 4 on page 120.

B **Work with a partner who applied for same job as you. Use the interview questions you developed above in A to interview your partner for the job. When you have finished, change roles.**

LANGUAGE

Asking questions at an interview

At the end of an interview candidates are usually asked whether they have any questions. It is important to have two or three that you can ask, such as:

- I would like to continue improving my skills. What in-service courses does the bank provide?
- Who would I report to?
- What are the prospects for promotion?
- What are the next stages of the selection process?
- When would the starting date be?
- Will I have the possibility to use my language skills?

KMK exam practice: Stufe III

12 Produktion

Sie sind auf der Suche nach einer festen Anstellung und finden folgendes Stellenangebot im Internet. Sie beschließen, sich auf die Stelle zu bewerben.

Verfassen Sie eine Bewerbung auf Englisch. Berücksichtigen Sie folgende Punkte:

- Verfassen Sie eine geeignete Einleitung.
- Erläutern Sie Ihre Motivation für die Stelle.
- Erklären Sie, warum Sie für die Stelle geeignet sind.
- Gehen Sie auf die geforderten Qualifikationen ein.
- Gehen Sie auf Ihre Englischkenntnisse ein.
- Erklären Sie, dass ein Umzug nach Frankfurt für Sie kein Problem ist.
- Bieten Sie ein persönliches Gespräch an.
- Beenden Sie das Anschreiben angemessen.

www.ibf.com/jobadvertisement

International Banking

Junior Adviser (m/w) International Banking, Frankfurt

Ihre Aufgaben:
- Unterstützung Ihrer Vorgesetzten bei der Betreuung von internationalen Kunden
- Durchführen von Bonitätsprüfungen
- Erstellen von Genehmigungsvorlagen
- Führen von Kunden- und Ratingsgesprächen auf Englisch
- Betreuung und Pflege der Datenbanken

Ihre Qualifikation:
- Abgeschlossene Ausbildung (Bankkaufmann/frau) oder entsprechende berufliche Qualifikation
- Professionalität, Belastbarkeit und Flexibilität
- Eigenverantwortliche, systematische und präzise Arbeitsweise
- Kommunikationsstärke
- Überdurchschnittliche Leistungsbereitschaft
- Verhandlungssicheres Englisch
- Hervorragende PowerPoint-Kenntnisse und sicherer Umgang mit MS-Office-Anwendungen

Interessiert? Dann senden Sie uns Ihre Bewerbungsunterlagen zu (bitte auf Englisch).

BEWERBEN

13 Interaktion

Partner A
Sie erhalten eine Einladung zum Vorstellungsgespräch. Sie wissen, dass das Gespräch auf Englisch stattfinden wird. Als Vorbereitung haben Sie eine Liste von Fragen zusammengestellt, die auf Sie zukommen könnten.

Schauen Sie File 3 auf S. 119 an und machen Sie als Vorbereitung für das Vorstellungsgespräch Notizen auf Englisch. Wie würden Sie die Fragen beantworten?

Partner B
Sie sind Personalleiter/in der Bank, die einen neuen Mitarbeiter / eine neue Mitarbeiterin sucht. Heute führen Sie ein Vorstellungsgespräch mit einem/einer Bewerber/in. Das Gespräch führen Sie auf Englisch, damit Sie die sprachlichen Fähigkeiten des Bewerbers / der Bewerberin feststellen können.

Schauen Sie File 5 auf S. 121 an und machen Sie als Vorbereitung für das Vorstellungsgespräch Notizen auf Englisch. Wie würden Sie Fragen stellen und Themen setzen? Wenn Sie und Partner A bereit sind, fangen Sie an.

14 Finding a job abroad

A **Read the text, then put paragraphs a–e in the most logical order.**

B **Explain the main message of each paragraph in a single sentence in German.**

C **In groups, discuss the benefits and drawbacks of working abroad.**

JOBS ADVICE

TOP TIPS FOR WORKING ABROAD

Interested in working abroad for two or three years? It can be good for your career and for your general development. Working abroad, you'll not only gain experience which will look good on your CV, you'll also get an insight into another culture which could be invaluable in later life. Getting that job abroad can be quite difficult. Here's a step-by-step guide about how to do it.

a

The next step is to find that job! Look on the internet at jobsites and at serious newspapers which carry advertisements for jobs in the country of your choice, or study the home pages of international banks and search for positions there.

b

Once you have secured your job offer, work permit and visa (if necessary) it's time to make sure that you have the right health insurance and pension cover to work in the country of your choice. The immigration services of the country in question should be able to help you with this.

c

But before you finally decide that you would like to work abroad, it's important to visit the country of your choice. You can only find out if a particular country is right for you if you spend some time there finding out if the climate will suit you and what the people are like.

It's especially important to find out about cultural differences. Remember that not every country offers equal opportunities for men and women. Some countries have strict laws regarding sexual orientation; some countries forbid the consumption of alcohol.

d

If you are thinking about working in another European Union country, you have the right to enter and live in the country in order to find work. However, countries outside the EU will generally require you to apply for a work permit and/or visa before entering the country as a resident. Remember that these documents are usually restricted to a certain length of time.

e

Once you have decided that you would like to spend some time working in another country, you should do some research into whether you can realistically expect to secure a job there. Search the internet for reliable information, e.g. from the embassy or consulate of the country in question. A direct enquiry to a local Chamber of Commerce may provide you with information about your chances of finding employment in their country.

You may be a good networker and already know people who work there. Use your connections and ask these people for advice.

1 Unit 10, Warm-up 1B, page 108

Ranking	Percentage of votes given (2107 trainees voted)
Having a good interview technique	47.4 %
Writing a good CV (BE) or résumé (AE)	20.6 %
Understanding job advertisements	17.8 %
Writing a good covering letter	8.2 %
Filling in application forms correctly	6.0 %

2 Unit 10, Exercise 3A, page 110

Partner A

Telephone Banking Adviser

We are a leading online bank. We have a vacancy for a telephone banking adviser for our call centre in Berlin.
Duties include: dealing with enquiries, helping customers with day-to-day transactions, promoting and selling financial products and services to customers.
The ideal candidate for the job will be a German native speaker and have an excellent working knowledge of English. Good telephone manner important.
You should have completed your training in a branch office, dealing with customers face-to-face.
Qualifications required: minimum of GCSE or equivalent
Starting salary: €20,000
Training opportunities and possibility of promotion
Please send your application together with your CV to beate.ross@officeone.com
If your application is successful, you will be invited to take part in a telephone interview.

3 Unit 10, Exercise 13, page 117

Partner A

Mögliche Fragen:

- Kurze eigene Vorstellung; Stärken und Schwächen
- Verantwortung in bisherigen Stellen
- Sprachkenntnisse – wie gut, wie viel praktische Erfahrung
- Gründe, warum man sich für diese Position bei dieser Bank beworben hat
- Eigene Fragen stellen, z.B. nach Fortbildungsmöglichkeiten oder unmittelbaren Vorgesetzten

4 Unit 10, Exercise 11A, page 116

Common interview questions	Tips
… about yourself ▪ Tell us about yourself. / How would you describe yourself? ▪ What are your strengths and weaknesses? ▪ What are your hobbies? ▪ Tell us about a mistake you made in the past and how you handled it. ▪ What question would you not like us to ask you?	▪ Be honest. ▪ Show that you are able to use your strengths and indicate that you are working on your "weaknesses". ▪ Always keep in mind that you are applying for a position. ▪ Be positive. Even if a mistake was made, remember to say that you learned from it. ▪ Say that you hope they do not ask you about a particular department / task (you choose) as you do not have much experience in that department / area yet. Keep your answer simple and say something positive.
… about your education, work experience and skills ▪ Why did you choose to train at vocational college? ▪ What responsibilities did you have / do you have during the work placement? / at work? ▪ Please tell me about your present job. ▪ What have you learned in your present job that you think would help you in the position you're applying for with us?	▪ Talk about the aspects of your education, work experience and skills that are relevant for the job in question. ▪ Be honest. Don't say you know how to do everything. Remember, the interviewer knows that you are a trainee at the moment. ▪ Talk about a particular project or task which you did successfully. ▪ Think of something that is relevant – don't avoid the question by saying something like: I'll have to think about that.
… about what you know ▪ What languages do you speak? ▪ What computer software are you familiar with?	▪ Answer honestly.
… about your motivation ▪ Why did you apply for this job? ▪ Why do you want to work for this bank? ▪ Why do you think you would be a good candidate for this job? ▪ Why do you want to work abroad? ▪ What would you like to achieve in the next five/ten years?	▪ Show that you have researched the bank and know what the job is about. ▪ Stress the positive aspects of the company and the job. ▪ Talk about realistic goals and describe how you would like to progress with your career.

... about negative things or gaps in your CV	
▪ You started to study rather late in life. Why is that? ▪ Why did you take a gap year after leaving school?	▪ Explain the situation honestly. ▪ Describe the positive lessons you have learned / the experience you have gained as a result.

5 Unit 10, Exercise 13, page 117

Partner B

Fragen Sie nach:

- Selbstbeschreibung mit eigenen Stärken und Schwächen
- Tätigkeiten und konkrete Verantwortungsbereiche in früheren Stellen
- Bisheriger praktischer Einsatz von Fremdsprachenkenntnissen
- Spezielles Interesse am konkreten Stellenangebot der Firma
- Der Bewerber hat Gelegenheit, Fragen zur Stelle zu stellen.

6 Unit 10, Exercise 3A, page 110

Partner B

Managerial Assistant

We have vacancies for a trainee managerial assistant for our international bank.
Training takes place on the job in one of our London branch offices. You will learn how to perform all routine banking operations including sales correspondence and customer service for personal, business and corporate clients. You will also be given training in personnel management.

Requirements

We are looking for a degree in a business-related field, preferably finance or economics or equivalent experience.
You should be a good communicator both orally and in writing. A good customer manner is essential. Standard software skills are a must. Excellent English required.
Salary: €24,000 p.a.
Apply online.
Successful applicants will be contacted by telephone.

1 Documentary credit application

To:

Application for Irrevocable Documentary Credit (DC)

Office: ______

DC No: .... (For Bank use only)

1. Applicant (Name and address):	2. Date: / / 4. DC not transferable or assignable unless ticked below: ☐ Transferable	3. DC to be available by negotiation (by default) unless another choice is made by ticking below: ☐ Sight Payment ☐ Deferred Payment ☐ Acceptance
5. Contact name: (For any clarification with regard to this application)	Tel. No.:	Fax No./Email:
6. Import Account No. ☐☐☐-☐☐☐☐☐☐-☐☐☐		
7. Beneficiary (Name and address): Contact Person: .... Phone No.: .... Fax No.:	8. Date of DC expiry 9. Place of DC expiry 10. Shipment / delivery not later than 11. Period for presentation of documents	Documents should be presented within .... (21 days by default unless specified otherwise) days after shipment but within validity of the credit.
12. Partial shipment / delivery ☐ Allowed ☐ Not allowed	13. Transshipment ☐ Allowed except in sanctioned or boycotted countries ☐ Not allowed	
14. Amount in figures and currency	15. Allowance of variance in amount and quantity, (if any)	
16. CCY & Amount in words		
17. Drafts required (N/A in case of deferred payment)	☐ At sight, drawn on the issuing bank for full invoice value of goods ☐ At .... days from .... ,drawn on the issuing bank for full invoice value of goods	
18. Description of goods (Be Brief but Specific): (the "Goods")		
19. Trade terms ☐ EXW ☐ FCA ☐ FOB ☐ CFR ☐ CIF ☐ CPT ☐ CIP ☐ DDP ☐ Other		
20. Insurance to be covered by ☐ Applicant ☐ Beneficiary ☐ Ultimate Buyer		
Fill up 21,22,23 and 24 for sea and road shipments only		
21. Place of taking in charge / shipment	22. Place of final destination	
23. Port of loading	24. Port of discharge [Port of Transshipment] [*]	
Fill up 25 and 26 for air shipments only		
25. Airport of departure	26. Airport of destination [Airport of Transshipment] [*]	
27. All banking charges outside the country of issuance of this Documentary Credit are on account of / In case of local DC, all charges other than issuance charges are on account of: ☐ Beneficiary ☐ Applicant		
28. In case the DC is usance, the acceptance commission to be borne by ☐ Beneficiary ☐ Applicant		
29. Confirmation ☐ Required ☐ Not required	30. Confirmation charges to be borne by ☐ Beneficiary ☐ Applicant	
31. Legalization charges as per the current law and regulations in UAE to be borne by ☐ Beneficiary ☐ Applicant		
32. Please debit DC opening commission, advising charges, SWIFT transmission and courier charges / margin if any to our account No .... (Give details under 37 if any of the above charges to be borne by beneficiary)		

Stand: 6.5.2105

2 Bill of lading

Bill of Lading for Combined Transport shipment or Port to Port shipment

Shipper
P&O NEDLLOYD LTD
BERTH 204/205/206
WESTERN DOCKS,
SOUTHAMPTON

B/L No.: PONLBHX23009678

Reference: LGM0099535

Consignee or Order (for U.S. Trade only: Not Negotiable unless consigned 'To Order')
YUSIF BIN YUSIF FAKHRO
P.O.BOX 214
MANAMA
BAHRAIN

Notify Party/Address (It is agreed that no responsibility shall attach to the carrier or his Agents for failure to notify (see clause 20 on reverse))
YUSIF BIN YUSIF FAKHRO
P.O.BOX 214
MANAMA
BAHRAIN

Place of Receipt (Applicable only when this document is used as a Combined Transport Bill of Lading)
SOUTHAMPTON

Vessel and Voy. No.
OOCL FREEDOM OFM0234

Place of Delivery (Applicable only when this document is used as a Combined Transport Bill of Lading)
PORT OF MINA SULMAN
STATE OF BAHRAIN

Port of Loading
SOUTHAMPTON

Port of Discharge
BAHRAIN

Undermentioned particulars as declared by Shipper, but not acknowledged by the Carrier (see clause 11)

Marks and Nos; Container Nos;	Number and kind of Packages; Description of Goods	Gross Weight (kg)	Measurement (cbm)
POCU0432963 SEAL: 000204	1x20'GP CONTAINER SAID TO CONTAIN		
	20 C/S FCL/FCL	6240.0000	
TEST DATA TEST DATA TEST DATA	TEST DATA FOR REMOTE BILL PRINTING FREIGHT COLLECT SHIPPERS LOAD, STOW & COUNT SHIPPED ON BOARD PER OCEAN VESSEL OOCL FREEDOM AT SOUTHAMPTON ON XXXXXXXXXXXXXXXX FOR P&O NEDLLOYD LIMITED		

TOTAL: PART OF 1x20' CONTAINER(S) ONLY

FREIGHT AND CHARGES:

ORIGIN INLAND HAULAGE CHARGE	P	HAI
ORIGIN TERMINAL HANDLING/LCL SERVICE CHARGE	P	HAI
OCEAN FREIGHT	C	BAH
DESTINATION TERMINAL HANDLING/LCL SERVICE CHARGE	C	BAH
DESTINATION INLAND HAULAGE CHARGE	C	BAH

* Total No. of Containers/Packages received by the carrier	Movement	Freight Payable at
1 PART	FCL/FCL	KANOO, BAHRAIN

Received by the Carrier from the Shipper in apparent good order and condition (unless otherwise noted herein) the total number or quantity of Containers or other packages or units indicated in the box above entitled "*Total No. of Containers/Packages received by the Carrier" for Carriage subject to all the terms and conditions hereof (INCLUDING THE TERMS AND CONDITIONS ON THE REVERSE HEREOF AND THE TERMS AND CONDITIONS OF THE CARRIER'S APPLICABLE TARIFF) from the Place of Receipt or the Port of Loading, whichever is applicable, to the Port of Discharge or the Place of Delivery, whichever is applicable. If the acknowledged tally is of Containers, this indicates that the Container has been packed and sealed by the Merchant at his premises without the Carrier being represented and able to check or verify either the tally of Goods or the stowage, which are consequently unknown to him (See Clause 8). The Merchant accepts that, except by special arrangement or pursuant to Clause 9 hereof, Containers are not weighed by the Carrier at any time. If the Carrier so requires, before he arranges delivery of the Goods one original Bill of Lading, duly endorsed, must be surrendered by the Merchant to the Carrier at the Port of Discharge or at some other location acceptable to the Carrier. In accepting this Bill of Lading the Merchant expressly accepts and agrees to all its terms and conditions whether printed, stamped or written, or otherwise incorporated, not withstanding the non-signing of this Bill of Lading by the Merchant. Without prejudice to the generality of this reference, attention is drawn, inter-alia, to Clause 12 (Shipper's/Merchant's Responsibility), 19 (Dangerous Goods) and 24 (Law & Jurisdiction).

Number of Original Bills of Lading	Place and Date of Issue	
2/TWO	PONL BIRMINGHAM	23/09/00

IN WITNESS of the contract herein contained the number of originals stated opposite has been issued, one of which being accomplished, the other(s) to be void.

EXCESS VALUATION: REFER TO CLAUSE 7(3) ON REVERSE SIDE (U.S. TRADE ONLY). . . . .

*** ORIGINAL ***

This Bill of Lading has been printed remotely via the Internet, at the customer's premises.

Business letters

THE EDINBURGH BANK
42-44 Princes Street
EDINBURGH
EH2 4EQ
Great Britain[1]

Cummings Medical Supplies[2]
22 Ferry Road
EDINBURGH
EH4 7TP

13 March 20..[3]

Our ref: NW/TT[4]

Attn. Mr David Cummings[5]

Dear Mr Cummings[6]

Your request for extension of overdraft facilities[7]

We refer to your request, dated 10 March 20.., for the extension of overdraft facilities.[8]

We have considered your request, and we are afraid that we cannot extend your overdraft facilities without further discussion with you.

As Cummings Medical Supplies is a long-time, valued customer of our bank, we would like to invite you to a meeting on Wednesday, 18th March at 10.30 when we will be happy to discuss other options with you.

For your information, we enclose a leaflet describing a range of our services that may be of interest to you.

We are sure that we will be able to come to a solution that is satisfactory for both parties and look forward to continuing to do business with you.

Yours sincerely[9]

Norah Wilson[10]

Norah Wilson[11]
Customer Services Manager

Enc.[12]

1. **Letterhead**
2. **Inside address:** Write the city in capital letters and the postcode on a separate line in a letter to the UK.
3. **Date:** Always write the month as a word to avoid confusion. Write the year with four digits.
4. **Reference initials:** NW = signatory's initials TT = secretary's intials
5. **Attention line**
6. **Salutation:** Linked with the complimentary close (no. 9).
7. **Subject line:** Underlined or bold
8. **Body of the letter:** Starts with a capital letter.
9. **Complimentary close:** Linked with the salutation (no. 6).
10. **Signature**
11. **Signatory's name** is written clearly under the signature. Signatory's initials are in no. 4.
12. **Enc./Encl.** = Enclosure **Encs./Encls.** = Enclosures

Salutation line and complimentary close

You open a letter with …	when you …	and you close with …
Dear Sir or Madam	don't know the person's name	Yours faithfully
Dear Mr/Mrs/Miss …	know the person	Yours sincerely
Dear Ms …	know that the person is female but are not sure whether she is *Miss* or *Mrs*	Yours sincerely

Incoterms® 2010

In international trade the eleven Incoterms® 2010 Rules (international commercial terms) are used in contracts of sale to define the rights and obligations of the buyer and seller as regards risk, transport, insurance, packing, customs duty and documentation. They are terms of delivery.

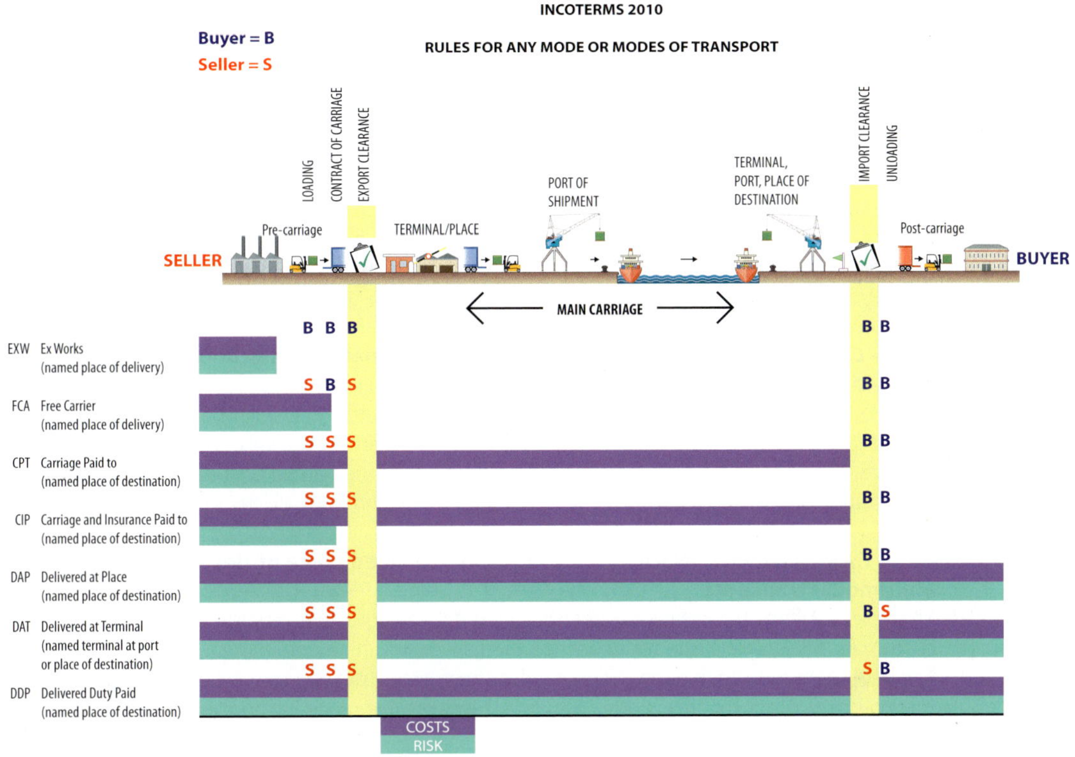

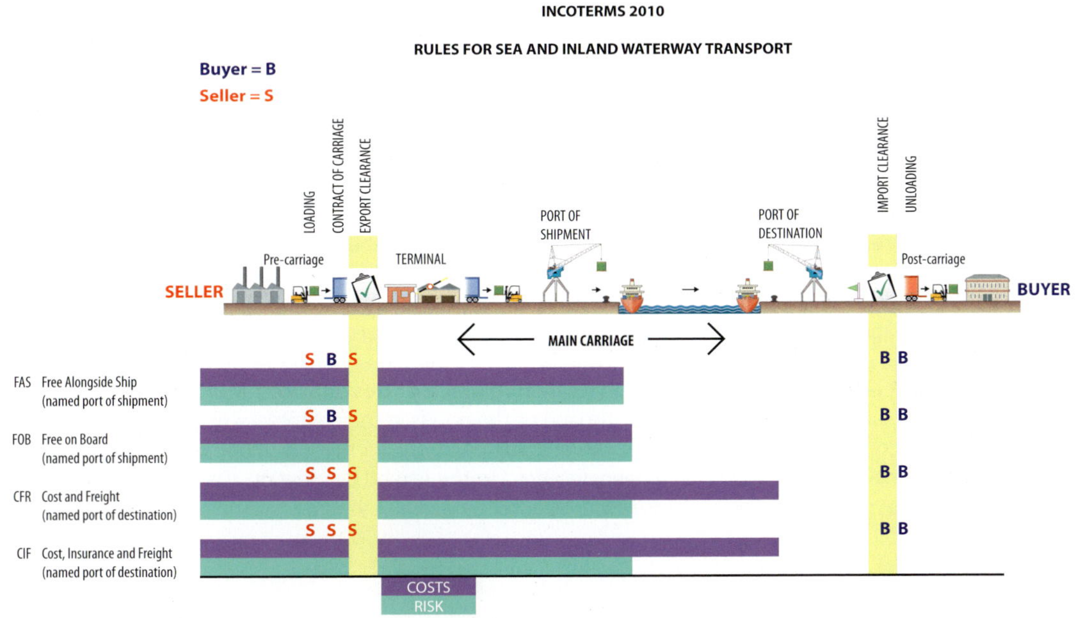

Rules for any mode or modes of transport

EXW – EX WORKS (... named place of delivery)
The seller makes the goods available at his premises in the customary packing. The seller assists the buyer in obtaining any documentation needed at the buyer's expense. The buyer is responsible for loading the goods, transporting them to their destination, customs clearance and insurance.

FCA – FREE CARRIER (... named place of delivery) Multimodal transport
The seller is not responsible for the main carriage of the goods. The seller delivers the goods at his own expense and risk, in the customary packing, cleared for export to the carrier nominated by the buyer. The seller provides the commercial invoice and, if requested, a certificate of origin at the buyer's expense. If the goods are collected at the seller's premises, the seller loads the goods. The seller bears the risks until the goods are in the custody of the first carrier. After that the buyer bears all the costs and risks of transporting the goods to their destination.

CPT – CARRIAGE PAID TO (... named place of destination) Multimodal transport
The seller pays for the main carriage of the goods. The seller delivers the goods, in the customary packing, cleared for export to the carrier which he nominates. The seller bears the risk until the goods have been delivered into the custody of the first carrier. The seller pays the transport costs for the goods, excluding transport insurance, up to the named destination. The buyer is responsible for insuring the goods for the main carriage and pays all import duties and taxes.

CIP – CARRIAGE AND INSURANCE PAID TO (... named place of destination) Multimodal transport
The seller pays for the main carriage of the goods. The seller delivers the goods in the customary packing, cleared for export to the carrier which he nominates. The seller bears the risk until the goods have been delivered into the custody of the first carrier. The seller pays the transport costs for the goods, including transport insurance, up to the named destination. The buyer pays all import duties and taxes.

DAP – DELIVERED AT PLACE (... named place of destination) Multimodal transport
The seller is responsible for the carriage of the goods in the customary packing, cleared for export to the named terminal at the destination by the carrier which he nominates. He bears the risk until the goods have been delivered to the named terminal. The buyer is responsible for unloading the goods at the place of destination and pays all import duties and taxes.

DAT – DELIVERED AT TERMINAL (... named terminal at port or place of destination) Multimodal transport
The seller is responsible for the carriage of the goods in the customary packing, cleared for export to the named terminal at the destination by the carrier which he nominates. He bears the risk until the goods have been delivered to the named terminal. The seller is responsible for unloading the goods at the place of destination. The buyer pays all import duties and taxes.

DDP – DELIVERED DUTY PAID (... named place of destination) Multimodal transport
The seller is responsible for the carriage of the goods in the customary packing, cleared for export to the named terminal at the destination by the carrier which he nominates. He bears the risk until the goods have been delivered to the named destination. The seller pays all import duties and taxes. The buyer is responsible for unloading the goods at the place of destination.

Rules for sea and inland waterway transport

FAS – FREE ALONGSIDE SHIP (... named port of shipment)
The seller is not responsible for the main carriage of the goods. The seller delivers the goods at his own expense and risk, in the customary packing, cleared for export, alongside the vessel selected by the buyer at the named port of shipment. Thereafter, the buyer bears all the costs and risks of transporting the goods to their destination.

FOB – FREE ON BOARD (... named port of shipment)
The seller is not responsible for the main carriage of the goods. The seller delivers the goods at his own expense and risk, in the customary packing, cleared for export, on board the vessel selected by the buyer unless otherwise agreed, at the named port of shipment. Thereafter, the buyer bears all the costs and risks of transporting the goods to their destination.

CFR – COST AND FREIGHT (... named port of destination)
The seller pays for the main carriage of the goods. The seller delivers the goods at his own expense and risk, in the customary packing, cleared for export, on board the vessel selected by the buyer, at the named port of shipment. The seller pays the transport costs for the goods, excluding transport insurance, up to the named port of destination. The buyer is responsible for insuring the goods for the main carriage and pays all import duties and taxes.

CIF – COST INSURANCE FREIGHT (... named port of destination)
The seller pays for the main carriage of the goods. The seller delivers the goods at his own expense and risk, in the customary packing, cleared for export, on board the vessel selected by the buyer, at the named port of shipment. The seller pays the transport costs for the goods, including transport insurance, up to the named port of destination. The buyer pays all import duties and taxes.

Terms of payment

payment in advance	Vorauszahlung/Vorkasse
cash with order (CWO)	Barzahlung bei Auftragserteilung
payment by irrevocable and confirmed documentary (letter of) credit	Zahlung durch unwiderrufliches und bestätigtes Dokumentenakkreditiv
documents against payment (D/P) / cash against documents (CAD)	Kasse gegen Dokumente
cash on delivery (COD)	gegen Nachnahme
1/3 with order, 1/3 on delivery, 1/3 within 30 days after delivery	1/3 bei Auftragserteilung, 1/3 bei Lieferung, 1/3 innerhalb von 30 Tagen nach Lieferung
payment within 60 days from date of invoice	Zahlung innerhalb von 60 Tagen nach Rechnungsdatum
10 days 2%, 30 days net	Zahlung innerhalb 10 Tagen abzüglich 2 % Skonto oder innerhalb 30 Tagen netto
payment on receipt of goods	Zahlung bei Erhalt der Waren
payment on receipt of invoice	Zahlung bei Rechnungserhalt
documents against (three months') acceptance (D/A)	Dokumente gegen (Dreimonats)akzept
open account terms with monthly/quarterly settlement	offenes Zahlungsziel mit monatlicher/vierteljährlicher Abrechnung

Schriftliche Prüfung

Zeit: 120 Minuten
Hilfsmittel: allgemeines zweisprachiges Wörterbuch
Maximale Punktzahl: 100 Punkte

Im Rahmen der schriftlichen Prüfung werden die Aufgabenanteile für die drei Kompetenzbereiche wie folgt gewichtet:

- **Rezeption – Hörverstehen 20 %**
- **Rezeption – Leseverstehen 20 %**
- **Produktion 30 %**
- **Mediation 30 %**

Im Folgenden werden vier Aufgaben vorgelegt, die Sie bearbeiten sollen. Die erste und die zweite Aufgabe beziehen sich auf Ihre Fähigkeit, englische Texte (gesprochene und geschriebene) zu verstehen = **Rezeption**. Bei der dritten Aufgabe sollen Sie ein Schriftstück erstellen = **Produktion** eines englischen Textes. Bei der vierten Aufgabe wird von Ihnen erwartet, dass Sie Texte von der deutschen oder englischen in die jeweils andere Sprache übertragen = **Mediation**.

Die Prüfung beginnt mit der Hörverstehensaufgabe.
Alle weiteren Aufgaben können in beliebiger Reihenfolge bearbeitet werden.

1 Rezeption: Hörverstehen — 20 Punkte

21

Situation: Sie nehmen an einer Fortbildungsveranstaltung zum Thema Beratung ausländischer Kunden teil. Dort werden Ihnen drei Dialoge in englischer Sprache vorgespielt. Demnächst werden Sie in Ihrer Filiale bei solchen Beratungsgesprächen assistieren und müssen daher in der Lage sein, wichtige Angaben festzuhalten. Dafür wurde ein Formular entwickelt (siehe unten).

Aufgabe: Notieren Sie sich die Angaben bzgl. der Wünsche oder Probleme der Kunden (Frau Morris, Herr Friday und Herr Coley) in deutscher Sprache.

Kundengespräch

Name des Kunden / der Kundin ______________________

Kundenwunsch/Problem ______________________
____

Beratung durch den Bankangestellten ______________________
____
____
____

2 Rezeption: Leseverstehen 20 Punkte

Situation: Sie nehmen an einer internationalen Fachtagung teil. Es geht um das Thema „Kontoführungsgebühren und deren Inklusivleistungen". Sie und ein Kollege wurden aufgefordert, eine Präsentation über die Situation in Großbritannien zu halten. Dazu ziehen Sie den untenstehenden Text von BBC News – Business heran. Ihr Kollege erstellte bereits Angaben bzgl. der wichtigen Aspekte, die im Text aufgeführt werden. Leider wurde er krank, sodass Sie die Tabelle mit Details allein vervollständigen müssen (siehe S. 130).

Aufgabe: Finden Sie die betreffenden Angaben für Ihre Präsentationsfolien mit Hilfe des Textes heraus und schreiben Sie diese in englischer Sprache stichwortartig auf.

Packaged accounts: How paid-for current accounts work

by David Black, Banking specialist, Defaqto

Packaged current accounts receive somewhat mixed publicity, so it is worth spending some time examining what is actually on offer before deciding whether or not to open one.

There is a choice of 69 packaged current accounts available in the UK, and many of the High Street banks offer a range of accounts from entry level through to premium accounts.

The monthly fees charged for them vary from £6.50 up to as much as £40, although the typical account charges about £15 per month.

In exchange for this monthly fee they offer various benefits. The typical high-value incentives are travel insurance, motor breakdown assistance and mobile phone insurance. [...]

Suitability

The Financial Services Authority (FSA) is currently in a consultation period looking at the insurance-based incentives offered by packaged current accounts. [...]

There will also be an annual statement setting out the benefits, with a recommendation that the customer reviews their suitability. This is a really salient issue and highlights the fact that differing circumstances dictate different needs.

But is it worth having a packaged account or should you just use a free in-credit current account?

It has long been the case that the informed consumer should look at the incentives on offer and decide whether they need the incentive.

If so, is it suitable for them, do they already have a similar product in place or could they buy it more cheaply – independently – elsewhere?

Examples of cover

To give you a flavour of the sort of things to consider, have a look at travel insurance where there is a wide variation in the cover details on offer. Some just cover European travel whereas others provide worldwide cover. [...]

(Source: abridged from BBC News – Business, http://www.bbc.co.uk/news/business-16596949)

1	Subject	…
2	Number of variations in the UK	…
3	Variations	▪ possible forms: … ▪ fees: …
4	Typical incentives for packaged accounts	▪ … ▪ …
5	Action taken by the FSA	▪ … ▪ …
6	Examples of cover	▪ … ▪ …
7	Recommendations	▪ … ▪ …

3 Produktion

30 Punkte

Situation: Sie sind seit einigen Wochen im Rahmen Ihrer Ausbildung in Ihrer Bank in der Anlageberatung eingesetzt. Nachdem der Umsatz von Fondsanlagen in der letzten Zeit stark rückläufig verlief, beauftragt Sie Ihre Vorgesetzte damit, für sie eine E-Mail in englischer Sprache an alle ausländischen Kunden zu entwerfen.

Aufgabe: Ihre Vorgesetzte schrieb: „Entwerfen Sie bitte umgehend eine E-Mail an unsere englischsprachigen Kunden. Bieten Sie den Kunden die Anlage in den Mischfonds NG-Invest an. Weisen Sie dabei auf unten aufgeführte Vorzüge des NG-Invest-Fonds hin:

- Zurzeit versprechen sehr günstige Einstiegskurse hohe zukünftige Gewinne
- Risikostreuung durch Anlage in verschiedenste Werte und dadurch geringe Fluktuation (Zusammensetzung des Fonds: 30 % europäische Aktien, 15 % US-Aktien, 25 % deutsche Unternehmensanleihen, 20 % deutsche Staatsanleihen, 10 % liquide Mittel)
- Professionelles Management
- Monatliche Anlage: bereits ab € 25
- Jederzeitige Rückgabemöglichkeit: hohe Liquidität
- Geringe Gebühren: Ausgabeaufschlag 2,5 %; Verwaltungsvergütung derzeit 1 % p. a.

Wählen Sie einen geeigneten Betreff sowie einen ansprechenden Einführungssatz und beenden Sie die E-Mail angemessen.

4 Mediation — 30 Punkte

Situation: Beratungsgespräche finden auch in Ihrer Filiale in zunehmendem Maße in englischer Sprache statt. Es gibt zwar Anweisungen für Anlageberatungsgespräche in deutscher Sprache (siehe unten), jedoch haben diese sich als nicht gerade kommunikationsfördernd bewiesen. Ihre Kollegen/Kolleginnen fänden es besser, einen Leitfaden mit knappen Anweisungen gleich auf Englisch zu haben.

Aufgabe: Verfassen Sie einen Leitfaden für Anlageberatungsgespräche in englischer Sprache. Dieser soll möglichst stichwortartige Anweisungen in Form einer Checkliste enthalten. Beachten Sie dazu die unten stehende Vorgabe zur Struktur.

Hier der in Ihrer Bank gebräuchliche Leitfaden in deutscher Sprache:

Phase I (ca. 1 Minute): Kontaktaufnahme

Begrüßen Sie den Kunden mit Handschlag, stellen sich dabei mit Ihrem Vor- und Nachnamen vor und nennen Ihre Abteilung sowie Ihr Aufgabengebiet.
Bieten Sie dem Kunden einen Sitzplatz an und fragen Sie ihn, ob er ein Getränk wünscht.
Beginnen Sie ein ungezwungenes Gespräch über das Wetter, seine Familie, Hobbys usw.

Phase II (maximal ca. 15 Minuten): Informationsaufnahme

Geben Sie dem Kunden das Gefühl, dass Sie sich intensiv mit seinem Anliegen beschäftigen möchten, indem Sie ihn fragen, ob Sie sich Notizen machen dürfen.
Erfragen Sie, welcher Betrag für welchen Zeitraum und wofür angelegt werden soll. Notieren Sie sich die Informationen.
Lassen Sie den Kunden über frühere Erfahrungen mit Anlagen berichten und versuchen Sie auf diese Weise, Details zu seiner Risikobereitschaft zu erfahren.
Sprechen Sie über das zu versteuernde Jahreseinkommen und lassen Sie den Kunden die Höhe seines „Notgroschens" nennen. Sprechen Sie auch das Thema Altersversorgung an.
Lenken Sie das Gespräch auf die Pläne des Kunden – z.B. Anschaffungen und Reisen.
Zum Abschluss dieser Phase fragen Sie, ob es noch etwas bei der Anlageplanung zu berücksichtigen gäbe.

Phase III (ca. 5 Minuten): Verkaufsphase

Fassen Sie die wichtigsten Punkte zusammen und fragen Sie, ob sie korrekt und vollständig sind.
Machen Sie nur zwei oder drei Vorschläge für die Geldanlage. Visualisieren Sie diese und erläutern Sie dabei die Vorteile.
Bitten Sie den Kunden um dessen Meinung zu den Produkten.
Informieren Sie ihn über die entstehenden Kosten, weisen auf die Vorschriften des Wertpapierhandelsgesetzes hin und bitten den Kunden um seine Unterschrift.

Phase IV (ca. 3 Minuten): Ausklang

Bitten Sie den Kunden um eine Rückmeldung zum Gespräch.
Bevor Sie sich verabschieden, sagen Sie ihm, dass er eine gute Entscheidung getroffen hat.

Erstellen Sie Ihren Leitfaden gemäß folgender Struktur:

Phase I (about 1 minute): Establishing contact

– ...
– ...

Mündliche Prüfung

Die Prüfung ist eine Gruppenprüfung, bei der Sie Gespräche persönlichen und fachlichen Inhalts in der Fremdsprache führen sollen. Es wird von Ihnen erwartet, dass Sie der vorgegebenen Situation entsprechend sprachlich agieren und reagieren. Es kommt dabei vor allem darauf an, dass Sie sich spontan äußern, dass Sie versuchen, sich verständlich zu machen und dass Sie gut zuhören.

Die Prüfung besteht aus zwei Teilen (ggf. noch einer dritten Zusatzaufgabe) und dauert insgesamt ca. 20 Minuten. Zur Vorbereitung haben Sie 20 Minuten Zeit.

Im ersten Teil der mündlichen Prüfung werden Sie gebeten, sich zu persönlichen oder beruflichen Themen zu äußern.

Im zweiten Teil sollen Sie zusammen mit einem anderen Kandidaten ein Rollenspiel durchführen. Dazu erhalten Sie vom Prüfer Rollenkarten, auf denen eine Situation beschrieben ist, die Sie vorspielen sollen. Eventuell nehmen Sie in einem dritten Teil zu einer vorgegebenen Situation Stellung.

Hilfsmittel: allgemeines zweisprachiges Wörterbuch.

5 Mündliche Prüfung (Teil II)

Situation: Sie werden demnächst im Rahmen eines europäischen Austauschprogramms vier Wochen mit mehreren deutschen Kolleginnen und Kollegen ein Praktikum in einer englischen Filiale absolvieren. Genau wie Ihre Bank plant auch die Bank in England, eine kleine Filiale in einem dünn besiedelten Vorort zu eröffnen. Alle Mitarbeiter werden aufgefordert, Gestaltungsvorschläge beizutragen.

Aufgabe: Diskutieren Sie zu Vorbereitungs- und Trainingszwecken gemeinsam mit Ihrer Kollegin / Ihrem Kollegen, die an diesem Austauschprogramm teilnehmen werden, in englischer Sprache verschiedene Möglichkeiten der Einrichtung der kleinen Filiale. Hier ist die Liste der Dinge, die platziert werden sollen:

Schalterbereich	SB-Zone
▪ Schalterbereich für 2 Personen ▪ 2 Schreibtische ▪ 1 Beratungsraum ▪ Kasse ▪ Tresorraum ▪ Kopiergerät	▪ Geldausgabeautomat ▪ Kontoauszugsdrucker ▪ Informationsbereich „Investment" (festverzinsliche Wertpapiere, Aktienkurse) ▪ Informationsbereich „Kredit" (Kreditzinsen, Immobilienangebote)

Hier ist der Grundriss:

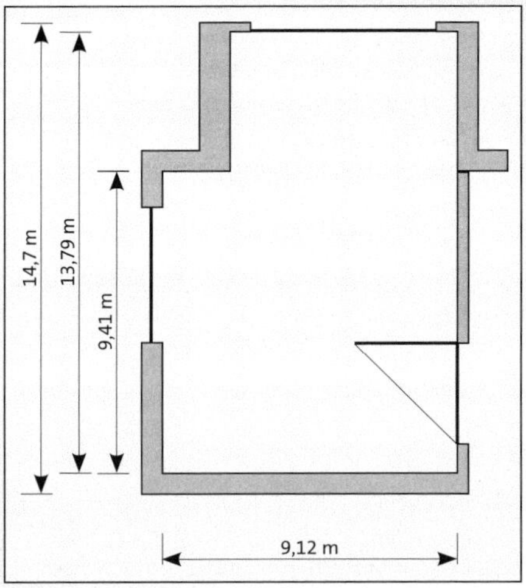

Weitere mögliche Aufgaben (auch geeignet für Phase III)

- Diskutieren Sie, wie wichtig **Spielecken** für Kinder in einer Bank sein können.
- Diskutieren Sie, ob Vorschriften für weitgehend vereinheitlichte Dienstkleidung zur Verbesserung der **„Corporate Identity"** beitragen können – wie z. B. die gleichen Krawatten für alle Mitarbeiter, die gleichen Farben für Hemden, Blusen usw.
- Diskutieren Sie, wie wichtig **Werbegeschenke** der Bank oder preiswerte Gegenstände des täglichen Gebrauchs (Becher usw.) **mit dem Banken-Logo** sind.
- Planen Sie gemeinsam einen **„Tag der offenen Tür"**, der an einem Samstag stattfinden soll. Sie haben dafür einen Etat von € 1.000 zur Verfügung. Einigen Sie sich auf einen thematischen Schwerpunkt.
- Betrachten Sie die **Internetseite** einer Bank und prüfen Sie diese mit Ihrem Partner / Ihrer Partnerin auf Kundenfreundlichkeit, farbliche Gestaltung, Übersichtlichkeit usw. (Alternativ: Gegenüberstellung zweier Internetseiten von englischen und/oder deutschen Banken).

Useful phrases

Making introductions

Greeting people you do not know	
Good morning/afternoon/evening. I'm …	*Guten Morgen/Tag/Abend. Ich bin …*
How do you do? My name is …	*Freut mich. Mein Name ist …*
Nice/Pleased to meet you.	*Es freut mich, Sie kennen zu lernen.*
Nice to meet you, too.	*Ganz meinerseits.*
Excuse me. Are you …?	*Entschuldigung. Sind Sie …?*
Yes, I am. / No, I'm not. I'm …	*Ja, das bin ich. / Nein, das bin ich nicht. Ich bin …*
Welcome to …	*Herzlich willkommen bei …*
Thank you. It's nice to be here.	*Dankeschön. Es ist schön, hier zu sein.*
Introducing people	
These are my colleagues, John and Mary.	*Das sind meine Kollegen, John und Mary.*
Allow me to / I'd like to introduce … from the … department.	*Darf ich Ihnen … aus der …-abteilung vorstellen?*

Making a phone call

Identifying yourself	
Good morning. My name's …	*Guten Morgen. Ich heiße …*
Good afternoon. This is … from (bank).	*Guten Tag. Hier spricht … von (Firma).*
Good evening. I work for …	*Guten Abend. Ich arbeite bei …*
Making small talk	
How are you?	*Wie geht es Ihnen?*
How's the weather today?	*Wie ist das Wetter bei Ihnen heute?*
Did you have a nice holiday?	*Haben Sie einen schönen Urlaub gehabt?*
Explaining the reason for your call	
I was wondering if you could help me …	*Wären Sie so nett, mir bei … zu helfen?*
I'm enquiring about …	*Ich wollte mich nach … erkundigen.*
I'd like some information on …	*Ich hätte gern nähere Informationen zu …*
Could you tell me about …?	*Könnten Sie mir etwas über … sagen?*
Asking for a person/department	
I'd like to speak to Mr/Ms …	*Ich hätte gern (mit) Herrn/Frau … gesprochen.*
Could you put me through to the … department, please?	*Könnten Sie bitte mich zur …-abteilung durchstellen?*
Saying what you want to do	
Can I leave a message?	*Kann ich eine Nachricht hinterlassen?*
I'll call again later.	*Ich rufe später noch einmal an.*
There's an urgent matter that I need to discuss with Mr/Ms …	*Ich muss mit Herrn/Frau … über eine dringende Angelegenheit sprechen.*
Ending the call	
Thank you for your help.	*Vielen Dank für Ihre Hilfe.*
You're welcome.	*Gern geschehen. / Bitte sehr.*
Goodbye.	*Auf Wiederhören.*
Have a nice day/evening.	*Einen schönen Tag/Abend noch.*

Writing emails

Salutation	
Dear Ms/Mrs/Miss/Mr Smith *(formal)*	*Sehr geehrte Frau / Sehr geehrter Herr Schmidt*
Dear Sirs / Dear Sir or Madam *(formal)*	*Sehr geehrte Damen und Herren*
Dear Paul and Paula	*Lieber Paul, Liebe Paula*
Good morning, Paul	*Guten Morgen, Paul*
Hi/Hello Paul/Paula	*Hi/Hallo Paul/Paula*

Complimentary close	
Regards / Best wishes / Yours sincerely *(formal)*	*Mit freundlichen Grüßen*
Cordially *(AE: formal)*	*Mit freundlichen Grüßen*
Yours faithfully *(formal)*	*Hochachtungsvoll*
Regards / Best regards	*Gruß/Grüße*
Best wishes	*Beste/Schöne/Liebe Grüße*
All the best / Take care	*Alles Gute*
Opening sentence	
I'm writing to … *(formal)*	*Ich schreibe Ihnen um zu …*
Just a quick note/message/line to …	*Nur eine kurze Mitteilung/Nachricht …*
Conclusion	
I look forward to your reply. *(formal)*	*Ich freue mich auf Ihre Antwort.*
Many thanks in advance. *(formal)*	*Vielen Dank im Voraus.*
I hope to hear from you soon.	*Ich freue mich darauf, bald von Ihnen zu hören.*

Making arrangements by email

Inviting somebody to a meeting	
Ms Smith would like to invite you to a meeting on (day) at (time).	*Frau Smith möchte Sie zu einem Treffen um (Zeit) Uhr am (Tag) einladen.*
I would like to invite you to lunch/dinner / a working breakfast on (day).	*Ich möchte Sie zum Essen / zum Abendessen / zu einem Arbeitsfrühstück am (Tag) einladen.*
The meeting will take place at my office / our premises in (town/city).	*Das Treffen findet in meinem Büro / in unseren Räumlichkeiten in (Ort/Stadt) statt.*
We have chosen the (name of restaurant) for our breakfast/lunch/dinner.	*Wir haben uns für (Name des Restaurants) für unser Frühstück/Mittagessen/Abendessen entschieden.*
Accepting the invitation	
Thank you for your invitation to meet you / to participate in discussions at (place). *(formal)*	*Vielen Dank für Ihre Einladung für das Treffen / zu der Besprechung in (Ort).*
I am pleased / We are delighted to accept your invitation/offer.	*Gern nehme ich / nehmen wir Ihre Einladung / Ihr Angebot an.*
Saying no	
I regret I cannot attend / I cannot come to the meeting/dinner because … *(formal)*	*Ich bedauere sehr, dass ich an dem Treffen/ Abendessen nicht teilnehmen kann, weil …*
I'm sorry, but I can't because (reason) on that date / at that time.	*Es tut mir leid, aber ich kann da nicht, weil ich an diesem Tag / zu dieser Zeit (Grund) …*
Making an alternative suggestion	
I would like to suggest postponing the meeting until (date/time). (formal)	*Ich möchte vorschlagen, den Termin auf (Datum/ Uhrzeit) zu verschieben.*
How about meeting for dinner on (day) at (time) instead?	*Wie wäre es, wenn wir uns stattdessen am (Tag) um (Uhrzeit) zum Abendessen treffen?*
Conclusion	
I look forward to your reply. *(formal)*	*Ich freue mich auf Ihre Antwort.*
I hope to hear from you soon.	*Ich hoffe, von Ihnen bald zu hören.*
Many thanks.	*Besten Dank.*

Writing business letters

Salutation	
Dear Madam or Sir *(BE: to a firm)*	*Sehr geehrte Damen und Herren*
Gentlemen *(AE: to a firm)*	*Sehr geehrte Damen und Herren*
Dear Mr Brown	*Sehr geehrter Herr Brown*
Dear Sharon	*Liebe Sharon*

Complimentary close	
Yours faithfully (*BE: to a firm*)	*Hochachtungsvoll*
Yours very truly / Cordially yours (*AE: to a firm*)	*Hochachtungsvoll*
Yours sincerely (*BE*)	*Mit freundlichen Grüßen*
Sincerely yours / Best personal regards (*AE*)	*mit freundlichen Grüßen / Beste Grüße*

Giving directions

How to get somewhere	
Go across the …	*Gehen Sie über …*
Go straight ahead.	*Gehen/Fahren Sie geradeaus.*
Turn left/right.	*Biegen Sie links/rechts ab.*
Take the first right/left.	*Nehmen Sie die erste Straße rechts/links.*
Keep to / Stay on the right/left.	*Halten Sie sich / Bleiben Sie rechts/links.*
It's just in front of/past/behind the …	*Es ist vor/nach/hinter …*
in the middle of the …	*mitten in … / in der Mitte von …*
in the distance	*in einiger Entfernung/ganz hinten*
on the right-hand side / on the left-hand side	*auf der rechten Seite / auf der linken Seite*

Attending meetings

Invitation to a meeting	
The monthly/quarterly/annual meeting of the team/ staff/group will be held / will take place on (date) at (time) in (place).	*Das monatliche/vierteljährliche/jährliche Treffen des Teams / der Mitarbeiter/Gruppe findet am (Datum) um (Uhrzeit) in (Ort) statt.*
Please confirm / let us know that you will / are able to attend.	*Bitte den Termin bestätigen / informieren Sie uns über Ihr Kommen.*
Starting a meeting	
Thank you all for coming.	*Danke, dass Sie alle gekommen sind.*
I'd like to welcome you all to this meeting.	*Ich möchte Sie alle zu dieser Besprechung willkommen heißen.*
Can we settle down, please?	*Darf ich um Ruhe bitten?*
Who is taking the minutes?	*Wer führt Protokoll?*
(Name of person) sends his/her apologies.	*(Name der Person) lässt sich entschuldigen.*
(Name of person) is going to chair this meeting.	*(Name der Person) wird diese Besprechung leiten/ moderieren.*
Introducing people	
This is (name of person). He/She is in charge of … (department).	*Das ist (Name der Person). Er/Sie leitet die … (Abteilung).*
(Name of person), this would be a good point for you to tell us about yourself and your position in the firm.	*(Name der Person), dies wäre ein guter Zeitpunkt, uns etwas über sich und Ihre Rolle in der Firma zu berichten.*
Setting the agenda	
Our meeting today is to discuss …	*Ziel unserer heutigen Besprechung ist …*
We have a lot to cover today, so I'd like to begin by looking at ...	*Wir haben viel vor heute, also möchte ich mit … anfangen.*
The first / most important item on today's agenda is …	*Der erste/wichtigste Tagesordnungspunkt für heute ist …*
Today, we're going to discuss last month's figures and see where we can make an improvement.	*Heute werden wir die Zahlen des vergangenen Monats besprechen und uns überlegen, wo noch Verbesserungspotenzial besteht.*
Let's get down to business.	*Also an die Arbeit.*

Giving a presentation

Introduction and structure	
This morning, I'm going to talk about …	*Heute morgen werde ich über … sprechen.*
Our topic today is …	*Das heutige Thema lautet …*
I've divided my talk / my presentation into three main parts, as follows: …	*Ich habe meinen Vortrag / meine Präsentation in drei Hauptthemen unterteilt, und zwar …*
First/Firstly, … ; second/secondly, … ; after that / then	*Erstens, … ; zweitens, … ; anschließend …*
The next topic I'm going to talk about is …	*Das nächste Thema, das ich behandeln möchte, lautet …*
Now I'd like to move on to …	*Jetzt möchte ich zum Thema … übergehen.*
Handouts	
I've prepared a few things/handouts for you to take away.	*Ich habe etwas / ein paar Handouts für Sie zum Mitnehmen vorbereitet.*
I hope you'll find these copies of the graphics useful.	*Ich hoffe, dass Sie diese Ausdrucke der Grafiken nützlich finden.*
Graphs	
The graph/chart shows/presents …	*Die Grafik / Das Diagramm zeigt … / stellt … dar.*
The horizontal/vertical axis has a scale from … to …	*Die waagrechte/senkrechte Achse hat eine Skala von … bis …*
The x axis / The y axis is divided into … units/ sections each representing …	*Die X-Achse / Die Y-Achse unterteilt sich in … Einheiten/Abschnitte, die … darstellen.*
Conclusion	
I'm now nearing the end of my talk.	*Ich komme nun zum Ende meines Vortrags.*
Before I finish my presentation, I'd just like to mention …	*Bevor ich meinen Vortrag beende, möchte ich kurz … erwähnen.*
Before I finish, I'd like to remind you of a few important facts and figures.	*Bevor ich meinen Vortrag beende, möchte ich (noch einmal) auf einige Daten und Fakten hinweisen.*
Finally, I'd like to say/stress how important these issues are.	*Abschließend möchte ich sagen/betonen, wie wichtig diese Themen/Fragen sind.*
I'd like to go over the main points/topics again.	*Ich möchte die Hauptpunkte/-themen nochmals kurz darlegen.*
Finally / In conclusion / To conclude / In summary, …	*Zum Schluss / Abschließend / Zusammenfassend …*
Questions	
Are there any questions?	*Gibt es / Haben Sie noch Fragen?*
We have time for a few questions / one last question.	*Wir haben noch Zeit für ein paar Fragen / eine letzte Frage.*
Thanking the audience	
Well, that's the end of my presentation.	*Damit bin ich am Ende meiner Präsentation angelangt.*
Thank you for your attention / for listening.	*Vielen Dank für Ihre Aufmerksamkeit / fürs Zuhören.*

Expressing politeness

Very polite forms	
May I ask you to email that to me?	*Darf ich Sie bitten, das an mich per E-Mail zu schicken?*
If I may/might make a suggestion, I would …	*Wenn ich einen Vorschlag machen dürfte, würde ich …*
Could you possibly email me a copy of that document, please?	*Könnten Sie mir bitte vielleicht eine Kopie des Dokuments per E-Mail schicken?*
I'm sorry to bother you but could you / would it be OK if you …	*Es tut mir leid, Sie zu stören, aber könnten Sie / wäre es OK, wenn Sie …*
Could you do me a favour and …?	*Würden Sie mir einen Gefallen tun und …?*

Useful phrases

Polite forms	
Could I have your surname, please?	*Könnten Sie mir bitte Ihren Nachnamen nennen?*
Could you spell your first name, please?	*Könnten Sie mir bitte Ihren Vornamen buchstabieren?*
All you have to do is fill in the form, please.	*Sie brauchen nur das Formular auszufüllen, bitte.*
Would/Could you sign here, please?	*Würden/Könnten Sie bitte hier unterschreiben?*
Would you please let me know (if) …?	*Würden Sie mir bitte mitteilen, (ob) …*
And if you would just like to sign here / fill in this form / give me a copy of your …	*Und wenn Sie bitte hier unterschreiben / dieses Formular ausfüllen / mir eine Kopie Ihrer … geben würden.*
I would be grateful if you could/would …	*Ich wäre Ihnen dankbar, wenn Sie … könnten/würden.*
Would you mind waiting a moment, please?	*Würden Sie bitte einen Moment warten?*

Saying and writing numbers and figures

763 – seven hundred and sixty-three	*763 – siebenhundertdreiundsechzig*
1,600 – one thousand six hundred	*1.600 – eintausendsechshundert*
145,000 – one hundred and forty-five thousand	*145.000 – einhundertfünfundvierzigtausend*
1,000,000 – one million	*1.000.000 – eine Million*
1,000,000,000 – one billion	*1.000.000.000 – eine Milliarde*
44.8 – forty-four point eight	*44,8 – vierundvierzig Komma acht*

Writing a covering letter/email

Opening phrases	
In reply to / With reference to your advertisement in … (newspaper) of … (date), …	*Bezugnehmend auf Ihre Ausschreibung in … (Zeitung) vom … (Datum), …*
I see that you are looking for a/an … (job).	*Wie ich sehe, sind Sie auf der Suche nach einem/einer … (Berufsbezeichnung).*
I would like / wish to apply for the above-mentioned position/post of … (job).	*Hiermit möchte ich mich für die oben genannte Stelle als … (Berufsbezeichnung) bewerben.*
Education/training / present employment	
I attended … (school/college) for … (length of time).	*Von … bis … (Jahr) besuchte ich (Schule).*
I studied … (subjects) at vocational school in … (town/city) from … (date) to … (date).	*An der Berufsschule in … (Ort) lernte/belegte ich … (Fächer) von … (Datum) bis … (Datum).*
At present I am working for a/an… (type of company) as a/an… (job).	*Zurzeit arbeite ich für eine / bei einer … (Firmenbezeichnung) als … (Berufsbezeichnung).*
I will complete my period of training on … (date).	*Am … (Datum) werde ich meine Ausbildung abschließen.*
Closing paragraph	
I enclose / Enclosed is my CV/résumé / a list of my qualifications and experience.	*Anbei finden Sie meinen Lebenslauf / eine Übersicht/Liste meiner Qualifikationen und Erfahrungen.*
I am available for interview at your earliest convenience.	*Für ein Vorstellungsgespräch stehe ich Ihnen jederzeit gern zur Verfügung.*
I hope you will consider my application favourably and (I) look forward to hearing from you in the near future.	*Ich hoffe, Sie werden meine Bewerbung positiv betrachten und (ich) freue mich darauf, von Ihnen bald zu hören.*

Basic word list

Diese Liste enthält ca. 1.000 Grundwörter, die in *Money Matters – 4th Edition* als bekannt vorausgesetzt werden. Nicht aufgeführt, jedoch vorausgesetzt, sind einige elementare Wörter, wie Pronomen, Zahlen, Wochentage sowie Wörter, die im Englischen und Deutschen die gleiche Bedeutung haben, wie z. B. *monitor, restaurant* und *hotel.*

A

a lot viel, sehr
a.m. vormittags
able fähig, in der Lage
about über, etwa
above über, oben
to **accept** annehmen, akzeptieren
accident Zufall, Unfall
accurate korrekt, exakt, fehlerfrei
across (quer) über
action Handlung
active aktiv, wirksam
actor Schauspieler/in
actual(ly) tatsächlich
to **add** zusammenzählen, hinzufügen
address Adresse
after nach
afternoon Nachmittag
again wieder
against gegen
age Zeitalter, Alter
aged alt
ago vor
to **agree** vereinbaren
to **agree to** zustimmen
air Luft
airport Flughafen
all alle(s)
to **allow** erlauben, (zu)lassen
allowed; to **be allowed to** erlaubt, dürfen
almost fast, beinahe
alone allein(e)
already schon, bereits
also auch, außerdem
alternative Alternative, alternativ
always immer
among zwischen, unter
amount Summe, Betrag
animal Tier
another noch eine
answer; to **answer** Antwort, Lösung; (be)antworten
any irgendetwas, -welche, jede, jegliche/r
anybody jemand, jede/r
anyone jemand, jede/r
anything etwas, alles
anyway also, jedenfalls, wie dem auch sei
apartment Wohnung
to **appear** erscheinen, auftauchen
to **apply** anwenden
around/round herum
to **arrive** ankommen
article Artikel
artist Künstler/in, Grafiker/in
as, ~ well auch (noch), ebenfalls; **such ~** wie (zum Beispiel)
to **ask** fragen, bitten
aspect Aspekt, Seite
at least mindestens
attractive attraktiv, reizvoll
to **avoid** vermeiden
away weg, entfernt
awful schrecklich

B

back zurück
background Hintergrund
bad schlecht, schlimm
bag Tasche
Baltic die Baltischen Staaten, die Ostsee
banker Bankier, Banker/in
banking Bankwesen, Bank-
basic Grund-, grundlegend, wesentlich
to **be** sein
to **be worried** fürchten
because weil
to **become** werden
bedroom Schlafzimmer
before vor(her)
to **begin** anfangen, beginnen
behind hinter, hinten
to **believe** glauben
below unter, unten; unterhalb, darunter
beside neben
best beste/r/s, am besten
better besser
between zwischen
BIC (= Business Identifier Code) BIC
big groß
bike Fahrrad
birthday Geburtstag
bit ein bisschen, etwas
black schwarz
book; to **book** Buch; buchen, bestellen
born geboren
to **borrow** borgen, leihen
both beide
both … and … sowohl … als auch …
bottle Flasche
bottom Boden, Unterseite
bottom, at the ~ unten
box Kasten, Kästchen, Schachtel
boy Junge
boyfriend (fester) Freund
brackets *(pl)* Klammern
to **break** (zer)brechen, kaputtgehen; kaputtmachen
break; to **break** Pause; brechen
bright hell
to **bring** bringen, holen
brochure Broschüre
brother Bruder
to **build** (auf)bauen
building Gebäude
business Geschäft, Firma
busy beschäftigt, besetzt
but aber, sondern
button Knopf, Taste
to **buy** kaufen
buyer Käufer/in
by an, bei, neben, von, bis
bye tschüs

C

cake Kuchen
call; to **call** Anruf; (an)rufen
called; to **be called** genannt; heißen
caller Anrufer/in
camera Fotoapparat, Kamera
can dürfen, können
cannot nicht können
captain Kapitän/in
car Auto
car park Parkhaus, -platz
card Karte
care, to **take ~ of** erledigen, sich kümmern um
career Kariere, Laufbahn
careful vorsichtig, sorgfältig
to **carry** tragen
cartoon Karikatur, Comic
case Fall
to **catch** fangen, erreichen
category Kategorie
central zentral
centre Zentrum
chance Gelegenheit, Möglichkeit
change; to **change** (Ver-) Änderung; (aus)wechseln, (sich) ändern
chat; to **chat** Unterhaltung; sich unterhalten
cheap billig, günstig
to **check** (über)prüfen
child, *pl* **children** Kind
chocolate Schokolade
choice Wahl, Auswahl
to **choose** (aus)wählen
Christmas Weihnachten, Weihnachtsfest
city (Groß-)Stadt
class Klasse
classic klassisch
clean; to **clean** sauber; reinigen, säubern
clear klar, deutlich
to **click** klicken
climate Klima
to **climb** klettern, steigen
close nah, dicht, eng
to **close** schließen
clothes *(pl)* Kleidung, Kleider

clothing Kleidung, Kleider
club Verein, Club
coast Küste
coat Mantel, Jacke
colleague Kollege/Kollegin
to **collect** sammeln
colour Farbe
coloured farbig
combination Kombination
to **come** kommen
commission Kommission
communication Kommunikation
company Firma, Unternehmen
to **compare** vergleichen
competent kompetent, fähig
complete; to **complete** vollständig; vervollständigen
complex kompliziert, komplex
complicated kompliziert
to **connect** (miteinander) verbinden, anschließen
connection Verbindung
constant konstant, gleichbleibend
contact; to **contact** Kontakt, Verbindung; sich in Verbindung setzen
to **continue** fortsetzen
control Beherrschung, Kontrolle
conversation Unterhaltung, Gespräch
cool ruhig, cool, kühl
cooperative kooperativ, hilfsbereit
copy; to **copy** Kopie; kopieren
correct; to **correct** richtig; korrigieren
cost; to **cost** Kosten; kosten
could konnte/n, könnte/n
to **count** zählen
country Land, Staat
couple Paar
course Kurs, Lehrgang; **of ~** natürlich, selbstverständlich
credit card Kreditkarte
crowded belebt
culture Kultur
cup Tasse
customer Kunde/Kundin
to **cut** schneiden

D

dad Papa, Vati
daily täglich
dance; to **dance** Tanz; tanzen
danger Gefahr
dangerous gefährlich
dark Dunkelheit; dunkel
data Daten
date Datum, Termin
daughter Tochter
day Tag
dead tot
deal Geschäft
dear liebe/r
to **decide** (sich) entscheiden, beschließen
decision Entscheidung
deep tief, nachhaltig
definition Definition
dentist Zahnarzt/-ärztin
to **depend on** abhängen von
to **describe** beschreiben
to **design** entwerfen, gestalten
desk Schreibtisch, Schalter
detail Detail
detective Detektiv/in, Kriminalpolizist/in
diagram Grafik, Abbildung
dialogue Dialog
difference Unterschied
different anders, verschieden
difficult schwer, schwierig
difficulty Schwierigkeit
digital digital
dinner *(festliches)* Abendessen
diploma Diplom, Abschlusszeugnis
direct(ly) direkt, unmittelbar
direction Richtung
to **discover** entdecken, herausfinden, feststellen
to **discuss** besprechen, diskutieren (über)
discussion Besprechung, Diskussion
to **do** tun, machen
document Dokument, Papier
door Tür
double doppelt
down (nach) unten
downstairs (nach) unten
dramatic dramatisch
to **draw** ziehen, zeichnen
dream; to **dream** Traum; träumen
dress; to **dress** Kleid; sich kleiden
drink; to **drink** Getränk; trinken
to **drive** (Auto) fahren
drop; to **drop** Fall; fallen (lassen)
during während

E

e.g. (for example) zum Beispiel
each jede/r/s
early früh
eastern östlich
easy leicht, einfach
to **eat** essen
effect (Aus-)Wirkung, Einfluss, Effekt
efficient effizient, rationell
electronic elektronisch, Elektronik-
element Element, (einzelner) Bestandteil
else sonst noch, andere/r/s
end; to **end** Ende, Schluss; (be)enden
energy Energie
to **enjoy** genießen, gefallen
enough ausreichend, genug
to **enter** eintreten, eingeben
especially besonders
etc. usw.
even sogar (noch)
evening Abend
event Veranstaltung, Ereignis
ever je(mals)
every jede/r/s
everybody jede/r
everyday alltäglich, Alltags-
everyone jede/r/s, alle
everything alles
everywhere überall
exact(ly) exakt, genau
example Beispiel
excellent ausgezeichnet, hervorragend
except (for) außer, bis auf
exciting aufregend, spannend
excuse me Verzeihung, Entschuldigung
exercise Übung
to **expect** erwarten, annehmen
expensive teuer
expert Fachmann/frau
to **explain** erklären
export Ausfuhr, Export
to **export** exportieren
extra zusätzlich; Zusatzleistung, Extra
extreme(ly) extrem, äußerst
eye Auge

F

face Gesicht
fact Tatsache; **in ~** tatsächlich, eigentlich
factor Faktor
fall; to **fall** Fall; fallen
false falsch
family Familie
famous berühmt
far weit (entfernt)
fashion Mode
fast schnell
father Vater
fax; to **fax** Fax(gerät); faxen
to **feed** füttern, ernähren
to **feel** (sich) fühlen
feeling Gefühl
few; a few wenig/e; ein paar
field Feld
figure Figur, Zahl, Ziffer
to **fill** füllen, einsetzen
finally schließlich
finance(s) Finanz(en)
to **find** finden, suchen
to **find out** herausfinden
fine gut, schön, fein
finish; to **finish** Ende; (be)enden
firm Firma; fest
first; at first erste/r/s, zuerst; am Anfang
fish, *pl* **fish** Fisch
flat flach; Wohnung
flexible flexibel
flight Flug
floor Etage, (Fuß-)Boden
to **fly** fliegen
folks *(pl)* Leute, Menschen
to **follow** (be)folgen
food Lebensmittel

foot, *pl* **feet** Fuß
football Fußball
to **forget** vergessen
form Form, Formular
form; to **form** Form; formen
freak Freak
free frei; gratis, kostenlos
friend Freund/in
friendly freundlich
front; in front of Vorderseite; vor *(räumlich)*
frustrated frustriert
full voll
fun Spaß
function Funktion
furniture *(no pl)* Möbel
further weitere
future Zukunft; (zu)künftig

G
gallery Galerie
garden Garten
gas Gas
general; generally allgemein, generell; im Allgemeinen, normalerweise
to **get** holen, bekommen, werden
to **get (to/into)** (hin-/hinein-) kommen, (hin-/hinein-)gelangen
girl Mädchen
girlfriend (feste) Freundin
to **give** geben
glass Glas
global global, weltweit
globalization Globalisierung
to **go** gehen, fahren
golden golden
good gut
good morning guten Morgen
goodbye auf Wiedersehen
good-looking gut aussehend
grammar school Gymnasium
granddaughter Enkelin
great groß(artig)
to **greet** (be)grüßen
greetings *(pl)* Grüße
group Gruppe
to **grow** wachsen, anbauen
to **guide** führen, (an)leiten
gun Schusswaffe
guy Bursche, Typ

H
hair Haar(e)
hairdresser Friseur/in
half, *pl* **halves** Hälfte; halb
to **happen** passieren, geschehen
happy glücklich, froh, zufrieden
hard schwer
to **hate** hassen, nicht mögen
to **have** haben
head Kopf
health Gesundheit
healthy gesund
to **hear** hören
heart Herz
help; to **help** Hilfe; helfen
helpful hilfsbereit
hero Held/in
to **hide (away)** (sich) verstecken, (sich) verbergen
high hoch
hit; to **hit** Schlager; schlagen, treffen
to **hold** halten
hole Loch
holiday(s) Ferien, Urlaub
home Zuhause, Heim; nach Hause
hope; to **hope** Hoffnung; hoffen
hospital Krankenhaus
hour Stunde
house Haus
how wie
however doch, jedoch
huge riesig
to **hurt** verletzen, wehtun, schaden
husband (Ehe-)Mann

I
IBAN (= International Bank Account Number) IBAN
idea Idee, Gedanke
if wenn, falls, ob
ill krank
illness Krankheit
I'm afraid leider
to **imagine** sich vorstellen
import Einfuhr, Import
importance Bedeutung, Wichtigkeit
important wichtig
impossible unmöglich
to **improve** verbessern, sich bessern
incorrect falsch, unrichtig
industry Industrie
inflation Inflation
to **inform** informieren
information Information(en), Angaben
inside (nach) drinnen, innerhalb (von)
instead stattdessen
instinct Instinkt
interested (in) interessiert (an)
interesting interessant
into in ... hinein
investor Investor/in
to **invite** einladen

J
jet Jet, Düsenflugzeug
job Arbeit(sstelle), Aufgabe; **on the ~** am Arbeitsplatz
to **join** beitreten, verbinden
to **jump** springen
just einfach, nur, genau

K
to **keep** (be)halten, aufbewahren
key Schlüssel, Taste
kid Kind
king König
kitchen Küche
to **know** kennen, wissen

L
land; to **land** Land; landen
language Sprache
large groß, umfangreich
last letzte/r/s, zuletzt
late (zu) spät
to **laugh (at)** lachen (über)
law Recht, Gesetz
leader Führer/in
to **learn** lernen, erfahren
least am wenigsten
to **leave** (ver)lassen
left linke/r/s, links; übrig
left, on the ~ links
to **lend** leihen
less weniger, abzüglich
to **let** erlauben, (zu)lassen, vermieten
letter Brief, Buchstabe
level Ebene
to **lie** liegen
life, *pl* **lives** Leben
lifestyle Lebensstil, Lifestyle
lift Fahrstuhl, Aufzug
like; to **like** (ähnlich) wie; mögen, gern tun
limit Grenze, Limit
line Linie, Zeile
list; to **list** Liste; aufzählen, nennen
to **listen** zuhören
listener Zuhörer/in
little klein, wenig
to **live** wohnen, leben
local örtlich, lokal
long lang
longer, no ~ nicht mehr
to **look** (aus)sehen, schauen, blicken
to **look at** ansehen
to **lose** verlieren
lots of / a lot of viel/e
love; to **love** Liebe; lieben, sehr gern mögen
low niedrig
loyal treu, loyal
luck Glück
lunch Mittagessen
lunchtime, (at) ~ (zur) Mittagszeit

M
machine Maschine
magazine Zeitschrift
main hauptsächlich, wichtigste/r/s
to **make** machen
man, *pl* **men** Mann, Mensch
manager Leiter/in, Direktor/in, Manager/in
many viele
market Markt; **~ square** Marktplatz
married verheiratet
match Spiel, Partie, Wettkampf
material Material, Stoff
maths Mathe(matik)

maximum, max. maximal, Maximum
may dürfen, können, mögen
maybe vielleicht
to **mean** bedeuten, meinen, heißen
meaning Bedeutung
media Medien
medium mittlere; Medium, Mittel
to **meet** (zusammen)treffen, begegnen
meeting Konferenz, Besprechung
member Mitglied
to **mention** erwähnen
message Mitteilung, Nachricht
method Methode, Verfahren
midday Mittag
middle Mitte
might könnte(n) (vielleicht)
mile Meile *(entspricht 1609 m)*
minimum Minimum; minimal
minute Minute
to **miss** verpassen, vermissen
missing fehlend
mistake Fehler
mix; to **mix** Mischung; (ver)mischen
mobile phone Mobiltelefon, Handy
moment Moment
money Geld
month Monat
more mehr
morning Morgen
most meist
mostly hauptsächlich, meistens
mother Mutter
motorbike Motorrad
to **move** (sich) bewegen, umziehen
Mrs/Ms Frau
much viel
must müssen; **a ~** ein Muss, eine Notwendigkeit

N

nail Nagel
name; to **name** Name; (be)nennen
nation Staat, Nation
national national, staatlich
near nahe
nearby nahe (gelegen)
nearly beinahe, fast
need; to **need** Bedarf, Bedürfnis; brauchen, benötigen
negative Verneinung; negativ
neighbour Nachbar/in
nervous nervös
network Sender, Netz(werk)
never nie(mals)
new neu
news Neuigkeit(en), Nachricht(en)
newspaper Zeitung
next nächst; danach
nice nett, freundlich; schön
night Nacht
no longer nicht mehr
nobody, no one niemand, keine/r
normal(ly) normal(erweise)
northern nördlich
note; to **note** Notiz; beachten, notieren
nothing nichts
notice; to **notice** Notiz; bemerken
now nun, jetzt; **right ~** zurzeit, im Augenblick
number Nummer, Zahl

O

o'clock ... Uhr
offer; to **offer** Angebot; (an)bieten
office Büro, Amt
officer Beamter/Beamtin
often oft, häufig
oil Öl
old alt
on the job am Arbeitsplatz
once einmal, einst, sobald
only nur, einzige/r/s
open; to **open** offen, geöffnet; öffnen, eröffnen
operation Operation
opinion Meinung, Einschätzung
opposite Gegenteil; gegensätzlich; gegenüber
option Option
order, in ~ to ... um ... zu
order; to **order** Bestellung, Reihenfolge; befehlen, bestellen, ordnen
organization Organisation
to **organize** organisieren
original original, ursprünglich; Original
other andere/r/s
out of ... aus ... (heraus/hinaus)
outdoor Outdoor-, im Freien, draußen
outside außerhalb (von), draußen
over über; **~ there** da drüben (hin), dort (drüben) (hin)
own; to **own** eigen; besitzen
owner Besitzer/in

P

p.m. nachmittags
to **pack** packen
page Seite *(Buch)*
pair Paar
paper Papier, Zeitung
paragraph Absatz, Abschnitt
parents *(pl)* Eltern
to **park** parken
parking space (einzelner) Parkplatz
part Teil, Rolle
to **pass** vorbeigehen, vergehen
passenger Passagier/in
passport Pass
past vorbei, nach; Vergangenheit
pay; to **pay** Gehalt; (be)zahlen
pen Kugelschreiber, Stift
people *(pl)* Leute, Volk
per cent Prozent
perfect perfekt
perhaps vielleicht, eventuell
period Zeit(raum)
person Mensch, Person
personal persönlich
petrol Benzin
phone call (Telefon-)Anruf
phone; to **phone** Telefon; anrufen
photo(graph) Foto(grafie)
to **photocopy** fotokopieren
picture Bild
piece Stück, Teil
pity: it's a ~ schade
place; to **place** Stelle, Platz; setzen, stellen
plan; to **plan** Plan; planen
plane Flugzeug
planet Planet
plant; to **plant** Pflanze; pflanzen
plastic Plastik
platform Plattform
to **play** spielen
please bitte
plenty (of) reichlich, viel
plus außerdem
pocket Tasche
pocket money Taschengeld
point Punkt; Komma
point of view Standpunkt, Ansicht
police Polizei
police officer Polizist/in
policy Politik, Richtlinie(n)
polite höflich
poor arm, schlecht, mangelhaft
popular beliebt, populär
population Bevölkerung
position Stellung, (Arbeits-)Stelle, Position
positive positiv
possible möglich, denkbar
post Post, Posten
pound Pfund (Sterling)
practice Praxis, Übung
to **practise** (ein)üben
to **prefer** vorziehen, bevorzugen
to **prepare** erstellen, verfassen *(Bericht etc.)*
present Geschenk, Gegenwart; gegenwärtig
to **present** vorstellen, präsentieren
presentation Vorstellung, Präsentation
to **press** drücken
pretty hübsch
price (Kauf-)Preis
to **print** drucken
printer Drucker
private privat, persönlich
probably wahrscheinlich
problem Problem
product Produkt, Erzeugnis
professional beruflich, Berufs-, professionell, Profi-
profit Profit, Gewinn
program (Computer-)Programm
programme Programm, (Fernseh-)Sendung
project Projekt

public öffentlich; Öffentlichkeit
to **pull** ziehen
to **push** schieben, drücken
to **put** setzen, stellen, legen

Q
quality Qualität
quantity Menge, Quantität
quarter Viertel
queen Königin
question Frage
queue Schlange
quick schnell, rasch
quite ziemlich, ganz

R
rain; to **rain** Regen; regnen
rainy regnerisch
to **reach** greifen, erreichen
to **read** lesen
reader Leser/in, Lektüre
ready fertig, bereit
real echt, wirklich
to **realize** erkennen, feststellen
really wirklich, eigentlich, tatsächlich
reason Grund, Begründung
record; to **record** Aufzeichnung, Beleg; Platte; Rekord-; aufzeichnen
region Region, Gebiet
regular(ly) regelmäßig, regulär
relationship Beziehung, Verhältnis
relative relativ
relevant relevant, wichtig
to **remember** sich erinnern, daran denken
rent; to **rent** Miete; mieten
to **repeat** wiederholen
report; to **report** Bericht; berichten
respect; to **respect** Respekt; respektieren
rest; to **rest** Pause, Rast, Rest; sich ausruhen
result; to **result** Resultat, Ergebnis; folgen
return; to **return** Rückkehr; zurückkehren, -gehen
revolution Revolution
rich reich, wohlhabend
to **ride** reiten, fahren (mit)
right rechts, rechte/r/s, richtig; Recht; **~ now** zurzeit, im Augenblick
right, on the ~ rechts
to **ring** anrufen
risk; to **risk** Risiko; riskieren
role Rolle
role-play Rollenspiel
room Zimmer, Raum
routine Routine-
rule Regel
to **run** laufen (lassen)

S
safe Safe; sicher
safety Sicherheit
sale (Schluss-)Verkauf
salesperson Verkäufer/-in
same gleiche/r/s, der-, die-, dasselbe
to **save** retten, sparen
to **say** sagen
scene Szene
school Schule
screen Bildschirm, Leinwand
sea See
search; to **search** Suche; (durch)suchen
seat Sitz(platz)
second zweite/r/s; Sekunde
to **see** sehen
to **seem** (er)scheinen
seldom selten
to **select** (aus)wählen
to **sell** (sich) verkaufen
seller Verkäufer/in
to **send** senden, schicken
sentence Satz
to **serve** servieren *(z.B. Essen)*, bedienen
service Kunden(dienst), Service
set; to **set** Satz; setzen
several etliche, einige, mehrere
to **share** (sich) teilen, gemeinsam (be)nutzen
sharp scharf
shirt Hemd
shock; to **shock** Schock, Schreck; schockieren, erschüttern
shoe Schuh
shop; to **shop** Laden, Geschäft; einkaufen
short kurz, klein, knapp
should solle/n, sollte/n
to **show** zeigen
to **shut** schließen
sign; to **sign** (An-)Zeichen; unterschreiben
signal; to **signal** Signal; signalisieren
silver Silber
simple einfach
since da, weil, seit
single einzig, einzeln
to **sink** sinken, sich senken
sister Schwester
to **sit** sitzen, sich hinsetzen
situation Situation, Lage
size Größe
sleep; to **sleep** Schlaf; schlafen
slow langsam
small klein
small talk Smalltalk, höfliche Unterhaltung
smile; to **smile** Lächeln; lächeln
smoke; to **smoke** Rauch; rauchen
smoker Raucher/in
snow Schnee
so also, damit, deshalb, so
social sozial
solid fest, solide
to **solve** lösen
some einige, etwas
somehow irgendwie
someone/somebody jemand
something etwas
sometime irgendwann
sometimes manchmal
somewhere irgendwo
son Sohn
soon bald
Sorry! Entschuldigung! Tut mir leid!
sort; to **sort** Art, Sorte; sortieren
sound; to **sound** Geräusch, Klang, Laut; klingen
southern südlich
space (Zwischen-)Raum, Abstand, Platz, Weltall
to **speak** sprechen, reden
speaker Sprecher/in
special besondere/r/s
specialist Spezialist
to **spell** buchstabieren, schreiben
spelling Schreibweise, Buchstabieren
to **spend** ausgeben, (Zeit) verbringen
sporty sportlich
square, market ~ Marktplatz
staff Angestellte, Mitarbeiter/innen
stairs *(pl)* Treppe(n)
to **stand** stehen
standard normal, üblich, Standard-
start; to **start** Beginn; anfangen, starten, beginnen
starter Neueinsteiger/in
state Land, Staat; staatlich
statement Aussage(satz), Erklärung
station, (train) ~ Bahnhof
stay; to **stay** Aufenthalt; bleiben
to **steal** stehlen
step Schritt, Stufe
still still, trotzdem, (immer) noch
stop; to **stop** Halt; (an) halten, aufhören (mit)
store Laden, Geschäft
story Geschichte
strategy Strategie, Taktik
street Straße
strict streng, strikt
strong stark, kräftig
student Student/in, Lernende/r
to **study** lernen, studieren
success Erfolg
successful erfolgreich
such so, solch; **~ as** wie (zum Beispiel)
suddenly plötzlich
sugar Zucker
sum Summe, Betrag
sunshine Sonnenschein
sure freilich, sicher
symbol Symbol

T
table Tisch, Tabelle

to **take** (mit)nehmen, bringen, dauern; **~ care of** erledigen, sich kümmern um
talk; to **talk** Gespräch, Unterhaltung, Vortrag; sprechen, reden
to **teach** unterrichten, lehren
technology Technik, Technologie
telephone; to **telephone** Telefon; anrufen
to **tell** sagen, erzählen
test Test, Untersuchung
text (message) SMS
than als *(Vergleiche)*
to **thank** danken
thanks, thank you danke
then dann
there da, dort(hin); **over ~** da drüben (hin), dort (drüben) (hin)
therefore deshalb, deswegen
these diese *(Plural)*
thing Sache, Ding, Gegenstand
to **think** denken, meinen, finden, glauben
third dritte/r/s
those jene *(Plural)*
though obwohl, allerdings
through durch
to **throw** werfen
ticket Karte, Fahrschein
tidy ordentlich, aufgeräumt
till bis
time Zeit, Mal
tip Hinweis, Tipp
title Bezeichnung
today heute
together zusammen
toilet Toilette, WC
tomorrow morgen
too zu, auch
top Spitze, Gipfel; Spitzen-
top, at the ~ oben
total (End-)Summe; völlig, (ins) gesamt
to **touch** berühren, anfassen
tourism Tourismus
towards auf ... zu
town Stadt
toy Spielzeug
tradition Tradition, Brauch
traditional traditionell, herkömmlich
train Zug
to **train** trainieren, ausbilden, ausgebildet werden
training Ausbildung
translation Übersetzung
transport Transport, Verkehr
travel; to **travel** Reisen; reisen, fahren
tree Baum
trip Ausflug, Reise, Besuch
trouble Ärger, Mühe, Umstände, Problem(e)
trousers *(pl)* Hose(n)
truck Lastwagen
true richtig, wahr
to **try** versuchen, probieren
turn; to **turn** Wendung; wenden; (sich) drehen, abbiegen
twice zweimal
type (of) Art, Sorte

U

under unter
to **underline** unterstreichen
to **understand** verstehen, begreifen
understanding Verständnis, Verständigung
unhappy unzufrieden, unglücklich
uniform Uniform
university Universität
unless wenn nicht, es sei denn
unlucky unglücklich, Unglücks-
until bis
unusual unüblich
up hinauf, hoch
upstairs oben
use; to **use** Gebrauch; benutzen, verwenden
useful nützlich
user Nutzer
usually normalerweise, gewöhnlich, meistens

V

very sehr
view; to **view** Ansicht, (Aus-)Sicht; anschauen
visit; to **visit** Besuch; besuchen, besichtigen
voice Stimme

W

to **wait** warten
walk; to **walk** Spaziergang; (zu Fuß) gehen
wall Wand, Mauer
to **want** wollen
warm warm
warm-up Aufwärmen, Vorprogramm
to **warn** warnen
warning Warnung
watch; to **watch** (Armband-)Uhr; beobachten, sehen
water Wasser
way Weg, Methode, Art (und Weise)
weak schwach
weather Wetter
web Netz, Internet
week Woche
weekday Wochentag
weekend Wochenende
welcome; to **welcome** Willkommen, willkommen; begrüßen
well gesund, gut, also; **as ~** auch (noch), ebenfalls
western westlich
what was, welche/r/s
when wenn, als, wann
whenever immer wenn
where wo(hin)
whether ob
which welche/r/s
while während; Weile
who wer, der/die/das, welche(r/s)
whole ganz
whose dessen, wessen
why warum
wide breit, weit
wife, *pl* **wives** (Ehe-)Frau
wild wild, ungezügelt, toll
will Wille; werde(n), wollen
to **win** gewinnen
wine Wein
wish; to **wish** Wunsch; wünschen
with mit, bei
within innerhalb (von), in
without ohne
woman, *pl* **women** Frau
wonderful wunderbar, wundervoll
won't wird nicht
word Wort
work; to **work** Arbeit, Werk; funktionieren, arbeiten
worker Arbeiter/in
world Welt
to **worry** sich Sorgen machen
worse schlechter, schlimmer
worst schlechteste/r/s, schlimmste/r/s
worth wert
would würde/n
to **write (down)** (auf)schreiben
writer Autor/in, Schreiber/in
wrong falsch

Y

year Jahr
yesterday gestern
yet ...?; not yet schon ...?; noch nicht
young jung

Chronological word list

Dieses Wörterverzeichnis enthält alle neuen Wörter aus *Money Matters – 4th Edition* in der Reihenfolge Ihres Erscheinens (Seitenzahlen sind angegeben). Nicht aufgeführt sind die Wörter aus dem Grundwortschatz (*Basic word list*). Wörter aus den Hörverständnisübungen sind mit einem **T** (*Transkript*) und Wörter aus den *Partner files* mit einem **P** gekennzeichnet. Die Zahl am linken Rand gibt die Seitenzahl an.

Abkürzungen	*AE* = amerikanisches Englisch	*jdm* = jemandem	*pl* = plural noun
	BE = britisches Englisch	*jdn* = jemanden	*sb* = somebody
	etw = etwas	*jds* = jemandes	*sth* = something

Unit 1

6	**impact (on)** ['ɪmpækt]	(Aus-)Wirkung, Folge
	to **make an impact** [ˌmeɪk ən 'ɪmpækt]	einen Eindruck hinterlassen
	branch [brɑːntʃ]	Zweig(stelle), Filiale
	impression [ɪm'preʃn]	Eindruck
	employee [ɪm'plɔɪiː]	Angestellte/r, Arbeitnehmer/in
	neat [niːt]	ordentlich, elegant, adrett
	appearance [ə'pɪərəns]	Aussehen, Äußeres
	serious ['sɪəriəs]	ernsthaft, seriös
	smart [smɑːt]	elegant, schick *(Kleidung)*
	overdressed [ˌəʊvə'drest]	zu elegant gekleidet
	underdressed [ˌʌndə'drest]	zu lässig/leger gekleidet
	appropriate [ə'prəʊpriət]	angemessen, passend, richtig
	inappropriate [ˌɪnə'prəʊpriət]	ungeeignet, unpassend, unangemessen
	acceptable [ək'septəbl]	annehmbar, akzeptabel
	unacceptable [ˌʌnək'septəbl]	unannehmbar, inakzeptabel
	casual ['kæʒuəl]	leger, sportlich, Freizeit-
	dress code ['dres kəʊd]	Kleiderordnung
	to **brainstorm** ['breɪnstɔːm]	Ideen (ungeordnet) sammeln
	topic ['tɒpɪk]	Punkt, Thema
	to **include** [ɪn'kluːd]	einbeziehen, einschließen
	heading ['hedɪŋ]	Überschrift
	(nail) varnish ['vɑːnɪʃ]	(Nagel-)Lack
	jewellery ['dʒuːəlri]	Schmuck
	to **impress** [ɪm'pres]	beeindrucken
	teller *AE* ['telə]	Kassierer/in
	customer service [ˌkʌstəmə 'sɜːvɪs]	Kundenberatung
	customer service representative [ˌkʌstəmə sɜːvɪs reprɪ'zentətɪv]	Kundenberater/in, Kundenservice-Vertreter/in
	investment [ɪn'vestmənt]	Anlage, Investition
	adviser [əd'vaɪzə]	Berater/in
	essential [ɪ'senʃl]	wesentlich
	guideline ['gaɪdlaɪn]	Richtlinie
	alike [ə'laɪk]	gleichermaßen, in gleicher Weise
7	to **require** [rɪ'kwaɪə]	benötigen, erfordern, verlangen
	presentable [prɪ'zentəbl]	vorzeigbar, respektabel
	skill [skɪl]	Fertigkeit, Fähigkeit
	people skills *pl* ['piːpl skɪlz]	soziale Kompetenz
	trainee [treɪ'niː]	Auszubildende/r, Praktikant/in
	rapport (with) [ræ'pɔː]	gutes Verhältnis (zu)
	trust [trʌst]	Vertrauen
	follow-through [ˌfɒləʊ 'θruː]	(konsequente) Durchführung
	request [rɪ'kwest]	Anfrage, Wunsch, Bitte
	to **handle** ['hændl]	umgehen mit, handhaben
	thorough ['θʌrə]	gründlich, sorgfältig
	meticulous [mə'tɪkjələs]	sorgfältig, gewissenhaft, gründlich
	to **afford** [ə'fɔːd]	(es) sich leisten (können)
	to **slip by** [ˌslɪp 'baɪ]	durchrutschen
	reliable [rɪ'laɪəbl]	zuverlässig, verlässlich
	account [ə'kaʊnt]	Konto
	whatever [wɒt'evə]	was auch immer
	to **need to do sth** [niːd]	etw tun müssen
	trustworthy ['trʌstwɜːði]	zuverlässig, vertrauenswürdig
	no matter what / how / who [ˌnəʊ 'mætə]	(ganz) egal, was / wie / wer
	matter ['mætə]	Angelegenheit, Sache
	patient ['peɪʃnt]	geduldig
	crucial ['kruːʃl]	äußerst wichtig, entscheidend
	to **create** [kri'eɪt]	(er)schaffen, erstellen
	atmosphere ['ætməsfɪə]	Atmosphäre, Stimmung
	courteous ['kɜːtiəs]	höflich

	phrase [freɪz]	(Rede-)Wendung, Ausdruck
	similar (to) ['sɪmələ]	ähnlich, vergleichbar
	agreement [ə'griːmənt]	Vereinbarung, Absprache, Zustimmung
	belief (in) [bɪ'liːf]	Glaube (an), Vertrauen (in)
	honesty ['ɒnəstɪ]	Ehrlichkeit
	dependable [dɪ'pendəbl]	zuverlässig, verlässlich
	demand (for) [dɪ'mɑːnd]	Forderung (nach), Bedarf (an), Nachfrage (an), Anforderung
	to **deal with** ['diːl wɪð]	sich beschäftigen mit, sich kümmern um, umgehen mit
	to **maintain** [meɪn'teɪn]	aufrecht erhalten
	loyalty ['lɔɪəlti]	Treue, Loyalität
	unfinished [ʌn'fɪnɪʃt]	unerledigt, unvollendet
	necessary ['nesəsəri]	nötig, erforderlich
	to **process** ['prəʊses]	(weiter)verarbeiten
	loan [ləʊn]	Darlehen, Kredit
	to **take (your) time** [ˌteɪk 'taɪm]	sich Zeit nehmen/lassen
	honest ['ɒnɪst]	ehrlich, aufrichtig
	employer [ɪm'plɔɪə]	Arbeitgeber/in
	to **pay (close) attention (to)** [peɪ ə'tenʃn]	(genau) aufpassen, achten (auf)
	attention [ə'tenʃn]	Aufmerksamkeit, Beachtung
	profile ['prəʊfaɪl]	Profil, Porträt
8	**requirement** [rɪ'kwaɪəmənt]	Voraussetzung, Bedingung, Anforderung
	entry ['entri]	Eintritt, Zutritt, Einstieg
	(at) entry level ['entri levl]	(auf) Einstiegsniveau
	interpersonal [ˌɪntə'pɜːsənl]	zwischenmenschlich
	keen [kiːn]	(sehr) interessiert, begeistert
	awareness [ə'weənəs]	Bewusstsein, Aufmerksamkeit
	degree [dɪ'griː]	Grad, Abschluss, Diplom
	highly ['haɪli]	höchst, äußerst
	applicant ['æplɪkənt]	Bewerber/in
	equivalent [ɪ'kwɪvələnt]	entsprechend
	certification [ˌsɜːtɪfɪ'keɪʃn]	Bestätigung, Zulassung
	college ['kɒlɪdʒ]	Fach(hoch)schule
	accounting [ə'kaʊntɪŋ]	Rechnungswesen, Buchhaltung
	related [rɪ'leɪtɪd]	zugehörig, verbunden, verwandt
	credit ['kredɪt]	Kredit *(Zahlungsaufschub)*
	analysis, *pl* **analyses** [ə'næləsɪs, ə'næləsiːz]	Analyse
	insurance [ɪn'ʃʊərəns]	Versicherung
	to **assist (with)** [ə'sɪst]	assistieren, helfen (bei)
	initial(ly) [ɪ'nɪʃl]	erste(r, s), Anfangs-, anfänglich
	to **hire** ['haɪə]	mieten, leihen
	to **seek** [siːk]	suchen (nach), anstreben
	promotion [prə'məʊʃn]	Beförderung, (beruflicher) Aufstieg
	dual ['djuːəl]	Doppel-, doppelt, dual
	traineeship [treɪ'niʃɪp]	Ausbildung, Praktikum
	expression [ɪk'spreʃn]	Ausdruck
	head office [ˌhed 'ɒfɪs]	Zentrale, Hauptstelle
	to **go on** [ˌgəʊ 'ɒn]	passieren, geschehen
	personal customer [ˌpɜːsənl 'kʌstəmə]	Privatkunde/-kundin
	wealthy ['welθi]	wohlhabend, reich
	business customer [ˌbɪznəs 'kʌstəmə]	Firmenkunde/-kundin, Geschäftskunde/-kundin
	foreign ['fɒrən]	ausländisch, Auslands-, fremd
	counter ['kaʊntə]	(Verkaufs-, Bank-) Schalter
	department [dɪ'pɑːtmənt]	Abteilung
	salary ['sæləri]	Gehalt, Lohn
	to **look forward to (doing sth)** [ˌlʊk 'fɔːwəd tə]	sich darauf freuen (etw zu tun)
	Take care. [ˌteɪk 'keə]	Pass auf dich auf.
9	**similarity** [ˌsɪmə'lærəti]	Ähnlichkeit, Gemeinsamkeit
	to **show sb (a)round** [ˌʃəʊ ə'raʊnd]	jdn herumführen
	to **introduce sb to sb/sth** [ˌɪntrə'djuːs]	jdm jdn/etw vorstellen
	floor plan ['flɔː plæn]	Grundriss, Lageplan
	to **refer to** [rɪ'fɜː]	sich beziehen auf
	ground floor [ˌgraʊnd 'flɔː]	Erdgeschoss
	lobby ['lɒbi]	Eingangshalle, Vorraum
	cash machine ['kæʃ məʃiːn]	Geldautomat
	ATM (automated teller machine) *AE* [ˌeɪ tiː 'em, ˌɔːtəmeɪtɪd 'telə məʃiːn]	Geldautomat
	cashpoint ['kæʃpɔɪnt]	Geldautomat
	nowadays ['naʊədeɪz]	heutzutage
	withdrawal [wɪð'drɔːəl]	Abhebung
	deposit [dɪ'pɒzɪt]	Einzahlung
	(bank) statement ['bæŋk steɪtmənt]	(Konto-)Auszug

	self-service [ˌself ˈsɜːvɪs]	Selbstbedienung(s-)
	security [sɪˈkjʊərəti]	Sicherheit
	issue [ˈɪʃuː]	(Streit-)Frage, Thema
	absolutely [ˈæbsəluːtli]	absolut, völlig
	to **stand/wait in line (for)** *AE* [ɪn ˈlaɪn]	Schlange stehen, sich anstellen (für/nach)
10	to **queue** [kjuː]	sich *(in einer Warteschlage)* anstellen, Schlange stehen
	till [tɪl]	Kasse
	assistance [əˈsɪstəns]	Hilfe, Unterstützung
	cashier [kæˈʃɪə]	Kassierer/in
	transaction [trænˈzækʃn]	(Geschäfts-)Vorgang, Transaktion
	currency [ˈkʌrənsi]	Währung
	cheque [tʃek]	Scheck
	to **fill in** [ˌfɪl ˈɪn]	eintragen, ausfüllen
	(bank) transfer [ˈtrænsfɜː]	(Bank-)Überweisung
	to **get sth** [get]	etw verstehen, mitbekommen
	by the way [baɪ ðə ˈweɪ]	übrigens, nebenbei (bemerkt)
	responsibility [rɪˌspɒnsəˈbɪləti]	Verantwortung, Aufgabe(nbereich)
	kind (of) [kaɪnd]	Art
	basement [ˈbeɪsmənt]	Keller, Untergeschoss
	strongroom [ˈstrɒŋruːm]	Banktresor, Tresor(raum)
	to **fascinate** [ˈfæsɪneɪt]	faszinieren
	vault *AE* [vɒlt]	Banktresor, Tresor(raum)
	to **take a look (at sth)** [teɪk ə ˈlʊk]	(sich) (etw) ansehen, betrachten
	safe deposit box, safety deposit box [ˌseɪf dɪˈpɒzɪt bɒks, ˌseɪfti dɪˈpɒzɪt bɒks]	Bankschließfach, Tresorfach
	advice [ədˈvaɪs]	Rat, Beratung
	say [seɪ]	zum Beispiel, beispielsweise
	to **invest** [ɪnˈvest]	anlegen, investieren
	capital [ˈkæpɪtl]	Kapital
	appointment [əˈpɔɪntmənt]	Termin
	generalist [ˈdʒenrəlɪst]	Generalist/in, Allrounder
	corporate client [ˌkɔːpərət ˈklaɪənt]	Firmenkunde/Firmenkundin, Geschäftskunde/Geschäftskundin
	to **look after** [lʊk ˈɑːftə]	sich kümmern um, betreuen
	headquarters, *pl* **headquarters** [ˌhedˈkwɔːtəz]	Zentrale, Hauptsitz
	elevator *AE* [ˈelɪveɪtə]	Lift, Aufzug
	to **hang on** [ˌhæŋ ˈɒn]	warten, dranbleiben *(Telefon)*
	bank manager [ˈbæŋk mænədʒə]	Bankdirektor/in, Filialleiter/in
	straight ahead [ˌstreɪt əˈhed]	geradeaus
11	**in charge (of)** [ɪn ˈtʃɑːdʒ]	verantwortlich (für), zuständig (für)
	responsible (for) [rɪˈspɒnsəbl]	verantwortlich, zuständig (für)
	to **wonder** [ˈwʌndə]	sich fragen
	to **be glad** [glæd]	sich freuen, froh sein
12	**restroom** *AE* [ˈrestruːm]	Toilette *(in öffentlichen Gebäuden)*
	first floor [ˌfɜːst ˈflɔː]	*(GB)* erste Etage, erster Stock, *(US)* Erdgeschoss
	valuables *(pl)* [ˈvæljuəblz]	Wertsachen
	executive [ɪgˈzekjətɪv]	leitend, Vorstands-, Führungs-
	to **save up (for)** [ˌseɪv ˈʌp]	(auf)sparen (für)
	to **see sb (about)** [siː]	jdn aufsuchen (wegen)
	limited [ˈlɪmɪtɪd]	begrenzt, beschränkt
	arrangement [əˈreɪndʒmənt]	Abmachung, Vereinbarung
13	**real estate** [ˈrɪəl ɪsteɪt]	Immobilien
	share [ʃeə]	Aktie, Anteil
	investment fund [ɪnˈvestmənt fʌnd]	Investmentfonds
	fund [fʌnd]	Fonds, Fundus
	branch manager [ˈbrɑːntʃ mænədʒə]	Filialleiter/in
	investment bank [ɪnˈvestmənt bæŋk]	Anlagebank, Investitionsbank
	day-to-day [ˌdeɪ tə ˈdeɪ]	tagtäglich
	enquiry [ɪnˈkwaɪəri]	Anfrage
	fixed [fɪkst]	fest, festgelegt, Fest-
	payment [ˈpeɪmənt]	(Be-)Zahlung
	stocks and shares *(pl)* [ˌstɒks ən ˈʃeəz]	Wertpapiere
	stock [stɒk]	Aktie, Anleihe
14	**challenging** [ˈtʃælɪndʒɪŋ]	anspruchsvoll, fordernd
T	**rewarding** [rɪˈwɔːdɪŋ]	lohnend, erfüllend
	term [tɜːm]	Begriff
	managerial [ˌmænəˈdʒɪəriəl]	Management-, Führungs-
	entry-level [ˈentri levl]	Einstiegs-, Anfangs-
	certified [ˈsɜːtɪfaɪd]	geprüft, diplomiert
	qualified [ˈkwɒlɪfaɪd]	mit Abschluss, qualifiziert
	in turn [ɪn ˈtɜːn]	wiederum
	to **lead (to)** [liːd]	führen (zu), leiten

employment opportunities *(pl)* [ɪmˌplɔɪmənt ɒpəˈtjuːnətiz]	Berufschancen
ability [əˈbɪləti]	Fähigkeit, Befähigung
to **attend to sth** [əˈtend tə]	sich um etw kümmern
client [ˈklaɪənt]	Kunde/Kundin
duty [ˈdjuːti]	Aufgabe, Pflicht
to **balance** [ˈbæləns]	ausgleichen, bilanzieren
cash drawer [ˈkæʃ drɔː]	Kassenlade
to **take in** [ˌteɪk ˈɪn]	einnehmen
to **hand out** [ˌhænd ˈaʊt]	aushändigen, herausgeben
typical [ˈtɪpɪkl]	typisch, charakteristisch
statement printer [ˈsteɪtmənt prɪntə]	Kontoauszugsdrucker
to **remove** [rɪˈmuːv]	entfernen
to **get stuck** [stʌk]	sich festfahren, stecken bleiben, sich (auf)stauen
to **replace** [rɪˈpleɪs]	ersetzen
ink cartridge [ɪŋk ˈkɑːtrɪdʒ]	Tintenpatrone
to **take place** [teɪk ˈpleɪs]	stattfinden
area [ˈeəriə]	Gebiet, Bereich
face-to-face [ˌfeɪs tə ˈfeɪs]	persönlich
to **pay in** [ˌpeɪ ˈɪn]	einzahlen, einlösen
to **provide** [prəˈvaɪd]	(an)bieten, zur Verfügung stellen
balance [ˈbæləns]	Kontostand, Bilanz, Saldo
monetary [ˈmʌnɪtri]	finanziell, Geld-
maintenance [ˈmeɪntənəns]	Wartung, Instandhaltung
to **key in** [ˌkiː ˈɪn]	eingeben, eintippen
to **arrange** [əˈreɪndʒ]	arrangieren, vereinbaren
range [reɪndʒ]	Palette, Auswahl
activity [ækˈtɪvəti]	Aktivität, Tätigkeit
15 **mobile** [ˈməʊbaɪl]	mobil, beweglich
benefit [ˈbenɪfɪt]	Nutzen, Vorteil, Pluspunkt
wheel [wiːl]	Rad
drawback [ˈdrɔːbæk]	Nachteil
urban-dwelling [ˈɜːbən dwelɪŋ]	städtisch
short of time [ˌʃɔːt əv ˈtaɪm]	in Zeitnot
majority [məˈdʒɒrəti]	größter Teil, Mehrheit
shape [ʃeɪp]	Form

crofter *BE* [ˈkrɒftə]	Kleinbauer/-bäuerin *(in Schottland)*
to **encounter sth** [ɪnˈkaʊntə]	auf etw stoßen/treffen
manifestation [ˌmænɪfeˈsteɪʃn]	Manifestation, Erscheinungsform
to **weave** [wiːv]	weben
popularity [ˌpɒpjuˈlærəi]	Beliebtheit, Popularität
affordability [əˌfɔːdəˈbɪləti]	Erschwinglichkeit, Bezahlbarkeit
to **dwindle** [ˈdwɪndl]	schwinden, nachlassen
to **announce** [əˈnaʊns]	ankündigen, bekanntgeben
closure [ˈkləʊʒə]	Schließung, Stilllegung
route [ruːt]	Route, Strecke
van [væn]	Lieferwagen, Transporter
additional [əˈdɪʃənl]	zusätzlich
excuse [ɪkˈskjuːs]	Ausrede
proper [ˈprɒpə]	richtig
at the wheel [ˌæt ðə ˈwiːl]	am Steuer
regular (customer) [ˌregjələ ˈkʌstəmə]	Stammkunde/-in, Bestandskunde/-in
off route [ˌɒf ˈruːt]	abseits
to **sweep** [swiːp]	fegen
doorstep [ˈdɔːstep]	Türschwelle
certain(ly) [ˈsɜːtn]	sicher(lich), bestimmt
to **appreciate** [əˈpriːʃieɪt]	würdigen, zu schätzen wissen
although [ɔːlˈðəʊ]	obwohl
to **bemoan** [bɪˈməʊn]	beklagen, betrauern
lack (of) [læk]	Mangel (an), Fehlen (von)
butcher [ˈbʊtʃə]	Metzger(ei), Fleischhauer(ei)
otherwise [ˈʌðəwaɪz]	ansonsten, andernfalls
community [kəˈmjuːnəti]	Gemeinschaft, Gemeinde, Bevölkerungsgruppe
to **insist** [ɪnˈsɪst]	darauf bestehen, beteuern
on a case-by-case basis [ˌkeɪs baɪ ˈkeɪs beɪsɪs]	durch/nach Einzelfallbetrachtung
basis, *pl* **bases** [ˈbeɪsɪs, ˈbeɪsiːz]	Basis, Grundlage
according to [əˈkɔːdɪŋ tə]	entsprechend, nach, gemäß
to **consider** [kənˈsɪdə]	erwägen, in Betracht ziehen
facilities *(pl)* [fəˈsɪlətiz]	Einrichtungen
nevertheless [ˌnevəðəˈles]	trotzdem, dennoch
to **personalize** [ˈpɜːsənəlaɪz]	persönlich/individuell gestalten

	to **roll out** [ˌrəʊl 'aʊt]	einführen, ausbauen
	fleet [fli:t]	Flotte
	to **exist** [ɪg'zɪst]	existieren
	practical ['præktɪkl]	praktisch, praxisbezogen
	to **equip** [ɪ'kwɪp]	ausrüsten, ausstatten
	satellite dish ['sætəlaɪt dɪʃ]	Satellitenschüssel
	to **crew** [kru:]	besetzen
	to **update** [ˌʌp'deɪt]	auf den neusten Stand bringen, aktualisieren
	base [beɪs]	Basis
	paperwork ['peɪpəwɜ:k]	Büroarbeit, Schreibarbeit
	thin [θɪn]	dünn
	indeed [ɪn'di:d]	in der Tat, wirklich
	supposedly [sə'pəʊzdli]	angeblich

Unit 2

16	**channel** ['tʃænl]	Kanal, Sender
	to **justify** ['dʒʌstɪfaɪ]	begründen, rechtfertigen
	via ['vaɪə]	über, durch, per, mittels
	to give sb a ring [ˌgɪv ə 'rɪŋ]	jdn anrufen
	luckily ['lʌkɪli]	glücklicherweise, zum Glück
	to **retire** [rɪ'taɪə]	in den Ruhestand gehen, in Rente gehen
	unfortunately [ʌn'fɔ:tʃənətli]	leider
	knee [ni:]	Knie
	to come in handy [ˌkʌm ɪn 'hændi]	sich als nützlich erweisen, gelegen kommen
	keyboard ['ki:bɔ:d]	Tastatur, Keyboard
	not … either ['aɪðə]	auch nicht
	to **reckon** ['rekən]	schätzen, glauben
	convenience [kən'vi:niəns]	Bequemlichkeit, Annehmlichkeit, Komfort
	to **graduate** ['grædʒueɪt]	den Abschluss machen, sein Examen machen
	lonely ['ləʊnli]	einsam
	… is not my cup of tea. [kʌp əv 'ti:]	… ist nicht mein Fall. / nach meinem Geschmack.
	particularly [pə'tɪkjələli]	besonders
	to **manage** ['mænɪdʒ]	(es) schaffen
	awkward ['ɔ:kwəd]	unangenehm, peinlich
	boring ['bɔ:rɪŋ]	langweilig
	money box ['mʌni bɒks]	Spardose
	to **advertise** ['ædvətaɪz]	werben (für), anbieten
	customer service officer [ˌkʌstəmə 'sɜ:vɪs ɒfɪsə]	Kundenberater/in
T	**cash** [kæʃ]	Bargeld
	rather ['rɑ:ðə]	ziemlich
	to **repair** [rɪ'peə]	reparieren
	financial [faɪ'nænʃl]	finanziell
	support [sə'pɔ:t]	Unterstützung
	cash dispenser [ˌkæʃ dɪ'spensə]	Bargeldautomat
	current account ['kʌrənt əkaʊnt]	Girokonto
	savings account ['seɪvɪŋz əkaʊnt]	Sparkonto
	savings book ['seɪvɪŋz bʊk]	Sparbuch
	identity card [aɪ'dentəti kɑ:d]	Personalausweis
	straightaway [ˌstreɪtə'weɪ]	sofort
	to **withdraw** [wɪð'drɔ:]	abheben
	terms and conditions *(pl)* [ˌtɜ:mz ənd kən'dɪʃnz]	Konditionen, (Allgemeine) Geschäftsbedingungen
	to take out (money) [ˌteɪk 'aʊt]	(Geld) abheben
	penalty ['penəlti]	Strafe
	to stick to sth ['stɪk tə]	bei etw bleiben, sich an etw halten
	penalized ['pi:nəlaɪzd]	bestraft
	I suppose [aɪ sə'pəʊz]	wohl

17	**line manager** ['laɪn mænɪdʒə]	(direkte/r) Vorgesetzte/r
	to **structure** ['strʌktʃə]	strukturieren
	logical order [ˌlɒdʒɪkl 'ɔ:də]	logische Reihenfolge
	follow-up ['fɒləʊ ʌp]	Anschlusstermin
	to **express** [ɪk'spres]	ausdrücken, äußern, zum Ausdruck bringen
	to get down to business [get ˌdaʊn tə 'bɪznəs]	zur Sache kommen
	refreshment [rɪ'freʃmənt]	Erfrischung, Stärkung, Imbiss
	to fix (a time / a date / an appointment) [fɪks]	(eine Uhrzeit / ein Datum / einen Termin) festlegen, vereinbaren
	available [ə'veɪləbl]	verfügbar; zu sprechen *(Telefon)*
	to **recommend** [ˌrekə'mend]	empfehlen
	pleased [pli:zd]	erfreut
	dreadful ['dredfl]	schrecklich, furchtbar

18	**dissatisfied** [dɪs'sætɪsfaɪd]	unzufrieden
	to **approach sb/sth** [ə'prəʊtʃ]	an jdn/etw herantreten
	task [tɑ:sk]	Aufgabe
	apology [ə'pɒlədʒi]	Entschuldigung
	complaint [kəm'pleɪnt]	Beschwerde, Klage, Reklamation
	disappointed (with sb/sth) [ˌdɪsə'pɔɪntɪd]	enttäuscht (von jdm/etw)
	free of charge [ˌfri: əv 'tʃɑ:dʒ]	gebührenfrei
	fee [fi:]	Entgelt, Gebühr
	to **switch** [swɪtʃ]	wechseln, umstellen
	frustrating [frʌ'streɪtɪŋ]	frustrierend
	recently ['ri:sntli]	jüngst, kürzlich, neulich
	to **reserve** [rɪ'zɜ:v]	buchen, reservieren
19	**freezing** ['fri:zɪŋ]	eisig, eiskalt
	cold [kəʊld]	Kälte
	reservation [ˌrezə'veɪʃn]	Reservierung, Buchung
	to **apologize (for)** [ə'pɒlədʒaɪz]	sich entschuldigen (für)
	inconvenience [ˌɪnkən'vi:niəns]	Unannehmlichkeit(en)
	triple ['trɪpl]	dreimalig, dreifach
	annoying [ə'nɔɪɪŋ]	ärgerlich, lästig, störend
	charge [tʃɑ:dʒ]	Gebühr
	fully ['fʊli]	völlig, vollkommen
	to **debit** ['debɪt]	belasten
	so-called [ˌsəʊ 'kɔ:ld]	sogenannt
	to **charge** [tʃɑ:dʒ]	berechnen
	not … anywhere ['eniweə]	nirgends, nirgendwo(hin)
	association [əˌsəʊʃi'eɪʃn]	Verband, Vereinigung
	to **prove** [pru:v]	beweisen
	to **suggest** [sə'dʒest]	vorschlagen
	partly ['pɑ:tli]	teils, teilweise
	fault [fɔ:lt]	Fehler, Schuld
	to **credit** ['kredɪt]	gutschreiben
	misunderstanding [ˌmɪsʌndə'stændɪŋ]	Missverständnis
	to **cause** [kɔ:z]	verursachen
20	**speaking** ['spi:kɪŋ]	am Apparat *(Telefon)*
T	to **hold the line** [ˌhəʊld ðə 'laɪn]	am Apparat bleiben
	to **leave a message** [ˌli:v ə 'mesɪdʒ]	eine Nachricht hinterlassen
	corporate customer [ˌkɔ:pərət 'kʌstəmə]	Firmenkunde/Firmenkundin, Geschäftskunde/Geschäftskundin
	to **put sb through** [ˌpʊt 'θru:]	jdn durchstellen
	to **cancel** ['kænsl]	absagen, stornieren
	would you mind … [wʊd ju 'maɪnd]	könnten Sie bitte …
	extension (number) [ɪk'stenʃn]	Durchwahl *(Telefon)*
	reception [rɪ'sepʃn]	Empfang *(auch beim Telefon)*, Rezeption
	you're welcome [jɔ: 'welkəm]	keine Ursache, gern geschehen
	short-term [ʃɔ:t 'tɜ:m]	kurzfristig
	overdraft ['əʊvədrɑ:ft]	Kontoüberziehung
	underscore [ˌʌndə'skɔ:]	Unterstrich
	not at all [nɒt ət 'ɔ:l]	keine Ursache
	engaged [ɪn'geɪdʒd]	besetzt *(Telefon)*
	terrible ['terəbl]	schrecklich, furchtbar
	crackly ['krækli]	knisternd
	dash [dæʃ]	Gedankenstrich
	dot [dɒt]	Punkt, Pünktchen
	to **identify** [aɪ'dentɪfaɪ]	identifizieren, nennen
	identification [aɪˌdentɪfɪ'keɪʃn]	Identifizierung, Nennung des Namens
	to **respond** [rɪ'spɒnd]	antworten, reagieren
21	**digit** ['dɪdʒɪt]	Ziffer
	separately ['seprətli]	einzeln
	oh [əʊ]	Null *(im gesprochenen Englisch)*
	zero ['zɪərəʊ]	Null
	country code ['kʌntrɪ kəʊd]	Ländervorwahl
	(dialling) code ['daɪəlɪŋ kəʊd]	Vorwahl
	area code *AE* ['eəriə kəʊd]	Vorwahl
	cell phone *AE* ['sel fəʊn]	Handy, Mobiltelefon
	landline ['lændlaɪn]	Festnetz
	unfamiliar [ˌʌnfə'mɪliə]	unbekannt, ungewohnt
	at your fingertips ['fɪŋgətɪps]	zur Hand
	capital letter ['kæpɪtl letə]	Großbuchstabe
	upper case [ˌʌpə 'keɪs]	großgeschrieben
	lower case [ˌləʊə 'keɪs]	kleingeschrieben
	punctuation [ˌpʌŋktʃu'eɪʃn]	Interpunktion, Zeichensetzung
	slash [slæʃ]	Schrägstrich
	backslash ['bækslæʃ]	Schrägstrich nach links
	hyphen ['haɪfn]	Bindestrich, Trennstrich
	minus ['maɪnəs]	Minus(zeichen)
	rarely ['reəli]	selten
	to **invent** [ɪn'vent]	erfinden
	to **dictate** [dɪk'teɪt]	diktieren

22	**coin** [kɔɪn]	Münze
	to **insure** [ɪn'ʃʊə]	versichern
23	to **suit sb** [su:t]	jdm passen, jdm recht sein
	convenient [kən'vi:niənt]	passend, praktisch, angenehm
	to **postpone** [pə'spəʊn]	verschieben
	to **apply (for)** [ə'plaɪ]	beantragen; sich bewerben (um)
	to **complain** [kəm'pleɪn]	sich beschweren, sich beklagen
	to **penalize** ['pi:nəlaɪz]	bestrafen
	to **regret** [rɪ'gret]	bedauern, bereuen
	to **reply (to)** [rɪ'plaɪ]	antworten (auf)
	corresponding (to) [ˌkɒrɪ'spɒndɪŋ]	entsprechend, passend (zu)
	favourable ['feɪvərəbl]	günstig, vorteilhaft
	satisfied ['sætɪsfaɪd]	zufrieden
	to **calm sb down** [ˌkɑ:m 'daʊn]	jdn beruhigen
	improvement [ɪm'pru:vmənt]	Verbesserung
	to **refund** [rɪ'fʌnd]	erstatten
	accordingly [ək'ɔ:dɪŋli]	(dem)entsprechend, folglich
24	**campaign** [kæm'peɪn]	Kampagne, Aktion
	work placement ['wɜ:k pleɪsmənt]	Praktikum
	bill [bɪl]	Rechnung
	go overdrawn [ˌgəʊ əʊvə'drɔ:n]	überziehen, ins Minus geraten
	details *pl* ['di:teɪlz]	Angaben
	prediction [prɪ'dɪkʃn]	Voraussage
	assumption [ə'sʌmpʃn]	Annahme
	traffic jam ['træfɪk dʒæm]	(Verkehrs-)Stau
25	to **found** [faʊnd]	gründen
	decision-maker [dɪ'sɪʒn meɪkə]	Entscheidungsträger
	on the move [ɒn ðə 'mu:v]	auf Achse, in Bewegung
	twenty-four seven (24/7) [ˌtwenti ˌfɔ: 'sevn]	rund um die Uhr
	brand [brænd]	Marke(nname)
	replacement [rɪ'pleɪsmənt]	Ersatz
	to **educate** ['edʒukeɪt]	erziehen
	advantage [əd'vɑ:ntɪdʒ]	Vorteil
	disadvantage [ˌdɪsəd'vɑ:ntɪdʒ]	Nachteil, Schaden
	regarding [rɪ'gɑ:dɪŋ]	bezüglich, betreffend
26	to **address** [ə'dres]	*(Problem etc.)* ansprechen, angehen, thematisieren
	behaviour [bɪ'heɪvjə]	Benehmen, Verhalten
	to **imply** [ɪm'plaɪ]	beinhalten, implizieren
	provision [prə'vɪʒn]	Bereitstellung
	access ['ækses]	Zugriff, Zugang
	feature ['fi:tʃə]	Merkmal, Eigenschaft, Kennzeichen
	to **increase** [ɪn'kri:s]	steigen, zunehmen; erhöhen
	consideration [kənˌsɪdə'reɪʃn]	Erwägung, Überlegung
	robust [rəʊ'bʌst]	widerstandsfähig, robust
	attitude (to/towards) ['ætɪtju:d]	Einstellung, (Geistes-) Haltung (zu/gegenüber)
	preference ['prefrəns]	Präferenz, Vorliebe
	pervasive [pə'veɪsɪv]	um sich greifend, durchdringend
	generation [ˌdʒenə'reɪʃn]	Generation
	primary ['praɪməri]	Haupt-, hauptsächlich
	financial services provider [faɪˌnænʃl 'sɜ:vɪsɪs prəvaɪdə]	Finanzdienstleister
	to **cite** [saɪt]	anführen, angeben
	to **evolve** [ɪ'vɒlv]	sich weiter entwickeln
	disruptive [dɪs'rʌptɪv]	(zer)störend, zerreißend
	innovation [ˌɪnə'veɪʃn]	Innovation, Neuerung
	proof [pru:f]	Beweis, Nachweis
	expectation [ˌekspek'teɪʃn]	Erwartung
	to **shape** [ʃeɪp]	formen
	experience [ɪk'spɪəriəns]	Erfahrung, Erlebnis
	content ['kɒntent]	Inhalt
	interaction [ˌɪntər'ækʃn]	Interaktion
	to **deliver** [dɪ'lɪvə]	überbringen, liefern
	engaging [ɪn'geɪdʒɪŋ]	fesselnd, spannend; verbindlich
	consumer [kən'sju:mə]	Verbraucher/in
	peer [pɪə]	Gleichaltrige/r, Altersgenosse
	word of mouth [ˌwɜ:d əv 'maʊθ]	Mundpropaganda
	independent [ˌɪndɪ'pendənt]	unabhängig
	influencer ['ɪnfluənsə]	Einflussnehmer/in
	rapid ['ræpɪd]	schnell, rasch
	emergence [i'mɜ:dʒəns]	Entstehen, Aufkommen
	in parallel [ɪn 'pærəlel]	nebeneinander
	rise [raɪz]	Aufschwung, Anstieg

mobility [məʊ'bɪləti]	Beweglichkeit, Mobilität
increasingly [ɪn'kri:sɪŋli]	zunehmend, in zunehmendem Maße
savvy ['sævi]	versiert
due to ['dju: tə]	wegen, aufgrund (von)
research [rɪ'sɜ:tʃ]	Forschung, Recherche
to **expose** [ɪk'spəʊz]	aussetzen, zeigen
differentiation [ˌdɪfəˌrenʃi'eɪʃn]	Differenzierung, Abgrenzung
provider [prə'vaɪdə]	Anbieter/in
self-directed [ˌself də'rektɪd]	selbstgesteuert
to **rely on/upon** [rɪ'laɪ ɒn]	sich stützen auf, sich verlassen auf
source [sɔ:s]	Quelle, Herkunft
comparison [kəm'pærɪsn]	Vergleich
purchase ['pɜ:tʃəs]	Einkauf, Kauf
straightforward [ˌstreɪt'fɔ:wəd]	einfach, klar (ausgedrückt)
widespread ['waɪdspred]	weit verbreitet, umfassend
boundary ['baʊndri]	Grenze, Begrenzung
rise [raɪz]	Erhöhung, Anstieg
to **amplify** ['æmplɪfaɪ]	verstärken
tremendous [trɪ'mendəs]	gewaltig
shy [ʃaɪ]	schüchtern, scheu
to **raise** [reɪz]	erhöhen, (an)heben
to **spread** [spred]	(sich) ausbreiten, (sich) verbreiten
irreparable [ɪ'repərəbl]	irreparabel
damage ['dæmɪdʒ]	Schaden
associated [ə'səʊʃieɪtɪd]	verbunden
27 **irate** [aɪ'reɪt]	zornig, wütend
located [ləʊ'keɪtɪd]	gelegen
to **face** [feɪs]	gegenüber stehen
flawed [flɔ:d]	fehlerhaft, mangelhaft
delivery [dɪ'lɪvəri]	Zustellung, (Aus-) Lieferung
inaccurate [ɪn'ækjərət]	ungenau, unrichtig
to **determine** [dɪ'tɜ:mɪn]	ermitteln, feststellen
to **gain** [geɪn]	erwerben, gewinnen, sammeln
confidence ['kɒnfɪdəns]	(Selbst-)Vertrauen, Zuversicht
to **diffuse** [dɪ'fju:z]	zerstreuen
volatile ['vɒlətaɪl]	explosiv, brisant
to **evoke** [ɪ'vəʊk]	auslösen, hervorrufen
outcome ['aʊtkʌm]	Ergebnis, Resultat
co-worker ['kəʊ wɜ:kə]	Arbeitskollege/-kollegin

supervisor ['su:pəvaɪzə]	Betreuer/in, Vorgesetzte/r
to **promote sb** [prə'məʊt]	jdn befördern
upset [ˌʌp'set]	verstimmt, verärgert
daunting ['dɔ:ntɪŋ]	einschüchternd, entmutigend, beängstigend
perspective [pə'spektɪv]	Perspektive, Blickwinkel
opportunity [ˌɒpə'tju:nəti]	Gelegenheit
blessing ['blesɪŋ]	Segen
be a blessing in disguise [ˌblesɪŋ ɪn dɪs'gaɪz]	sich im Nachhinein als gut herausstellen, Glück im Unglück sein
disguise [dɪs'gaɪz]	Verkleidung, Tarnung
flaw [flɔ:]	Schwachstelle, Fehler, Mangel
revenue ['revənju:]	Einkünfte, Einnahmen
critical ['krɪtɪkl]	entscheidend
interest ['ɪntrəst]	Interesse
to **lay blame** [ˌleɪ 'bleɪm]	Schuld zuweisen
blame [bleɪm]	Schuld
regardless of [rɪ'gɑ:dləss əv]	ungeachtet
to **be at fault** [ət 'fɔ:lt]	im Unrecht sein, schuldig sein
to **put yourself in sb's place** [pleɪs]	sich in jds Lage versetzen
to **care about sb/sth** ['keər əbaʊt]	sich um jdn/etw kümmern, am Herzen liegen
concern [kən'sɜ:n]	Befürchtung, Bedenken, Sorge
upsetting [ʌp'setɪŋ]	ärgerlich
to **blame sb** [bleɪm]	jdm die Schuld geben
pertinent ['pɜ:tɪnənt]	sachdienlich, relevant
caring ['keərɪŋ]	fürsorglich, warmherzig
concerned [kən'sɜ:nd]	betroffen, besorgt
manner ['mænə]	Art (und Weise)
angry ['æŋgri]	aufgebracht, ungehalten
patience ['peɪʃns]	Geduld
tact [tækt]	Takt(gefühl)
outrageous [aʊt'reɪdʒəs]	empörend, schockierend, unerhört
in essence [ɪn 'esns]	im Grunde genommen
to **throw a fit** [ˌθrəʊ ə 'fɪt]	einen Anfall haben, durchdrehen
to **remain** [rɪ'meɪn]	bleiben
calm [kɑ:m]	ruhig, gelassen
to **empathize** ['empəθaɪz]	sich einfühlen

	to reward [rɪ'wɔ:d]	belohnen
	to highlight ['haɪlaɪt]	hervorheben, markieren
	equivalent [ɪ'kwɪvələnt]	Äquivalent, Gegenstück

UNIT 3

29	**item** ['aɪtəm]	Artikel, Gegenstand, Punkt
	various ['veəriəs]	(mehrere) verschiedene
	expenses *(pl)* [ɪk'spensɪz]	Kosten, Auslagen
	to confirm [kən'fɜ:m]	bestätigen
	residence registration ['rezɪdəns redʒɪstreɪʃn]	Meldebescheinigung
	to attach [ə'tætʃ]	anfügen, anhängen *(an ein E-Mail)*
	to enclose [ɪn'kləʊz]	beifügen, beilegen
	navigation link [ˌnævɪ'geɪʃn lɪŋk]	(Navigations-)Link, Hyperlink
	to hesitate ['hezɪteɪt]	zögern
	Best regards [best rɪ'gɑ:dz]	Beste Grüße
30	**printout** ['prɪntaʊt]	Ausdruck
	joint account [ˌdʒɔɪnt ə'kaʊnt]	Gemeinschaftskonto
	debit card ['debɪt kɑ:d]	Bankkarte, ec-Karte
	direct debit [dəˌrekt 'debɪt]	Einzugsermächtigung, Lastschrift(verfahren)
	standing order [ˌstændɪŋ 'ɔ:də]	Dauerauftrag
	overdraft facility [ˌəʊvədrɑ:ft fə'sɪləti]	Dispositionskredit
	description [dɪ'skrɪpʃn]	Beschreibung, Schilderung
	to enable [ɪ'neɪbl]	ermöglichen, befähigen
	flexibility [ˌfleksə'bɪləti]	Flexibilität
	to purchase ['pɜ:tʃəs]	kaufen
	in addition to [ɪn ə'dɪʃn tə]	zusätzlich zu
	immediate [ɪ'mi:diət]	sofortig, sofort, umgehend
	variable ['veəriəbl]	variabel, veränderlich, wechselnd
	goods *(pl)* [gʊdz]	Güter, Ware(n)
	tradesperson, *pl* **tradespeople** ['treɪdzpɜ:sn]	Gewerbetreibende/r, Handwerker/in
	to be aware [bi ə'weə]	sich bewusst sein
	hefty ['hefti]	satt, saftig *(Betrag)*
	to clear a cheque [ˌkliə ə 'tʃek]	einen Scheck gutschreiben (lassen)
	combined [kəm'baɪnd]	kombiniert
	to authorize ['ɔ:θəraɪz]	autorisieren, ermächtigen
	to vary ['veəri]	variieren, schwanken
	on a regular basis [ɒn əˌregjələ 'beɪsɪs]	regelmäßig
31	**permanent** ['pɜ:mənənt]	ständig, fest, dauerhaft
	certificate [sə'tɪfɪkət]	Zeugnis, Urkunde, Bescheinigung
	residents' registration office [ˌrezɪdənts ˌredʒɪ'streɪʃn ɒfɪs]	Einwohnermeldeamt
	reference ['refərəns]	Auskunft, Referenz
	agency ['eɪdʒənsi]	Agentur, Organisation
	to tick [tɪk]	ankreuzen
	to indicate ['ɪndɪkeɪt]	anzeigen, angeben
	to set up [ˌset 'ʌp]	einstellen, einrichten, eröffnen
	for the time being [fə ðə ˌtaɪm 'bi:ɪŋ]	vorläufig, für den Moment
	to receive [rɪ'si:v]	erhalten, empfangen, bekommen
	working day ['wɜ:kɪŋ deɪ]	Werktag
	separate ['seprət]	getrennt, separat
	to get settled ['setld]	sich einleben
	to activate ['æktɪveɪt]	aktivieren
	sole [səʊl]	alleinig
	account holder [ə'kaʊnt həʊldə]	Kontoinhaber/in
	(third party) mandate [ˌθɜ:d pɑ:ti 'mændeɪt]	Vollmacht
	power of attorney [ˌpaʊər əv ə'tɜ:ni]	Handlungsvollmacht
	to designate ['dezɪgneɪt]	benennen, bestimmen
	incapacitated [ˌɪnkə'pæsɪteɪtɪd]	arbeitsunfähig, außer Gefecht
	restriction [rɪ'strɪkʃn]	Beschränkung, Einschränkung
	to safeguard ['seɪfgɑ:d]	schützen
	regulation [ˌregju'leɪʃn]	Vorschrift
32	**driving licence** ['draɪvɪŋ laɪsns]	Führerschein
33	**credit interest** *(no pl)* [ˌkredɪt 'ɪntrəst]	Guthabenzins(en)
	credit transfer [ˌkredɪt 'trænsfɜ:]	Überweisung
	to transfer [træns'fɜ:]	überweisen
	permission [pə'mɪʃn]	Erlaubnis
	to overdraw [ˌəʊvə'drɔ:]	überziehen
	to exceed [ɪk'si:d]	überschreiten
	versus ['vɜ:səs]	gegen
	paperless ['peɪpələs]	papierlos
	monthly ['mʌnθli]	monatlich

	via regular mail [vaɪə 'regjələ meɪl]	auf dem Postweg
	pros and cons *(pl)* [ˌprəʊz ənd 'kɒnz]	Für und Wider, Pro und Contra
	based on ['beɪst ɒn]	basierend auf, auf der Grundlage von
	to **possess** [pə'zes]	besitzen
	power outage *AE* ['paʊə aʊtɪdʒ]	Stromausfall
	environmental [ɪnˌvaɪrən'mentl]	Umwelt-
	overall [ˌəʊvər'ɔːl]	Gesamt-
	decade ['dekeɪd]	Jahrzehnt
	considerable [kən'sɪdərəbl]	erheblich, beträchtlich
	to **claim** [kleɪm]	angeben, behaupten
	likely ['laɪkli]	wahrscheinlich, geeignet
	to **tamper with** ['tæmpə]	manipulieren
34	to **number** ['nʌmbə]	nummerieren
	explanation [ˌeksplə'neɪʃn]	Erläuterung, Erklärung
	current ['kʌrənt]	derzeitig, aktuell
	interest rate [ˌɪntrəst 'reɪt]	Zinssatz
	previous ['priːviəs]	vorherig, früher
35	**entry** ['entri]	Buchung
	pre-printed [ˌpriː'prɪntɪd]	vorgedruckt
	credit slip ['kredɪt slɪp]	Einzahlungsschein
	to **specify** ['spesɪfaɪ]	angeben, spezifizieren
	internship ['ɪntɜːnʃɪp]	Praktikum
	to **register** ['redʒɪstə]	(sich) anmelden, (sich) registrieren, (sich) eintragen
	user ID [ˌjuːzər aɪ 'diː]	Nutzerkennung
	to **contain** [kən'teɪn]	enthalten
	activation [ˌæktɪ'veɪʃn]	Aktivierung
	tour [tʊə]	Rundgang, Führung
	to **log in** [ˌlɒg 'ɪn]	sich einloggen
	procedure [prə'siːdʒə]	Vorgang, Verfahren
36	to **enrol** [ɪn'rəʊl]	(sich) eintragen, (sich) registrieren
	secure [sɪ'kjʊə]	sicher
	enrolment [en'rəʊlmənt]	Registrierung
	memorable ['memərəbl]	einprägsam
	at hand [ət 'hænd]	zur Hand
	character ['kærəktə]	Zeichen
	instructions *pl* [ɪn'strʌkʃnz]	Anleitung, Anweisung(en)
	(right/left-hand) side [saɪd]	(rechte/linke) Seite
	frequently asked questions (FAQ) [ˌef eɪ 'kjuː]	häufig gestellte Fragen
	tool [tuːl]	Werkzeug, Tool
37	**GMT (Greenwich Mean Time)** [ˌdʒiː em 'tiː]	mittlere Greenwich-Zeit *(koordinierte Weltzeit)*
	survey ['sɜːveɪ]	Umfrage
	to **question** ['kwestʃən]	befragen
	painful ['peɪnfl]	schmerzhaft
	recommendation [ˌrekəmen'deɪʃn]	Empfehlung
	competition [ˌkɒmpə'tɪʃn]	Wettbewerb
	guarantee [ˌgærən'tiː]	Garantie
	common ['kɒmən]	verbreitet, üblich
	high street bank ['haɪ striːt bæŋk]	Großbank
	to **trade** [treɪd]	handeln, Handel (be)treiben
	automatic(ally) [ˌɔːtə'mætɪk]	automatisch
	to **cover** ['kʌvə]	(be-, ab-)decken
	to **notify** ['nəʊtɪfaɪ]	benachrichtigen, mitteilen
	to **acknowledge** [ək'nɒlɪdʒ]	bestätigen, anerkennen
	application [ˌæplɪ'keɪʃn]	Antrag
	sort code ['sɔːt kəʊd]	Bankleitzahl
	to **miss a payment** [ˌmɪs ə 'peɪmənt]	eine Zahlung versäumen
	to **be down to sb** ['daʊn tə]	jds Sache sein, jds Aufgabe sein
	to **decrease** [dɪ'kriːs]	senken, reduzieren; sinken, abnehmen
	to **participate (in)** [pɑː'tɪsɪpeɪt]	teilnehmen (an), sich beteiligen (an)
	scheme [skiːm]	Plan, Programm
	to **involve** [ɪn'vɒlv]	(mit) betreffen, (mit) einbeziehen
	to **take part (in)** [ˌteɪk 'pɑːt]	teilnehmen (an)
	new entrant [njuː 'entrənt]	Neueinsteiger
	building society ['bɪldɪŋ səsaɪəti]	Bausparkasse
38	**stepping stone** ['stepɪŋ stəʊn]	Sprungbrett
	smart [smɑːt]	intelligent, pfiffig, geschickt
	specialized ['speʃəlaɪzd]	Spezial-
	welcome kit ['welkʌm kɪt]	Begrüßungspaket
	ID card [ˌaɪ 'diː kɑːd]	Ausweis
	along with [ə'lɒŋ wɪð]	zusammen mit

	necessity [nə'sesəti]	Notwendigkeit
	photographic membership card [ˌfəʊtəˌgræfɪk 'membəʃɪp kɑːd]	Lichtbild-Mitgliedsausweis
	discount ['dɪskaʊnt]	Rabatt, Skonto, Nachlass
	voucher ['vaʊtʃə]	Gutschein
	entertainment [ˌentə'teɪnmənt]	Unterhaltung
	cover ['kʌvə]	Deckung
	subject to ['sʌbdʒekt tə]	vorbehaltlich
	approval [ə'pruːvl]	Zustimmung
	repayable [rɪ'peɪəbl]	rückzahlbar
	on demand [ɒn dɪ'mɑːnd]	auf Verlangen
	grace period ['greɪs pɪəriəd]	Schonzeit, Karenzzeit
	to **lodge money** [ˌlɒdʒ 'mʌni]	Geld einlegen
	to **be incurred** [ɪn'kɜːd]	anfallen
39	**incentive** [ɪn'sentɪv]	Anreiz, Bonus
	to **attract** [ə'trækt]	anlocken, anziehen
	to **sign up** [ˌsaɪn 'ʌp]	sich anmelden
	gift [gɪft]	Geschenk
	beyond [bɪ'jɒnd]	darüber hinaus, über etw hinaus
	household ['haʊshəʊld]	Haushalt, Haushalts-
	appliance [ə'plaɪəns]	Gerät, Haushaltsgerät
	specification [ˌspesɪfɪ'keɪʃn]	Spezifikation
	to **tempt** [tempt]	in Versuchung führen, verleiten
	fantastic [fæn'tæstɪk]	fantastisch
	hairy ['heəri]	haarig, brenzlig
	the taxman *(infml)* ['tæksmæn]	das Finanzamt
	to **come a-calling** [kʌm ə'kɔːlɪŋ]	vorbeischauen
	to **mail** [meɪl]	(zu)schicken, (zu) senden, mailen
	IRS (= Internal Revenue Service) [ˌaɪ ɑːr 'es]	*US-Finanzbehörde*
	income ['ɪnkʌm]	Einkommen
	government ['gʌvənmənt]	Regierung
	to **remind (sb of sth)** [rɪ'maɪnd]	(jdn an etw) erinnern
	recipient [rɪ'sɪpiənt]	Empfänger/in
	to **be obliged to do sth** [bi ə'blaɪdʒd tə]	etw tu müssen
	tax [tæks]	Steuer
	lucrative ['luːkrətɪv]	lukrativ
	reminder [rɪ'maɪndə]	(Zahlungs-)Erinnerung, Mahnung
	rifle ['raɪfl]	Gewehr
	movie ['muːvi]	Film
	to **depict** [dɪ'pɪkt]	darstellen, aufzeigen
	to **hunt** [hʌnt]	jagen
	time deposit account [ˌtaɪm dɪ'pɒzɪt əkaʊnt]	Festgeldkonto
	to **await** [ə'weɪt]	erwarten, abwarten
	jokingly ['dʒəʊkɪŋli]	scherzhaft
	to **hand over** [ˌhænd 'əʊvə]	übergeben, überantworten
	to **deposit** [dɪ'pɒzɪt]	*(Geld)* einzahlen
	shotgun ['ʃɒtgʌn]	Schrotflinte
	limited edition [ˌlɪmɪtɪd ɪ'dɪʃn]	limitierte Auflage/Serie
	if ..., that is. [ðæt 'ɪz]	wenn … überhaupt / auch wirklich …
	to **represent** [ˌreprɪ'zent]	ausmachen, darstellen
	prepaid [ˌpriː'peɪd]	im Voraus bezahlt
	interest *(no pl)* ['ɪntrəst]	Zins(en)
	instant ['ɪnstənt]	sofortig, unmittelbar
	gratification [ˌgrætɪfɪ'keɪʃn]	Befriedigung, Genugtuung
	spectacular [spek'tækjələ]	sensationell, spektakulär
	to **entice** [ɪn'taɪs]	locken
	to **amount to** [ə'maʊnt tə]	betragen
	instead of [ɪn'sted əv]	anstelle von, (an)statt
	excited [ɪk'saɪtɪd]	(freudig) aufgeregt, begeistert
	per [pə]	pro
	front-row [ˌfrʌnt 'rəʊ]	in vorderster Reihe
	to **attend** [ə'tend]	besuchen
	...-based [beɪst]	in … stattfindend/ansässig
	concert ['kɒnsət]	Konzert
	prestige [pre'stiːʒ]	Prestige
	on average [ɒn 'ævərɪdʒ]	im Durchschnitt
	value ['væljuː]	Wert
	to **translate (as sth)** [træns'leɪt]	sich (mit etw) übersetzen lassen
	return [rɪ'tɜːn]	Rendite
	era ['ɪərə]	Ära, Epoche
	austerity [ɒ'sterəti]	wirtschaftliche Einschränkung, Entbehrung

UNIT 4

40	to **prevent** [prɪ'vent]	(ver)hindern, vorbeugen
	misuse [ˌmɪs'juːs]	Missbrauch
	cashless ['kæʃləs]	bargeldlos
	journey ['dʒɜːni]	Fahrt, Reise

	to **prompt** [prɒmpt]	veranlassen
	contactless ['kɒntæktləs]	kontaktlos
	bus pass ['bʌs pɑ:s]	Busticket *(Zeitkarte)*
	transition [træn'zɪʃn]	Übergang, Umstellung
	check *AE* [tʃek]	Scheck
	sixteen-year-olds *(pl)* ['sɪks jɪə əʊldz]	Sechzehnjährige
41	**payee** [ˌpeɪ'i:]	Zahlungsempfänger/in
	underneath [ˌʌndə'ni:θ]	darunter; unterhalb
	flyer ['flaɪə]	Flugblatt, Flyer
42	**map** [mæp]	Landkarte, Stadtplan
	to **miss off** [ˌmɪs 'ɒf]	auslassen, nicht aufführen
43	**handout** ['hændaʊt]	Flugblatt, Merkblatt
	participant [pɑ:'tɪsɪpənt]	Teilnehmer/in
	to **standardize** ['stændədaɪz]	standardisieren
	cross-border [ˌkrɒs 'bɔ:də]	grenzüberschreitend
	denominated in euros [dɪˌnɒmɪneɪtɪd ɪn 'jʊərəʊz]	in Euro ausgewiesen, auf Euro lautend
	to **achieve** [ə'tʃi:v]	erreichen
	council ['kaʊnsl]	Rat
	legal ['li:gl]	gesetzlich, juristisch, legal
	technical ['teknɪkl]	technisch
	organizational [ˌɔ:gənaɪ'zeɪʃənl]	organisatorisch
	solution [sə'lu:ʃn]	Lösung
	at present [ət 'preznt]	momentan, derzeit, zurzeit
	to **comprise** [kəm'praɪz]	umfassen, bestehen aus
	economic [ˌi:kə'nɒmɪk]	wirtschaftlich, Wirtschafts-
	to **develop** [dɪ'veləp]	(sich) entwickeln
	core [kɔ:]	Basis(-), Kern(-), Schwerpunkt(-)
	framework ['freɪmwɜ:k]	Rahmen, Rahmenbedingungen
	to **regulate** ['regjuleɪt]	regeln, regulieren
	institution [ˌɪnstɪ'tju:ʃn]	Institution
	to **affect** [ə'fekt]	beeinflussen, sich auswirken auf
	insurance premium [ɪnˌʃʊərəns 'pri:miəm]	Versicherungsbeitrag, -prämie
	instalment [ɪn'stɔ:lmənt]	Rate
	membership fee ['membəʃɪp fi:]	Mitgliedsbeitrag
	mortgage ['mɔ:gɪdʒ]	Hypothek, Hypothekendarlehen
	repayment [rɪ'peɪmənt]	Tilgung
	savings plan ['seɪvɪŋz plæn]	Sparplan
	savings *(pl)* ['seɪvɪŋz]	Ersparnisse
	season ticket ['si:zn tɪkɪt]	Zeit-, Jahreskarte; Abonnement
	utility bill [ju:'tɪləti bɪl]	Betriebskostenabrechnung
	electricity [ɪˌlek'trɪsəti]	Strom, Elektrizität
	tenant ['tenənt]	Mieter/in
	property loan ['prɒpəti ləʊn]	Baudarlehen
44	**chart** [tʃɑ:t]	Diagramm, Tabelle
	fellow student [ˌfeləʊ 'stju:dnt]	Mitschüler/in
T	to **be scared** [skeəd]	Angst haben
	to **hack** [hæk]	hacken
	to **experience** [ɪk'spɪəriəns]	erleben, erfahren
	clue [klu:]	Hinweis, Anhaltspunkt
	property ['prɒpəti]	(Grund-)Besitz, Immobilie
	urgent ['ɜ:dʒənt]	dringend
	final ['faɪnl]	endgültig, abschließend
	to **alter** ['ɔ:ltə]	ändern, abändern
	quarterly ['kwɔ:təli]	vierteljährlich
	onwards ['ɒnwədz]	an
45	to **crash** [kræʃ]	abstürzen (lassen)
	taken ill [ˌteɪkən 'ɪl]	erkrankt
	temporary ['temprəri]	vorübergehend, befristet
	down [daʊn]	außer Betrieb, heruntergefahren *(Computer)*
	to **advise** [əd'vaɪz]	(be)raten, empfehlen
	flatly ['flætli]	rundweg, entschieden
	to **refuse** [rɪ'fju:z]	ablehnen, sich weigern
	to **claim** [kleɪm]	einziehen, verlangen
	due [dju:]	fällig
	to **release** [rɪ'li:s]	freigeben, einlösen
	to **recur** [rɪ'kɜ:]	sich wiederholen, wiederkehren
	due date [ˌdju: 'deɪt]	Fälligkeit(sdatum)
	advance notice [ədˌvɑ:ns 'nəʊtɪs]	Vorankündigung
	to **restrict** [rɪ'strɪkt]	beschränken, einschränken
	to **revoke** [rɪ'vəʊk]	widerrufen
	identifier [aɪ'dentɪfaɪə]	Kennung, Identifikationsnummer
	reference ['refərəns]	(Akten-)Zeichen, Referenznummer
	whatsit *(infml)* ['wɒtsɪt]	Dings
46	**creditor** ['kredɪtə]	Gläubiger/in
	to **issue** ['ɪʃu:]	ausgeben, ausstellen

	protection [prə'tekʃn]	Schutz
	punctual ['pʌŋktʃuəl]	pünktlich
	to **draw** [drɔ:]	einziehen
	to **order** ['ɔ:də]	anweisen
	refund ['ri:fʌnd]	Erstattung
48	**unable** [ʌn'eɪbl]	nicht in der Lage
	leaflet ['li:flət]	Broschüre, Merkblatt
	(safety) precaution [prɪ'kɔ:ʃn]	Sicherheitsvorkehrung
	significant(ly) [sɪg'nɪfɪkənt]	deutlich, signifikant
	to **store** [stɔ:]	speichern
	encrypted [ɪn'krɪptɪd]	verschlüsselt
	to **verify** ['verɪfaɪ]	überprüfen
	unlike [,ʌn'laɪk]	anders als, im Gegensatz zu
	signature ['sɪgnətʃə]	Unterschrift
	to **forge** ['fɔ:dʒ]	fälschen
	point of sale [,pɔɪnt əf 'seɪl]	Verkaufsstelle
	consecutive [kən'sekjətɪv]	in Folge, aufeinander folgend
	to **lock** [lɒk]	sperren
	failed attempt [,feɪld ə'temt]	fehlgeschlagener Versuch, Fehlversuch
	to **access** ['ækses]	zugreifen auf
	to **disclose** [dɪs'kləʊz]	offenlegen, mitteilen
	key pad ['ki: pæd]	Eingabefeld, Tastatur
	in case [ɪn 'keɪs]	falls
	emergency [ɪ'mɜ:dʒənsi]	Notfall, Not-
	agent *(gramm)* ['eɪdʒənt]	Agens, der/die Handelnde
49	**to stop payment (on)** [,stɒp 'peɪmənt]	sperren
	to **protect** [prə'tekt]	schützen
	fraud [frɔ:d]	Betrug
	to **summarize** ['sʌməraɪz]	zusammenfassen
	to **rush** [rʌʃ]	eilen, sich beeilen
	to **insert** [ɪn'sɜ:t]	einführen, (hin)einstecken
	to **grab** [græb]	packen, greifen, *sich etw* schnappen
	to **pop out** [,pɒp 'aʊt]	herauskommen, herausspringen
	to **drop** [drɒp]	fallen (lassen), verlieren
	panic ['pænɪk]	Panik
	to **relax** [rɪ'læks]	(sich) entspannen
	thief [θi:f]	Dieb/in
	receipt [rɪ'si:t]	Beleg
	forgery ['fɔ:dʒəri]	Fälschung
	proof of identity [,pru:f əv aɪ'dentəti]	Legitimation, Ausweis
	to **deduct** [dɪ'dʌkt]	abbuchen
	police station [pə'li:s steɪʃn]	Polizeiwache, Polizeirevier
	serial number ['sɪəriəl nʌmbə]	Seriennummer
	magnetic strip [mæg,netɪk 'strɪp]	Magnetstreifen
	visible ['vɪzəbl]	sichtbar
	to **obtain** [əb'teɪn]	erhalten, bekommen
	relating to [rɪ'leɪtɪŋ tə]	in Zusammenhang mit, bezüglich
	retail outlet ['ri:teɪl aʊtlet]	Ladengeschäft, Einzelhandelsgeschäft
	loss [lɒs]	Verlust
	strange [streɪndʒ]	seltsam, merkwürdig
	debit ['debɪt]	Lastschrift, Abbuchung
	entire [ɪn'taɪə]	gesamte/r/s, ganz, vollständig
	to **clear** [klɪə]	räumen
	to **bombard** [bɒm'bɑ:d]	bombardieren
	unpaid [,ʌn'peɪd]	unbezahlt
	hassle ['hæsl]	Ungelegenheiten, Stress
	in the meantime [ɪn ðə 'mi:ntaɪm]	in der Zwischenzeit
50	**invoice** ['ɪnvɔɪs]	Rechnung
	no., *pl* **nos.** ['nʌmbə]	Nr.
	unit price [,ju:nɪt 'praɪs]	Stückpreis
	total ['təʊtl]	Gesamtbetrag, Summe
51	**graph** [grɑ:f]	Diagramm, Kurve
	to **comment (on)** ['kɒment]	kommentieren
	development [dɪ'veləpmənt]	Entwicklung
	surprising [sə'praɪzɪŋ]	überraschend, erstaunlich
	to **fancy sth** ['fænsi]	auf etw Lust haben
	bakery ['beɪkəri]	Bäckerei
	to **bear** [beə]	tragen
	subsidiary [səb'sɪdiəri]	Tochterunternehmen, Filiale
	slice [slaɪs]	Scheibe, Stück *(Kuchen)*
	giant ['dʒaɪənt]	Riese
	to **boom** [bu:m]	blühen, boomen
	wallet ['wɒlɪt]	Brieftasche, Geldbörse
	accessible [ək'sesəbl]	erreichbar, zugänglich
	to **integrate** ['ɪntɪgreɪt]	integrieren
	to **bind** [baɪnd]	binden
	to **reduce** [rɪ'dju:s]	senken, reduzieren, verringern
	miss the boat [,mɪs ðə 'bəʊt]	den Anschluss verpassen
	major ['meɪdʒə]	bedeutend, wichtig
	to **launch** [lɔ:ntʃ]	*(Produkt)* auf den Markt bringen, einführen

	to **pronounce** [prə'naʊns]	aussprechen
	to **bother with** ['bɒðə wɪð]	sich kümmern um
	to **estimate** ['estɪmeɪt]	schätzen
	billion ['bɪliən]	Milliarde
	to **embed** [ɪm'bed]	integrieren, einbetten, einbauen
	to **cooperate** [kəʊ'ɒpəreɪt]	kooperieren, zusammenarbeiten
	to **produce** ['prɒdju:s]	produzieren, herstellen
	widely ['waɪdli]	weit (verbreitet), in großem Umfang
	throughout [θru:'aʊt]	überall (in), in ganz
	to **locate** [ləʊ'keɪt]	ausfindig machen, orten, lokalisieren
	potential [pə'tenʃl]	potenziell, möglich, künftig
	recent ['ri:snt]	jüngst, aktuell
	target group ['tɑ:gɪt gru:p]	Zielgruppe
	female ['fi:meɪl]	Frau; weiblich
	to **be within walking distance** [wɪˌðɪn ˌwɔ:kɪŋ 'dɪstəns]	in Laufentfernung
	infected [ɪn'fektɪd]	infiziert
	malicious [mə'lɪʃəs]	bösartig
	burden of proof [ˌbɜ:dn əv 'pru:f]	Beweislast
	in the event of [ɪ'vent]	im Falle
	theft [θeft]	Diebstahl
	in the light of [ɪn ðə 'laɪt əv]	angesichts
	leak [li:k]	Leck, undichte Stelle
	to **boil down to** [ˌbɔɪl 'daʊn tə]	darauf hinauslaufen

UNIT 5

52	**gimmick** ['gɪmɪk]	Schnickschnack, Spielerei; (Werbe-)Trick
	to **dig** [dɪg]	graben
	to **be tired of sth** [bi 'taɪəd əv]	etw satt haben
	to **bounce** *(infml)* [baʊns]	platzen *(Scheck)*
T	**on top of that** [ɒn 'tɒp əv ðæt]	darüber hinaus, außerdem
	to **submit** [səb'mɪt]	einreichen, vorlegen, zusenden
	anonymous [ə'nɒnɪməs]	anonym
	approach [ə'prəʊtʃ]	Ansatz, Herangehensweise
	to **top up** [ˌtɒp 'ʌp]	aufladen
	to **upload** [ˌʌp'ləʊd]	hochladen, aufladen
	one-off [ˌwʌn 'ɒf]	einmalig
	anonymity [ˌænə'nɪməti]	Anonymität
	validity [və'lɪdəti]	Gültigkeit, Echtheit
	valid ['vælɪd]	gültig
	attraction [ə'trækʃn]	Anziehung(spunkt)
	reduction [rɪ'dʌkʃn]	Nachlass, Rabatt
53	to **head** [hed]	*(in Richtung von etw)* gehen, fahren
	down under [ˌdaʊn 'ʌndə]	in/nach Australien
	to **assume** [ə'sju:m]	annehmen, davon ausgehen
	obvious ['ɒbviəs]	offensichtlich
	expenditure [ɪk'spendɪtʃə]	Ausgabe
	to **misuse** [ˌmɪs'ju:s]	missbrauchen
	purpose ['pɜ:pəs]	Absicht, Zweck, Ziel
	frequent ['fri:kwənt]	häufig, oft
	traveller ['trævələ]	Reisende/r
	baggage ['bægɪdʒ]	Gepäck
	apart from [ə'pɑ:t frəm]	abgesehen von, außer
	annual ['ænjuəl]	jährlich
	percentage [pə'sentɪdʒ]	Anteil, Prozentsatz
	better off [ˌbetər 'ɒf]	besser dran, besser bedient
54	**identity** [aɪ'dentəti]	Identität
	advanced [əd'vɑ:nst]	entwickelt, fortgeschritten
	assured [ə'ʃʊəd]	sicher
	reassuring [ˌri:ə'ʃʊərɪŋ]	beruhigend
	to **repay** [rɪ'peɪ]	zurückzahlen
	to **owe** [əʊ]	schulden
	revolving credit [rɪ'vɒlvɪŋ kredɪt]	revolvierender Kredit *(Konto, das nur im Minus geführt wird)*
	debt [det]	Schuld(en)
	application form [ˌæplɪ'keɪʃn fɔ:m]	Antragsformular
	definitely ['defɪnətli]	bestimmt, sicher, definitiv
	compromise ['kɒmprəmaɪz]	Kompromiss
	syllable ['sɪləbl]	Silbe
	equal ['i:kwəl]	gleich
55	**competitive** [kəm'petətɪv]	umkämpft, wettbewerbsintensiv
	suitable ['su:təbl]	geeignet, passend
	risky ['rɪski]	riskant
	sensible ['sensəbl]	vernünftig
	to **make sense** [ˌmeɪk 'sens]	sinnvoll sein
	Yours sincerely [jɔ:z sɪn'sɪəli]	Mit freundlichen Grüßen
58	**reply** [rɪ'plaɪ]	Antwort
	to **assure** [ə'ʃʊə]	versichern, zusichern

	creditworthiness ['kredɪtwɜːðinəs]	Kreditwürdigkeit
	history ['hɪstri]	Geschichte *(vergangene Zeiten)*
	to **pay off** [ˌpeɪ 'ɒf]	tilgen
	i.e. [ˌaɪ 'iː]	d.h.
	to **subtract** [səb'trækt]	abziehen, subtrahieren
	minimum payment [ˌmɪnɪməm 'peɪmənt]	Mindestzahlung
	to **revolve** [rɪ'vɒlv]	rotieren, sich drehen
	advertisement [əd'vɜːtɪsmənt]	Werbung, Reklame
59	to **decline** [dɪ'klaɪn]	ablehnen
	billing cycle ['bɪlɪŋ saɪkl]	Abrechnungszeitraum
	to **invoice** ['ɪnvɔɪs]	berechnen, in Rechnung stellen
	ongoing ['ɒngəʊɪŋ]	laufend
	time frame ['taɪm freɪm]	Zeitrahmen
	to **tie (to)** [taɪ]	verbinden (mit), anbinden (an), verknüpfen (mit)
	usual ['juːʒuəl]	üblich, normal
	creditworthy ['kredɪtwɜːði]	kreditwürdig
	premium ['priːmiəm]	erstklassig, Premium-
	economics *(pl)* [ˌiːkə'nɒmɪks]	(Volks-)Wirtschaft, Wirtschaftskunde
	to **rack up** [ˌræk 'ʌp]	anhäufen, akkumulieren *(hier: Schulden bis zum Limit auf einem Kreditkartenkonto)*
	to **go over the top** [gəʊ ˌəʊvə ðə 'tɒp]	ausufern
	luxury ['lʌkʃəri]	Luxus
	stuff [stʌf]	Zeug, Sache(n)
	vacation *AE* [və'keɪʃn]	Urlaub
	to **keep up (with)** [ˌkiːp 'ʌp]	Schritt halten (mit)
	a real killer [ə rɪəl 'kɪlə]	mörderisch
	groceries *(pl)* ['grəʊsəriz]	Lebensmittel
	outstanding [aʊt'stændɪŋ]	ausstehend
	altogether [ˌɔːltə'geðə]	insgesamt, zusammen
60	**in full** [ɪn 'fʊl]	in voller Höhe, vollständig
	slippery slope [slɶpəri 'sləʊp]	Schlitterpfad, Weg nach unten
	to **weigh up** [ˌweɪ 'ʌp]	abwägen, einschätzen, beurteilen
	introductory offer [ɪntrəˌdʌktəri 'ɒfə]	Einführungsangebot
	to **trick** [trɪk]	täuschen, hereinlegen
	nasty ['nɑːsti]	Gemeinheit
	reality [ri'æləti]	Realität, Wirklichkeit
	to **fail** [feɪl]	(es) nicht schaffen, scheitern
	to **promise** ['prɒmɪs]	versprechen
	to **knock (on)** [nɒk]	anklopfen (an)
	to **default** [dɪ'fɔːlt]	zahlungsunfähig werden
	advance [əd'vɑːns]	Vorschuss
	budget ['bʌdʒɪt]	Budget, Haushalt, Etat
61	**off you go!** [ˌɒf jə 'gəʊ]	los geht's!
	no messing (about …) [nəʊ 'mesɪŋ]	locker (ohne …)
	note [nəʊt]	Geldschein, Banknote
	to **keep track of** [kiːp 'træk əv]	verfolgen
	to **mark** [mɑːk]	kennzeichnen, markieren, angeben
	to **get in touch with** [get ɪn 'tʌtʃ wɪð]	(sich) in Verbindung setzen mit
62	to **earn** [ɜːn]	verdienen, erwerben
	representative [ˌreprɪ'zentətɪv]	repräsentativ
	APR (= annual percentage rate) [ˌeɪ piː 'ɑː, ˌænjuəl pə'sentɪdʒ ret]	effektiver Jahreszins
	overview ['əʊvəvjuː]	Überblick, Übersicht
63	**inquiry** [ɪn'kwaɪəri]	Untersuchung, Nachforschung
	marketing ['mɑːkɪtɪŋ]	Marketing, Vermarktung
	conduct ['kɒndʌkt]	Verhalten, Gebaren
	authority [ɔː'θɒrəti]	Behörde
	transparency [træns'pærənsi]	Transparenz
	bn (= billion) ['bɪljən]	Milliarde
	m (= million) ['mɪljən]	Million
	cardholder ['kɑːdhəʊldə]	Inhaber/n einer Kreditkarte
	to **investigate** [ɪn'vestɪgeɪt]	untersuchen
	to **market** ['mɑːkɪt]	vermarkten
	amid [ə'mɪd]	inmitten, mitten unter
	investigation [ɪnˌvestɪ'geɪʃn]	Forschung, Untersuchung
	sector ['sektə]	Sektor, Bereich
	to **reveal** [rɪ'viːl]	enthüllen
	scope [skəʊp]	Umfang
	complexity [kəm'pleksəti]	Komplexität, Vielschichtigkeit
	regulator ['regjuleɪtə]	Regulierungsbehörde
	to **inquire (into)** [ɪn'kwaɪə]	untersuchen, erkunden
	to **resist** [rɪ'zɪst]	widerstehen
	lure [lʊə]	Verlockung
	eventually [ɪ'ventʃuəli]	letztendlich, schließlich

to **wear down** [ˌweə ˈdaʊn]	zermürben, mürbe machen
continual [kənˈtɪnjuəl]	ständig, ununterbrochen, kontinuierlich
targeted [ˈtɑːɡɪtɪd]	gezielt
mailing shot [ˈmeɪlɪŋ ʃɒt]	Werbesendung
to **pre-approve** [ˌpriː əˈpruːv]	vorab bestätigen, im Voraus genehmigen
unaffordable [ˌʌnəˈfɔːdəbl]	unerschwinglich
to **flag up sth** [ˌflæɡ ˈʌp]	auf etw aufmerksam machen
payday [ˈpeɪdeɪ]	Zahltag
well established [ˌwel ɪˈstæblɪʃt]	gut eingeführt
huge [hjuːdʒ]	gewaltig, riesig
director [dəˈrektə]	Geschäftsführer/in, Chef/in
official [əˈfɪʃl]	offiziell
in-depth [ˌɪn ˈdepθ]	ausführlich
to **publish** [ˈpʌblɪʃ]	veröffentlichen
chief executive (officer), CEO [ˌtʃiːf ɪɡˈzekjətɪv]	Geschäftsführer/in, Vorstandsvorsitzende/r
charity [ˈtʃærəti]	Wohltätigkeitsorganisation
announcement [əˈnaʊnsmənt]	Mitteilung, Bekanntgabe
net [net]	Netz
trap [træp]	Falle
to **struggle** [ˈstrʌɡl]	kämpfen, sich abmühen
multiple [ˈmʌltɪpl]	mehrere, vielfach
to **cope** [kəʊp]	zurechtkommen
ups and downs [ˌʌps ən ˈdaʊnz]	Höhen und Tiefen
to **ensure** [ɪnˈʃʊə]	sicherstellen
to **operate** [ˈɒpəreɪt]	arbeiten, in Betrieb sein, funktionieren
vulnerable [ˈvʌlnərəbl]	verletzlich, verwundbar
observation [ˌɒbzəˈveɪʃn]	Beobachtung
long-standing [ˌlɒŋ ˈstændɪŋ]	langjährig, schon lange bestehend
commitment [kəˈmɪtmənt]	Verpflichtung
to **reprice** [ˌriːˈpraɪs]	den Preis neu festlegen
forbearance [fɔːˈbeərəns]	Nachsicht, Geduld
head [hed]	Leiter/in
trade body [ˈtreɪd bɒdi]	Handelsinstitution
to **outline** [ˈaʊtlaɪn]	skizzieren, beschreiben, darstellen
aim [eɪm]	Ziel, Zweck, Absicht

Unit 6

64	**stock market** [ˈstɒk mɑːkɪt]	(Wertpapier-)Börse
	billionaire [ˌbɪljəˈneə]	Milliardär/in
	quote [kwəʊt]	Zitat
	sooner or later [ˌsuːnə ɔː ˈleɪtə]	früher oder später, über kurz oder lang
	to **compete** [kəmˈpiːt]	konkurrieren
	to **encourage** [ɪnˈkʌrɪdʒ]	ermuntern, fördern, unterstützen
	individual [ˌɪndɪˈvɪdʒʊəl]	einzeln, individuell
	saver [ˈseɪvə]	Sparer/in
	subsidy [ˈsʌbsədi]	Subvention
	asset-building [ˈæset bɪldɪŋ]	vermögensbildend
	life assurance [ˈlaɪf əʃʊərəns]	Lebensversicherung
	policy [ˈpɒləsi]	(Versicherungs-)Police
65	to **give notice** [ˌɡɪv ˈnəʊtɪs]	ankündigen; kündigen
	rate [reɪt]	Rate, Quote
	to **tie up** [ˌtaɪ ˈʌp]	festmachen
	bond [bɒnd]	Anleihe, Rentenpapier, Obligation
	notice account [ˈnəʊtɪs əkaʊnt]	Konto mit Kündigung(sfrist), Termingeldkonto
66	**tax-free** [ˌtæks ˈfriː]	steuerfrei
	despite [dɪˈspaɪt]	trotz
	to **tend to** [ˈtend]	dazu neigen
	male [meɪl]	Mann; männlich
	counterpart [ˈkaʊntəpɑːt]	Gegenstück, Pendant
	adult [ˈædʌlt]	Erwachsene/r
	retirement [rɪˈtaɪəmənt]	Pensionierung, Ruhestand
	pension [ˈpenʃn]	Rente
	to **belong (to)** [bɪˈlɒŋ]	gehören (zu)
	defined [dɪˈfaɪnd]	festgelegt
	contribution [ˌkɒntrɪˈbjuːʃn]	Beitrag
	to **contribute** [kənˈtrɪbjuːt]	beitragen
	inequality [ˌɪnɪˈkwɒləti]	Ungleichheit
	earnings *(pl)* [ˈɜːnɪŋz]	Einkünfte, Verdienst
	statistics *(pl)* [stəˈtɪstɪks]	Statistik(en), statistische Angabe(n)
	median [ˈmiːdiən]	mittlere/r/s, durchschnittlich
	gross [ɡrɒs]	brutto
	whereas [ˌweərˈæz]	während, wohingegen
	to **rise** [raɪz]	(an)steigen
	to **guarantee** [ˌɡærənˈtiː]	garantieren

	economical [ˌiːkə'nɒmɪkl]	sparsam, wirtschaftlich
67	**advisable** [əd'vaɪzəbl]	ratsam
68	**shortly** ['ʃɔːtli]	bald, in Kürze
	attachment [ə'tætʃmənt]	Anhang *(E-Mail)*
	asap (= as soon as possible) [ˌeɪ es eɪ 'piː]	so bald wie möglich
	Inc. (= incorporated) [ɪŋk, ɪn'kɔːpəreɪtɪd]	(als Kapitalgesellschaft) eingetragen
	high [haɪ]	Hoch
	analyst ['ænəlɪst]	Analyst/in
	to **leap** [liːp]	springen
	record ['rekɔːd]	Rekord
	to **fluctuate** ['flʌktʃueɪt]	fluktuieren, schwanken
	slightly ['slaɪtli]	leicht, geringfügig
	gain [geɪn]	Gewinn, Vorteil
	all-time high [ˌɔːl taɪm 'haɪ]	Allzeithoch
	outlook ['aʊtlʊk]	*(Zukunfts-)* Aussicht(en)
	retention [rɪ'tenʃn]	Beibehaltung, Erhaltung
	round the corner [ˌraʊnd ðə 'kɔːnə]	um die Ecke
	findings *(pl)* ['faɪndɪŋz]	Ergebnisse
69	**long-term** [ˌlɒŋ 'tɜːm]	langfristig
	contract ['kɒntrækt]	Vertrag
	congratulations [kənˌgrætʃu'leɪʃnz]	herzlichen Glückwunsch
	disaster [dɪ'zɑːstə]	Katastrophe, Unglück, Desaster
	not necessarily [nɒt ˌnesə'serəli]	nicht unbedingt
	to **yield** [jiːld]	erwirtschaften
	basically ['beɪsɪkli]	grundsätzlich, im Grunde
	to **pool** [puːl]	zusammenlegen, bündeln
	units *(pl)* ['juːnɪts]	Investmentanteile
	knowledge ['nɒlɪdʒ]	Wissen, Kenntnis(se)
	on sb's behalf [ɒn bɪ'hɑːf]	in jds Namen
	initial charge [ɪˌnɪʃl 'tʃɑːdʒ]	Ausgabeaufschlag, Agio
	management fee ['mænɪdʒmənt fiː]	Verwaltungsgebühr
	to **reinvest** [ˌriːɪn'vest]	reinvestieren, neu investieren
	lump sum [ˌlʌmp 'sʌm]	Einmalzahlung, Pauschale
	fluctuation [ˌflʌktʃʊ'eɪʃn]	Schwankung
	yield [jiːld]	Ertrag
	diversified [daɪ'vɜːsɪfaɪd]	diversifiziert, gefächert, gestreut
	portfolio [pɔːt'fəʊliəʊ]	Depot, Wertpapierbestand, Portfolio
	particular [pə'tɪkjələ]	besonders, speziell
	emerging markets *(pl)* [ɪˌmɜːdʒɪŋ 'mɑːkɪts]	Schwellenländer
	fund of funds [fʌnd əv 'fʌndz]	Dachfonds
	to **spread** [spred]	verteilen
	selection [sɪ'lekʃn]	Auswahl
	prospect ['prɒspekt]	Aussicht
	growth [grəʊθ]	Wachstum
70	**exception** [ɪk'sepʃn]	Ausnahme
	hardly ['hɑːdli]	kaum
	lately ['leɪtli]	neulich, in letzter Zeit
	to **behave** [bɪ'heɪv]	sich benehmen, sich verhalten
	to **perform** [pə'fɔːm]	abschneiden, Leistung bringen, Erträge erzielen
	forecast ['fɔːkɑːst]	Vorhersage
	fluent ['fluːənt]	fließend
	share price ['ʃeə praɪs]	Aktienkurs
	steep [stiːp]	steil
	eco-friendly [ˌiːkəʊ 'frendli]	umweltfreundlich
	to **react (to)** [ri'ækt]	reagieren (auf)
	to **plunge** [plʌndʒ]	fallen, stürzen
	performance [pə'fɔːməns]	Leistung; Abschneiden
	drastic ['dræstik]	drastisch
	abrupt [ə'brʌpt]	abrupt, plötzlich
	decline [dɪ'klaɪn]	Rückgang
	to **decline** [dɪ'klaɪn]	zurückgehen, fallen, sinken
71	**maternity leave** [mə'tɜːnəti liːv]	Mutterschaftsurlaub
	to **divide up** [dɪ'vaɪd ʌp]	unterteilen
	assets *(pl)* ['æsets]	Aktiva, Vermögen(swerte)
	upturn ['ʌptɜːn]	Kursanstieg
	to **soar** [sɔː]	steigen
	downturn ['daʊntɜːn]	Kursrückgang
	to **slump** [slʌmp]	zurückgehen, fallen
	precise [prɪ'saɪs]	genau, präzise
	gradual ['grædʒuəl]	schrittweise, allmählich
	steady ['stedi]	gleichmäßig, stetig
	volatile ['vɒlətaɪl]	unbeständig
	to **rally** ['ræli]	sich erholen
	to **rebound** [rɪ'baʊnd]	wieder steigen
	to **recover** [rɪ'kʌvə]	sich erholen
	stable ['steɪbl]	stabil, konstant
	unchanged [ʌn'tʃeɪndʒd]	unverändert

	to predict [prɪ'dɪkt]	voraussagen, vorhersagen
72	**tax-free allowance** [ˌtæks friː ə'laʊəns]	Steuerfreibetrag
	application for tax exemption [æplɪˌkeɪʃn fə ˌtæks ɪg'zempʃn]	Freistellungsantrag
73	**to raise capital** [reɪz 'kæpɪtl]	Kapital aufbringen
	government bonds ['gʌvənmənt bɒndz]	Staatsanleihen
	stock exchange ['stɒk ɪkstʃeɪndʒ]	Börse
	to consult [kən'sʌlt]	hinzuziehen, zu Rate ziehen
	to intend [ɪn'tend]	beabsichtigen
	to mature [mə'tʃʊə]	fällig werden
	a long way off [ə ˌlɒŋ weɪ 'ɒf]	(noch) ein weiter Weg
	inexperienced [ˌɪnɪk'spɪəriənst]	unerfahren
	willing ['wɪlɪŋ]	bereit, willens, gewillt
	to tolerate ['tɒləreɪt]	tolerieren
	cautious ['kɔːʃəs]	vorsichtig
	coupon ['kuːpɒn]	Zinsschein, Genussschein
	to combine [kəm'baɪn]	verbinden, kombinieren
74	**cash deposit** [ˌkæʃ dɪ'pɒzɪt]	Bareinlage
75	**paltry** ['pɔːltri]	armselig, erbärmlich
	to stash [stæʃ]	bunkern
	typically ['tɪpɪkli]	typischerweise
	minuscule ['mɪnəskjuːl]	unbedeutend, winzig
	affront [ə'frʌnt]	Affront, Beleidigung
	consternation [ˌkɒnstə'neɪʃn]	Bestürzung, Fassungslosigkeit
	treatment ['triːtmənt]	Behandlung
	presumably [prɪ'zjuːməbli]	vermutlich
	to nudge [nʌdʒ]	schubsen, anstoßen
	liquid ['lɪkwɪd]	flüssig, liquide
	lot [lɒt]	Menge, Haufen
	to shun [ʃʌn]	scheuen, meiden
	trillion [trɪljən]	Billion
	ordinary ['ɔːdnri]	gewöhnlich, normal
	to flog *(infml)* [flɒg]	verscherbeln, verramschen
	to speculate ['spekjuleɪt]	spekulieren
	shameful ['ʃeɪmfl]	schändlich
	gambling ['gæmblɪŋ]	Glücksspiel
	excess [ɪk'ses]	Überschuss
	sceptical ['skeptɪkl]	skeptisch
	loose [luːs]	locker
	to spur [spɜː]	anspornen
	thus [ðʌs]	so, somit, dadurch
	fiscal ['fɪskl]	finanzpolitisch, Steuer-
	structural ['strʌktʃərəl]	strukturell
	reform [rɪ'fɔːm]	Reform
	to accuse (of) [ə'kjuːz]	anklagen (wegen)
	inevitable [ɪn'evɪtəbl]	unvermeidlich, unvermeidbar
	relation [rɪ'leɪʃn]	Beziehung, Verhältnis
	hawkish ['hɔːkɪʃ]	einen harten Kurs vertretend
	in the dumps *(infml)* [ɪn ðə 'dʌmps]	im Keller
	intention [ɪn'tenʃn]	Absicht. Intention
	productive [prə'dʌktɪv]	produktiv
	to mirror ['mɪrə]	(wider)spiegeln
	underinvestment [ˌʌndərɪn'vestmənt]	Unterinvestition(en)
	to recognise ['rekəgnaɪz]	erkennen
	thrifty ['θrɪfti]	sparsam, geizig
	to shirk [ʃɜːk]	umgehen, sich (vor etw) drücken
	gist [dʒɪst]	das Wesentliche
	to mistrust [ˌmɪs'trʌst]	misstrauen
	to approve of sth [ə'pruːv əv]	etw gut finden

Unit 7

76	**personal loan** [ˌpɜːsənl 'ləʊn]	Kleinkredit, Privatkredit
	to assess [ə'ses]	einschätzen, beurteilen, bewerten
	overnight [ˌəʊvə'naɪt]	über Nacht, Nacht-
	borrower ['bɒrəʊə]	Kreditnehmer/in
	to deal in ['diːl ɪn]	handeln mit
	bureau, *pl* **bureaux** *or* **bureaus** ['bjʊərəʊ, 'bjʊərəʊz]	Büro
	commercial [kə'mɜːʃl]	gewerblich, kommerziell
	alongside [əˌlɒŋ'saɪd]	neben
	dozen ['dʌzn]	Dutzend
	(card) issuer ['ɪʃuə]	Kartenunternehmen, (Karten-)Aussteller
	individual [ˌɪndɪ'vɪdʒuəl]	Einzelne/r, Individuum
	to supply [sə'plaɪ]	bereitstellen, zur Verfügung stellen, anbieten
	credit record ['kredɪt rekəd]	Bonitätsauskunft
	credit-scoring [ˌkredɪt 'skɔːrɪŋ]	Kreditwürdigkeitsbewertung

	Citizens Advice Bureau [ˌsɪtɪznz ədˈvaɪs bjʊərəʊ]	Bürgerbüro, Bürgerberatungsstelle
77	to **carry out** [ˌkæri ˈaʊt]	ausführen, durchführen
	holiday of a lifetime [ˌhɒlədeɪ əv ə ˈlaɪftaɪm]	einmaliger Urlaub
	to **consolidate** [kənˈsɒlɪdeɪt]	konsolidieren
	repayment loan [rɪˈpeɪmənt ləʊn]	Annuitätsdarlehen
	tailored [ˈteɪləd]	maßgeschneidert
	interest-only loan [ˈɪntrəst əʊnli ləʊn]	endfälliges Darlehen
	endowment insurance [ɪnˈdaʊmənt ɪnʃʊərəns]	Kapitalversicherung
	term [tɜːm]	Laufzeit
	competitive [kəmˈpetətɪv]	konkurrenzfähig, günstig *(Preis)*
	peace of mind [ˌpiːs əv ˈmaɪnd]	Sicherheit, innere Ruhe
	unemployed [ˌʌnɪmˈplɔɪd]	arbeitslos
	to **pass away** [ˌpɑːs əˈweɪ]	sterben
	loan application [ˌləʊn æplɪˈkeɪʃn]	Kreditantrag, Darlehensantrag
78	**masses** *(pl)* [ˈmæsɪz]	Massen, Mengen
	junior [ˈdʒuːniə]	Junioren-, Nachwuchs-
	champion [ˈtʃæmpiən]	Meister/in
	kayaking [ˈkaɪækɪŋ]	Kajakfahren
	fortune [ˈfɔːtʃuːn]	Vermögen
	to **ship** [ʃɪp]	verschicken, versenden
	roof rack [ˈruːf ræk]	Dachgepäckträger
	equipment [ɪˈkwɪpmənt]	Ausrüstung
	file [faɪl]	Datei, Ordner, Akte
	to **extend** [ɪkˈstend]	erweitern, ausdehnen
	to **score** [skɔː]	bewerten
	arrangement fee [əˈreɪndʒmənt fiː]	Bearbeitungsgebühr
79	to **secure** [sɪˈkjʊə]	sichern
	land register [ˌlænd ˈredʒɪstə]	Grundbuch
	meaningful [ˈmiːnɪŋfl]	sinnvoll
81	**joint** [dʒɔɪnt]	gemeinschaftlich, gemeinsam
	rough [rʌf]	grob, ungefähr
	approximately [əˈprɒksɪmətli]	ungefähr, annähernd
	to **average sth** [ˈævərɪdʒ]	etw durchschnittlich erreichen
T	**net** [net]	netto, Netto-
	pay slip [ˈpeɪ slɪp]	Gehaltsabrechnung
	living expenses *(pl)* [ˌlɪvɪŋ ɪkˈspensɪz]	Lebenshaltungskosten
	hire purchase [ˌhaɪə ˈpɜːtʃəs]	Ratenkauf
	disposable income [dɪˌspəʊzəbl ˈɪnkʌm]	verfügbares Einkommen
	mobile home [ˌməʊbaɪl ˈhəʊm]	(großer) Wohnwagen, Wohnmobil
	bargain [ˈbɑːɡɪn]	Schnäppchen
	camper van [ˈkæmpə væn]	Wohnmobil
	to **cash in** *(infml)* [ˌkæʃ ˈɪn]	zu Geld machen
	to **total** [ˈtəʊtl]	sich summieren auf, sich belaufen auf
	to **rent out** [ˌrent ˈaʊt]	vermieten
	to **deduct** [dɪˈdʌkt]	abziehen
	mainly [ˈmeɪnli]	hauptsächlich, vor allem
	alimony *AE* [ˈælɪməni]	Unterhalt, Alimente
	maintenance payment [ˈmeɪntənəns peɪmənt]	Unterhaltungszahlung
82	to **grant** [ɡrɑːnt]	bewilligen
	to **dispose of** [dɪˈspəʊz əv]	verfügen über
	confirmation [ˌkɒnfəˈmeɪʃn]	Bestätigung
	to **state** [steɪt]	erklären, angeben
	terms *(pl)* [tɜːmz]	Bedingungen, Bestimmungen
	formality [fɔːˈmæləti]	Formalität
	model [ˈmɒdl]	Muster-
	largely [ˈlɑːdʒli]	weitgehend, überwiegend
	opening hours *(pl)* [ˈəʊpənɪŋ aʊəz]	Geschäftszeiten, Öffnungszeiten
	economy [ɪˈkɒnəmi]	Wirtschaft, Volkswirtschaft
	to **promote** [prəˈməʊt]	fördern, unterstützen
	savings scheme [ˈseɪvɪŋz skiːm]	Sparplan
	to **double** [ˈdʌbl]	(sich) verdoppeln
	payday loan [ˈpeɪdeɪ ləʊn]	Kurzzeitkredit
83	to **make ends meet** [meɪk ˌendz ˈmiːt]	über die Runden kommen
	to **analyse** [ˈænəlaɪz]	analysieren
	to **suffer** [ˈsʌfə]	leiden, erleiden
	to **account for** [əˈkaʊnt fə]	ausmachen, ergeben
	youngster [ˈjʌŋstə]	Jugendliche/r
	in debt [ɪn ˈdet]	verschuldet
	mainstream [ˈmeɪnstriːm]	konventionell, regulär
	severe [sɪˈvɪə]	ernst, schwerwiegend

	education [ˌedʒu'keɪʃn]	Ausbildung
	to **get by** [ˌget 'baɪ]	auskommen *(mit Geld)*, über die Runden kommen
	in your teens [ɪn jə 'ti:nz]	im Teenageralter, zwischen 13 und 19
	significant [sɪg'nɪfɪkənt]	bedeutend, wichtig
	to **damage** ['dæmɪdʒ]	(be)schädigen, schaden
	consequence ['kɒnsɪkwəns]	Konsequenz, Folge
	guarantor loan [ˌgærən'tɔ: ləʊn]	Bürgschaftskredit
	logbook loan ['lɒgbʊk ləʊn]	Pfandkredit *(bei dem ein Kfz das Pfand darstellt)*
	liable ['laɪəbl]	haftbar
	lender [lendə]	Kreditgeber/in
	up to ['ʌp tə]	bis zu
	fellow ['feləʊ]	Mit-, andere
84	**graduate** ['grædʒuət]	Absolvent/in
T	to **inherit** [ɪn'herɪt]	erben
	unmet [ˌʌn'met]	unerfüllt, unbefriedigt
	to **customize** ['kʌstəmaɪz]	*(individuell)* anpassen, zuschneiden, einrichten
	component [kəm'pəʊnənt]	Bestandteil, Komponente
	gap [gæp]	Lücke
	cash flow ['kæʃ fləʊ]	Einnahmen, Geldzufluss
	sales *pl* [seɪlz]	Verkäufe
	proposition [ˌprɒpə'zɪʃn]	Vorschlag
	realistic [ˌri:ə'lɪstɪk]	realistisch
	committed (to) [kə'mɪtɪd]	engagiert (für)
	circumstances *(pl)* ['sɜ:kəmstənsɪz]	Umstände
	to **demonstrate** ['demənstreɪt]	vorstellen, vorführen
	to **persuade** [pə'sweɪd]	überzeugen
	eventuality [ɪˌventʃu'æləti]	Möglichkeit, Eventualität
85	**vital** ['vaɪtl]	unerlässlich
	collateral [kə'lætərəl]	Sicherheit(en)
	to **fulfil** [fʊl'fɪl]	erfüllen
	criterion, *pl* **criteria** [kraɪ'tɪəriən, kraɪ'tɪəriə]	Kriterium
	whereby [weə'baɪ]	wobei, wodurch, womit
	to **act** [ækt]	handeln, sich verhalten
	assignment [ə'saɪnmənt]	Abtretung
	to **assign** [ə'saɪn]	abtreten
	assignment by bill of sale [əˌsaɪnmənt baɪ ˌbɪl əv 'seɪl]	Sicherungsübereignung
	to **pledge** [pledʒ]	pfänden
	to **take out a mortgage** [ˌteɪk aʊt ə 'mɔ:gɪdʒ]	Hypothek aufnehmen
	land charge ['lænd tʃɑ:dʒ]	Grundschuld
	commonly ['kɒmənli]	häufig, üblicherweise
	pledge [pledʒ]	Pfand
	valuable ['væljuəbl]	wertvoll
	fine art [ˌfaɪn 'ɑ:t]	schöne Künste, bildende Kunst
	antique [æn'ti:k]	Antiquität
	art [ɑ:t]	Kunst
	to **install** [ɪn'stɔ:l]	einbauen, einrichten, aufbauen
	security system [sɪ'kjʊərəti sɪstəm]	Sicherheitssystem
	break-in ['breɪk ɪn]	Einbruch
	painting ['peɪntɪŋ]	Bild, Gemälde
	to **value** ['vælju:]	bewerten, schätzen
	cottage ['kɒtɪdʒ]	kleines Haus, Hütte
	veterinary ['vetnri]	Tierarzt/Tierärztin
	currently ['kʌrəntli]	derzeit, zurzeit, aktuell

Unit 8

86	**credit reference** [ˌkredɪt 'refrəns]	Kreditauskunft
	liquidity [lɪ'kwɪdəti]	Liquidität
	to **sponsor** ['spɒnsə]	finanziell unterstützen, fördern
	to **aim to do sth** [eɪm]	bestrebt sein etw zu tun, etw tun wollen
	to **interview** ['ɪntəvju:]	befragen, interviewen
	communications *(pl)* [kəˌmju:nɪ'keɪʃnz]	Kommunikationsnetz, Verbindung(en)
	formula ['fɔ:mjələ]	Formel
87	**medium-sized** ['mi:diəm saɪzd]	mittelgroß
	documentary credit [ˌdɒkju'mentri kredɪt]	Akkreditiv
	treasury services ['treʒəri sɜ:vɪsɪz]	Treasury Services *Vermögensverwaltung*
	to **finance** ['faɪnæns]	finanzieren
	takeover ['teɪkəʊvə]	Übernahme
	merger ['mɜ:dʒə]	Fusion
	to **focus (on)** ['fəʊkəs]	sich konzentrieren (auf)
	to **acquire** [ə'kwaɪə]	erwerben
	hospitality [ˌhɒspɪ'tæləti]	Gastfreundschaft
	expat *(infml)* [ˌeks'pæt]	Auswanderer/in

	negotiation [nɪˌɡəʊʃiˈeɪʃn]	Verhandlung, Vermittlung
	syndicated loan [ˈsɪndɪkeɪtɪd ləʊn]	Konsortialkredit
	turnover [ˈtɜːnəʊvə]	Umsatz, Absatz
88	**native speaker** [ˌneɪtɪv ˈspiːkə]	Muttersprachler/in
	to **treat** [triːt]	behandeln
	emphasis [ˈemfəsɪs]	Betonung, Schwerpunkt, Akzent
89	**invitation** [ˌɪnvɪˈteɪʃn]	Einladung
	corporate business [ˈkɔːpərət bɪznəs]	Firmenkunden
	confidential [ˌkɒnfɪˈdenʃl]	vertraulich
	timber [ˈtɪmbə]	(Nutz-)Holz
	thereby [ˌðeəˈbaɪ]	dabei, dadurch
	grateful [ˈɡreɪtfl]	dankbar
	balance (sheet) [ˈbæləns, ˈbæləns ʃiːt]	Bilanz
	cooperation [kəʊˌɒpəˈreɪʃn]	Zusammenarbeit, Zusammenwirken
	Yours faithfully [ˌjɔːz ˈfeɪθfəli]	Mit freundlichen Grüßen
	enclosure, encl. [ɪnˈkləʊʒə]	Anlage *(Brief)*
	influence [ˈɪnfluəns]	Einfluss
	status [ˈsteɪtəs]	Status
90	**subject** [ˈsʌbdʒɪkt]	Thema
	to **omit** [əˈmɪt]	auslassen, weglassen
	as of … [ˈæz əv]	Stand …
	liabilities *(pl)* [laɪəˈbɪlətiz]	Passiva, Verbindlichkeiten
	machinery [məˈʃiːnəri]	Maschinen, Geräte
	vehicle [ˈviːəkl]	Fahrzeug
	current assets *(pl)* [ˌkʌrənt ˈæsets]	Umlaufvermögen, -kapital
	accounts receivable *(pl)* [əˌkaʊnts rɪˈsiːvəbl]	Forderungen, Außenstände
	retained profits *(pl)* [rɪˌteɪnd ˈprɒfɪts]	thesaurierte Gewinne
	accounts payable *(pl)* [əˌkaʊnts ˈpeɪəbl]	Verbindlichkeiten
	payable [ˈpeɪəbl]	fällig
	credit balance [ˈkredɪt bæləns]	Guthaben, Habensaldo
	raw material [ˌrɔː məˈtɪəriəl]	Rohstoff
	work-in-progress [ˌwɜːk ɪn ˈprəʊɡres]	unfertig, in Arbeit
	finished [ˈfɪnɪʃt]	fertiggestellt
	debtor [ˈdetə]	Schuldner/in
	supplier [səˈplaɪə]	Lieferant, Zulieferer, Anbieter *(Firma)*
	reinvestment [ˌriːɪnˈvestmənt]	Wiederanlage, Reinvestition
	possession [pəˈzeʃn]	Besitz, Besitztum
91	**Middle Eastern** [ˌmɪdl ˈiːstən]	aus dem nahen Osten
	energetic [ˌenəˈdʒetɪk]	energisch, kraftvoll
	disorganized [dɪsˈɔːɡənaɪzd]	chaotisch
	incompetent [ɪnˈkɒmpɪtənt]	inkompetent, unfähig
	silence [ˈsaɪləns]	Stille, Schweigen
	embarrassing [ɪmˈbærəsɪŋ]	peinlich, unangenehm
	upside down [ˌʌpsaɪd ˈdaʊn]	umgekehrt, auf den Kopf gestellt
	line of credit [ˌlaɪn əv ˈkredɪt]	Kreditlinie, Kreditrahmen
	as regards [əz rɪˈɡɑːdz]	in puncto, hinsichtlich
	creativity [ˌkriːeɪˈtɪvəti]	schöpferische Begabung, Kreativität
	to **seize** [siːz]	ergreifen
	to **arise** [əˈraɪz]	sich ergeben, entstehen, auftreten
	to **reuse** [ˌriːˈjuːz]	wiederverwenden
	fundamental [ˌfʌndəˈmentl]	wesentlich, grundsätzlich
	enterprise [ˈentəpraɪz]	Unternehmen, Unternehmung
	smooth [smuːð]	glatt, reibungslos, problemlos
	marketplace [ˈmɑːkɪtpleɪs]	Markt
	cycle [ˈsaɪkl]	Zyklus, Kreislauf
	bulk [bʌlk]	Masse, Menge
	reputation [ˌrepjuˈteɪʃn]	Ansehen, Ruf
	receivables *(pl)* [rɪˈsiːvəbl]	Forderungen
	prompt [prɒmpt]	umgehend
	to **expand** [ɪkˈspænd]	expandieren, (sich) erweitern, (sich) vergrößern
92	**specific** [spəˈsɪfɪk]	bestimmt, speziell, spezifisch
93	to **concentrate (on)** [ˈkɒnsntreɪt]	sich konzentrieren (auf)
	to **support** [səˈpɔːt]	unterstützen, tragen, stützen
	afterwards [ˈɑːftəwədz]	nachher, danach
	to **repossess** [ˌriːpəˈzes]	beschlagnahmen
	lump sum repayment [ˌlʌmp ˌsʌm rɪˈpeɪmənt]	einmalige Rückzahlung
	to **incur** *fml* [ɪnˈkɜː]	anfallen lassen *(Gebühren)*
94	**condition** [kənˈdɪʃn]	Bedingung, Zustand
	concession [kənˈseʃn]	Konzession, Zugeständnis
	production [prəˈdʌkʃn]	Produktion
	premises [ˈpremɪsɪz]	Geschäftsräume

Chronological word list

	bankrupt ['bæŋkrʌpt]	bankrott
	dividend ['dɪvɪdend]	Dividende
	capacity [kə'pæsəti]	Kapazität, Leistung
	to **communicate** [kə'mju:nɪkeɪt]	sich verständigen, kommunizieren
	overseas [,əʊvə'si:z]	Auslands-
95	**entrepreneur** [,ɒntrəprə'nɜ:]	Unternehmer/in
	sole trader [,səʊl 'treɪdə]	Einzelunternehmer/in
	proprietor [prə'praɪətə]	Inhaber/in
	corporation [,kɔ:pə'reɪʃn]	Konzern
	abbreviation [ə,bri:vi'eɪʃn]	Abkürzung
	Ltd (private limited company) *(UK)* ['lɪmɪtɪd]	*entspricht* Gesellschaft mit beschränkter Haftung (GmbH)
	shareholder ['ʃeəhəʊldə]	Aktionär/in, Teilhaber/in, Gesellschafter/in
	liability [,laɪə'bɪləti]	Haftung
	PLC (= public limited company) *(UK)* [,pi: el 'si:]	Aktiengesellschaft, AG
	LLP (= limited liability partnership) [,el el 'pi:]	Personengesellschaft
T	**prestigious** [pre'stɪdʒəs]	renommiert, angesehen
	chain [tʃeɪn]	Kette
	substantial [səb'stænʃl]	beträchtlich, ansehnlich
	profit and loss account [,prɒfɪt ənd 'lɒs əkaʊnt]	Gewinn- und Verlustrechnung
	to **overstretch** [,əʊvə'stretʃ]	überfordern
	expansion [ɪk'spænʃn]	Ausweitung, Expansion
	tax-deductible [,tæks dɪ'dʌktəbl]	steuerlich absetzbar
	to **dilute** [daɪ'lu:t]	verdünnen, abschwächen
96	**fighter pilot** ['faɪtə paɪlət]	Jagdflieger
	can [kæn]	Dose
	RAF (= Royal Air Force) [,ɑ: eɪ 'ef]	*britische Luftwaffe*
	to **recruit sb** [rɪ'kru:t]	jdn anwerben
	vision ['vɪʒn]	Sehkraft
	angle ['æŋgl]	Winkel
	to **strain** [streɪn]	überlasten, zerren
	muscle ['mʌsl]	Muskel
	to **devastate** ['devəsteɪt]	zerstören, verwüsten
	in tatters [ɪn 'tætəz]	in Fetzen
	chemistry ['kemɪstri]	Chemie

spell [spel]	Abschnitt, Weile, kurze Zeit
accountant [ə'kaʊntənt]	Buchhalter/in
to **audit** ['ɔ:dɪt]	*(die Bücher)* prüfen
rank [ræŋk]	Dienstrang
industrial [ɪn'dʌstriəl]	industriell, Industrie-
aircraft, *pl* **aircraft** ['eəkrɑ:ft]	Flugzeug
wing [wɪŋ]	Flügel
latterly ['lætəli]	in letzter Zeit, am Ende
to **knock sth into shape** [,nɒk ɪntə 'ʃeɪp]	etw auf Vordermann bringen
to **manufacture** [,mænju'fæktʃə]	herstellen, produzieren
canned [kænd]	in Dosen, Dosen-
consumption [kən'sʌmpʃn]	Verbrauch, Konsum
recession [rɪ'seʃn]	Rezession
retailer ['ri:teɪlə]	Einzelhändler/in
to **slash** [slæʃ]	*(drastisch)* reduzieren, senken
to **preserve** [prɪ'zɜ:v]	bewahren, erhalten
to **beg** [beg]	flehen, eindringlich bitten
rating ['reɪtɪŋ]	Bewertung, Beurteilung, Klassifizierung
borrowing ['bɒrəʊɪŋ]	Darlehen, Kreditaufnahme
shopper ['ʃɒpə]	Käufer/in, Kunde/Kundin
plastics *(pl)* ['plæstɪks]	Kunststoff(e)
packaging ['pækɪdʒɪŋ]	Verpackung
cosmetics *(pl)* [kɒz'metɪks]	Kosmetikprodukte, Kosmetika
medicine ['medsn]	Medikament(e), Medizin
to **bottle** ['bɒtl]	in Flaschen abfüllen
tap [tæp]	Wasserhahn
impassive [ɪm'pæsɪv]	unbewegt
leather ['leðə]	Leder
to **recall** [rɪ'kɔ:l]	sich erinnern
challenge ['tʃælɪndʒ]	Herausforderung, (große/schwierige) Aufgabe
core [kɔ:]	Kern-, Haupt-
tough [tʌf]	hart, grob, brutal
conglomerate [kən'glɒmərət]	Konzern
to **pose** [pəʊz]	darstellen, posieren
vast [vɑ:st]	riesig, sehr groß
to **consume** [kən'sju:m]	verbrauchen, konsumieren
fizzy drink ['fɪzi drɪŋk]	Erfrischungsgetränk (mit Kohlensäure)
to **pour** [pɔ:]	gießen, schütten

	factory ['fæktəri]	Fabrik
	sage [seɪdʒ]	klug, weise
	downtime *AE* ['daʊntaɪm]	Freizeit, Auszeit
	self-confessed [ˌself kən'fest]	erklärt, nach eigener Aussage
	motorhead ['məʊtəhed]	Autonarr
	race [reɪs]	Rennen
	plane spotter [ˌpleɪn 'spɒtə]	Flugzeugbeobachter/in *(Hobby)*
	tail [teɪl]	Heck
	cellar ['selə]	Keller
97	**IPO (initial public offering)** [ˌaɪ piː 'əʊ]	Börsengang, Erstemission
	to **go public** [gəʊ 'pʌblɪk]	an die Börse gehen
	to **subscribe to** [səb'skraɪb tə]	zeichnen
	to **meet** [miːt]	erfüllen
	to **price sth** [praɪs]	für etw den Preis festsetzen
	tech (= technology) [tek]	Technologie
	prospectus [prə'spektəs]	Emissionsprospekt
	institutional [ˌɪnstɪ'tjuːʃnl]	institutionell
	underwriter ['ʌndəraɪtə]	Anleger/in, Zeichner/in
	allotment [ə'lɒtmənt]	Zuteilung
	to **exercise** ['eksəsaɪz]	ausüben
	surge [sɜːdʒ]	Welle, starker Anstieg
	to **fizzle** ['fɪzl]	im Sande verlaufen, missglücken
	kick-off ['kɪk ɒf]	Anstoß, Start
	to **give up** [ˌgɪv 'ʌp]	aufgeben, abgeben
	debut ['deɪbjuː]	Debüt
	meager *AE*, **meagre** *BE* [miːgə]	mager, dürftig
	to **contrast (with sth)** [kən'trɑːst]	gegenüberstehen, im Gegensatz stehen (zu etw)

Unit 9

98	**foreign trade** [ˌfɒrən 'treɪd]	Außenhandel
	Incoterm ['ɪnkəʊtɜːm]	*Internationale Handelsklausel*
	volume of trade [vɒljuːm əv 'treɪd]	Handelsvolumen
	emerging market economies *(pl)* [iˌmɜːdʒɪŋ ˌmɑːkɪt ɪ'kɒnəmiz]	Schwellenländer
	trade deficit [ˌtreɪd 'defɪsɪt]	Handelsdefizit, Handelsbilanzdefizit
	trade surplus [ˌtreɪd 'sɜːpləs]	Handelsüberschuss, Handelsbilanzüberschuss
99	to **chair (a discussion)** [tʃeə]	(eine Diskussion) leiten
	conclusion [kən'kluːʒn]	Schlussfolgerung, Schluss
	to **clarify** ['klærəfaɪ]	klären, verdeutlichen
	to **recap** ['riːkæp]	rekapitulieren, (kurz) zusammenfassen
	terms of payment *(pl)* [ˌtɜːmz əv 'peɪmənt]	Zahlungsbedingungen
	acceptance [ək'septəns]	Annahme
	on open account [ɒn ˌəʊpn ə'kaʊnt]	gegen Rechnung
	in advance [ɪn əd'vɑːns]	im Voraus, gegen Vorkasse
	after sight [ɑːftə 'saɪt]	nach Sicht
	letter of credit [ˌletər əv 'kredɪt]	Akkreditiv
	exporter [ɪk'spɔːtə]	Exporteur/in
	to **dispatch** [dɪ'spætʃ]	versenden, (aus)liefern
	shipment ['ʃɪpmənt]	Sendung, Ladung, Lieferung
	importer [ɪm'pɔːtə]	Importeur/in
	bill of exchange [ˌbɪl əv ɪks'tʃeɪndʒ]	Wechsel
100	**glue** [gluː]	Klebstoff, Leim
	consultation [ˌkɒnsl'teɪʃn]	Beratung
	sample ['sɑːmpl]	Probe, Muster
	to **enquire (about)** [ɪn'kwaɪə]	fragen, sich erkundigen (nach/wegen)
	to **place an order** [ˌpleɪs ən 'ɔːdə]	eine Bestellung aufgeben
	Goodness no! [ˌgʊdnəs 'nəʊ]	Um Himmels willen!
	to **doubt** [daʊt]	bezweifeln
	collection of documents [kəˌlekʃn əv 'dɒkjumənts]	Dokumenteninkasso
	bill of lading [ˌbɪl əv 'leɪdɪŋ]	Konnossement
	commercial invoice [kəˌmɜːʃl 'ɪnvɔɪs]	Handelsrechnung
	certificate of origin [səˌtɪfɪkət əv 'ɒrɪdʒɪn]	Ursprungszeugnis
	packing list ['pækɪŋ lɪst]	Packliste, Packzettel
	freight forwarder ['freɪt fɔːwədə]	Spediteur/in, Spedition
101	to **dislike** [dɪs'laɪk]	nicht mögen
	possibility [ˌpɒsə'bɪləti]	Möglichkeit
	in italics [ɪn ɪ'tælɪks]	kursiv (gedruckt)

	to specialize in ['speʃəlaɪz ɪn]	sich spezialisieren auf
	to consist of [kən'sɪst əv]	bestehen aus
102	**shipper** ['ʃɪpə]	Versender/in, Spediteur/in
	consignee [ˌkɒnsaɪ'ni]	(Waren-)Empfänger/in
	irrevocable [ɪ'revəkəbl]	unwiderruflich
	in favour of [ɪn 'feɪvər əv]	zugunsten
	to advise [əd'vaɪz]	avisieren, ankündigen
	to conform (with) [kən'fɔːm]	entsprechen, übereinstimmen (mit)
	to forward ['fɔːwəd]	senden, befördern, weiterleiten
103	**ethnic group** ['eθnɪk gruːp]	Volksgruppe
	to offend sb [ə'fend]	jdn beleidigen, verletzen; jdm zu nahe treten
	confrontation [ˌkɒnfrʌn'teɪʃn]	Auseinandersetzung
	to resolve [rɪ'zɒlv]	lösen, auflösen
	indirect [ˌɪndə'rekt]	indirekt
	implicit [ɪm'plɪsɪt]	implizit, stillschweigend
	destination [ˌdestɪ'neɪʃn]	Bestimmungsort
	loading ['ləʊdɪŋ]	Verladung
	discharge ['dɪstʃɑːdʒ]	Entladung, Löschen
	port of loading [ˌpɔːt əv 'ləʊdɪŋ]	Verladehafen
	port [pɔːt]	Hafen
	vessel ['vesl]	Schiff
	consignment [kən'saɪnmənt]	Frachtgut, Lieferung, Sendung
104	**transferable** [træns'fɜːrəbl]	übertragbar, transferierbar
	beneficiary [ˌbenɪ'fɪʃəri]	Zahlungsempfänger/in
	date of expiry [ˌdeɪt əv ɪk'spaɪəri]	Verfallsdatum, Ablaufdatum
	partial shipment ['pɑːʃl ʃɪpmənt]	Teillieferung
	transshipment [ˌtræns'ʃɪpmənt]	Umschlag, Umladung
	draft [drɑːft]	Wechsel, Tratte
	ultimate buyer [ˌʌltɪmət 'baɪə]	Endabnehmer, Endkäufer
	issuance charge ['ɪʃuənts tʃɑːdʒ]	Ausstellungsgebühr
	acceptance commission [ək'septəns kəmɪʃn]	Akzeptprovision
105	**carrier** ['kæriə]	Spedition, Frachtführer *(Firma)*
	transportation [ˌtrænspɔː'teɪʃn]	Beförderung, Transport(wesen)
	weight [weɪt]	Gewicht
	on board [ɒn 'bɔːd]	an Bord
	unclean [ʌn'kliːn]	unsauber
	identical [aɪ'dentɪkl]	identisch
	title document [ˌtaɪtl 'dɒkjumənt]	Traditionspapier
	forwarding agent ['fɔːwədɪŋ eɪdʒənt]	Spediteur/in
	negotiable [nɪ'gəʊʃiəbl]	übertragbar
	to endorse [ɪn'dɔːs]	indossieren
	mode [məʊd]	Modus, Art
	multi-modal transport [ˌmʌltiməʊdl 'trænspɔːt]	kombinierte Beförderung, multimodaler Transport
	waybill ['weɪbɪl]	Frachtbrief
	domestic [də'mestɪk]	Inlands-, inländisch
	contract of sale [ˌkɒntrækt əv 'seɪl]	Kaufvertrag
	to load [ləʊd]	verladen, laden, füllen
107	**Islamic** [ɪz'læmɪk]	islamisch
	conference ['kɒnfərəns]	Konferenz, Tagung
	Muslim ['mʊzlɪm]	muslimisch; Moslem, Muslima
	compliant [kəm'plaɪənt]	konform, verträglich
	worldwide ['wɜːldwaɪd]	weltweit
	yearly ['jɪəli]	jährlich
	principle ['prɪnsəpl]	Grundsatz, Prinzip
	to stipulate ['stɪpjuleɪt]	festlegen
	intrinsic [ɪn'trɪnsɪk]	immanent, eigentlich
	as a matter of faith [æz ə ˌmætə əv 'feɪθ]	aus Glaubensgründen
	faith [feɪθ]	Glaube
	prohibition [ˌprəʊɪ'bɪʃn]	Verbot
	debenture [dɪ'bentʃə]	Obligation
	permitted [pə'mɪtɪd]	erlaubt, gestattet
	pork [pɔːk]	Schweinefleisch
	weapon ['wepən]	Waffe
	speculation [ˌspekjʊ'leɪʃn]	Spekulation
	to rule out [ˌruːl 'aʊt]	ausschließen
	derivative [dɪ'rɪvətɪv]	Derivat
	futures *(pl)* ['fjuːtʃəz]	Termingeschäfte
	swap [swɒp]	Tauschgeschäft
	to resell [ˌriː'sel]	weiterverkaufen
	backed [bækt]	gedeckt
	physical ['fɪzɪkl]	materiell, konkret
	nominal value [ˌnɒmɪnl 'væljuː]	Nominalwert
	maturity [mə'tʃʊərəti]	Fälligkeit

	crisis, *pl* **crises** ['kraɪsɪs, 'kraɪsi:z]	Krise
	sixfold ['sɪksfəʊld]	sechsfach
	tendency ['tendənsi]	Neigung, Tendenz
	to **ignore** [ɪg'nɔ:]	hinwegsehen über, ignorieren

Unit 10

108	**CV (= curriculum vitae)** *BE* [,si: 'vi, kə,rɪkjələm 'vi:taɪ]	Lebenslauf
	poll [pəʊl]	Umfrage
	covering letter [,kʌvərɪŋ 'letə]	Anschreiben, Begleitschreiben
	to **rank** [ræŋk]	einstufen, anordnen
P	**vote;** to **vote** [vəʊt]	Stimme; abstimmen, wählen
	technique [tek'ni:k]	Methode, Technik
	résumé *AE* ['rezjumeɪ]	Lebenslauf
	confident ['kɒnfɪdənt]	(selbst)sicher
	to **complement** ['kɒmplɪmənt]	ergänzen
	prospective [prə'spektɪv]	(zu)künftig, potenziell
	at a glance [æt ə 'glɑ:ns]	auf einen Blick
	educational [,edʒu'keɪʃənl]	Erziehungs-, Bildungs-
109	**job advertisement** [,dʒɒb əd'vɜ:tɪsmənt]	Stellenanzeige
	abroad [ə'brɔ:d]	im/ins Ausland
	to begin with [tə bɪ'gɪn wɪð]	anfänglich
	qualification [,kwɒlɪfɪ'keɪʃn]	Qualifikation, Zeugnis, Fähigkeit
	characteristics *pl* [,kærəktə'rɪstɪks]	typische Merkmale, Eigenschaften
	shortlist ['ʃɔ:tlɪst]	(engere) Auswahlliste
	per annum [pər 'ænəm]	pro Jahr
	location [ləʊ'keɪʃn]	Standort, Ort
	computerized [kəm'pju:təraɪzd]	Computer-
	to **exchange** [ɪks'tʃeɪndʒ]	austauschen, eintauschen, umtauschen
	administration [əd,mɪnɪ'streɪʃn]	Verwaltung
	drive [draɪv]	Antrieb, Tatkraft, Energie
	to **think on your feet** [θɪŋk ɒn jə 'fi:t]	schnell reagieren
	willingness ['wɪlɪŋnəs]	Bereitschaft
	reliability [rɪ,laɪə'bɪləti]	Zuverlässigkeit, Verlässlichkeit
	discretion [dɪ'skreʃn]	Diskretion
	incremental [,ɪŋkrə'mentl]	schrittweise
	to **recognize** ['rekəgnaɪz]	anerkennen
	commitment (to) [kə'mɪtmənt]	Engagement (für), Bekenntnis (zu)
	superb [su:'pɜ:b]	ausgezeichnet
	enthusiastic [ɪn,θju:zi'æstɪk]	begeistert
110	**vacancy** ['veɪkənsi]	offene Stelle
P	**candidate** ['kændɪdət]	Bewerber/in
	manner ['mænə]	Umgangsform(en)
	GCSE (= General Certificate of Secondary Education) [,dʒi: si: es 'i:]	Prüfung für Schüler ab 15, mittlerer Schulabschluss
	managerial assistant [,mænə,dʒɪəriəl ə'sɪstənt]	Führungsassistent
	correspondence [,kɒrə'spɒndəns]	Briefwechsel, Korrespondenz
	personnel management [,pɜ:sənel 'mænɪdʒmənt]	Personalmanagement
	preferably ['prefrəbli]	vorzugsweise, am liebsten
	communicator [kə'mju:nɪkeɪtə]	Kommunikator/in
	oral ['ɔ:rəl]	mündlich
	in writing [ɪn 'raɪtɪŋ]	schriftlich, in Schriftform
	exclusive [ɪk'sklu:sɪv]	exklusiv
111	**summary** ['sʌməri]	Zusammenfassung
	set [set]	festgelegt, festgesetzt
	factual ['fæktʃuəl]	sachlich
	motivated ['məʊtɪveɪtɪd]	motiviert
	reverse [rɪ'vɜ:s]	umgekehrt, entgegengesetzt
	chronological [,krɒnə'lɒdʒɪkl]	chronologisch, zeitlich
	achievement [ə'tʃi:vmənt]	Errungenschaft, Leistung
	brief [bri:f]	kurz, knapp
	academic [,ækə'demɪk]	Schul-, akademisch
	rounded ['raʊndɪd]	abgerundet
	personality [,pɜ:sə'næləti]	Persönlichkeit
	to **socialize** ['səʊʃəlaɪz]	sich treffen, unter Leute gehen
	referee [,refə'ri:]	Referenzgeber/in
112	**vocational colalege** [vəʊ,keɪʃənl 'kɒlɪdʒ]	Fachoberschule, Berufskolleg
	vocational school [vəʊ,keɪʃənl 'sku:l]	Berufsschule, berufsbildende Schule
	exam [ɪg'zæm]	Prüfung

	A levels *(BE, pl)* ['eɪ levlz]	Abitur, Berufsreifeprüfung
	pressure ['preʃə]	Druck
113	**formal** ['fɔːml]	formell, förmlich
	tailor-made ['teɪlə meɪd]	maßgeschneidert
	ref. no. (= reference number) ['refrəns nʌmbə]	Referenznummer, Aktenzeichen
	to **employ** [ɪm'plɔɪ]	beschäftigen, einstellen *(Personal)*
	database ['deɪtəbeɪs]	Datenbank
	to **be an asset (to)** ['æset]	von Wert sein (für)
114	**length** [leŋθ]	Länge, Dauer
	communicative [kə'mjuːnɪkətɪv]	kommunikativ
	availability [əˌveɪlə'bɪləti]	Verfügbarkeit
115	**strength** [streŋθ]	Stärke
	bullet point ['bʊlɪt pɔɪnt]	Stichpunkt
	concise [kən'saɪs]	kurzgefasst, prägnant
	as the saying goes [æz ðə ˌseɪɪŋ 'gəʊz]	wie man so sagt
	saying ['seɪɪŋ]	Sprichwort, Redensart
	suggestion [sə'dʒestʃən]	Vorschlag
116	**HR (= human resources) manager** [ˌhjuːmən rɪ'sɔːsɪz mænɪdʒə]	Personalleiter/in
	introduction [ˌɪntrə'dʌkʃn]	Einleitung, Einführung, Vorstellung
	stage [steɪdʒ]	Phase, Abschnitt
T	to **come along** [ˌkʌm ə'lɒŋ]	vorbeikommen
	My pleasure. [maɪ 'pleʒə]	Es ist mir ein Vergnügen. *(höfliche Erwiderung)*
	preparation [ˌprepə'reɪʃn]	Vorbereitung
	argument ['ɑːgjumənt]	Argument, Streit
	for the sake of sth [seɪk]	einer Sache zuliebe, einer Sache wegen
	handshake ['hændʃeɪk]	Händedruck
	to **shake hands** [ˌʃeɪk 'hændz]	sich die Hand geben, die Hände schütteln
	bound to be ['baʊnd tə biː]	zu erwarten sein, (dass)
	horrible ['hɒrəbl]	fürchterlich
	habit ['hæbɪt]	Gewohnheit
	to **conduct** [kən'dʌkt]	leiten
	panel ['pænl]	Gremium, Ausschuss
	weakness ['wiːknəs]	Schwäche
	to **relate to sth** [rɪ'leɪt tə]	sich auf etw beziehen
	section ['sekʃn]	Abteilung, Abschnitt
	to **occur** [ə'kɜː]	vorfallen, geschehen
	to **concern** [kən'sɜːn]	betreffen, angehen, beunruhigen
	assessment [ə'sesmənt]	Beurteilung, Einstufung
	evaluation [ɪˌvælju'eɪʃn]	Auswertung, Bewertung
	coach [kəʊtʃ]	Trainer/in
P	**familiar** [fə'mɪliə]	vertraut
	to **research** [rɪ'sɜːtʃ]	recherchieren
	to **stress** [stres]	betonen, hervorheben
	goal [gəʊl]	Ziel
	to **progress** [prə'gres]	vorankommen, weiterkommen
118	**insight (into)** ['ɪnsaɪt]	Einblick (in), Verständnis (von)
	invaluable [ɪn'væljuəbl]	unbezahlbar, von unschätzbarem Wert
	jobsite ['dʒɒbsaɪt]	*Internetauftritt, auf dem Stellen angeboten werden*
	work permit ['wɜːk pɜːmɪt]	Arbeitserlaubnis
	visa [viːzə]	Visum
	immigration [ˌɪmɪ'greɪʃn]	Einwanderung
	cultural ['kʌltʃərəl]	kulturell
	sexual ['sekʃuəl]	sexuell
	orientation [ˌɔːriən'teɪʃn]	Orientierung
	to **forbid** [fə'bɪd]	verbieten, untersagen
	resident ['rezɪdənt]	Einwohner/in
	embassy ['embəsi]	Botschaft
	consulate ['kɒnsjələt]	Konsulat
	chamber of commerce [ˌtʃeɪmbər əv 'kɒmɜːs]	Handelskammer
	networker ['netwɜːkə]	Netzwerker/in

Alphabetical word list

Dieses Wörterverzeichnis enthält alle neuen Wörter aus *Money Matters – 4th Edition* in alphabetischer Reihenfolge. Nicht aufgeführt sind Wörter, die zum Grundwortschatz (*Basic word list*) gehören. Wörter aus den Hörverständnisübungen sind zusätzlich mit einem **T** (*Transkript*) und Wörter aus den *Partner files* mit einem **P** gekennzeichnet.

A

A levels *(BE, pl)* *112* Abitur, Berufsreifeprüfung
abbreviation *95* Abkürzung
ability *14T* Fähigkeit, Befähigung
abroad *109* im/ins Ausland
abrupt *70* abrupt, plötzlich
absolutely *9* absolut, völlig
academic *111* Schul-, akademisch
a-calling, to **come ~** *39* vorbeischauen
acceptable *6* annehmbar, akzeptabel
acceptance *99* Annahme; **~ commission** *104* Akzeptprovision
to **access** *48* zugreifen auf
access *26* Zugriff, Zugang
accessible *51* erreichbar, zugänglich
according to *15* entsprechend, nach, gemäß
accordingly *23* (dem)entsprechend, folglich
to **account for** *83* ausmachen, ergeben
account *7* Konto; **on open ~** *99* gegen Rechnung; **time deposit ~** *39* Festgeldkonto
account holder *31* Kontoinhaber/in;
accountant *96* Buchhalter/in
accounting *8* Rechnungswesen, Buchhaltung
accounts, ~ payable *(pl)* *90* Verbindlichkeiten; **~ receivable** *(pl)* *90* Forderungen, Außenstände
to **accuse (of)** *75* anklagen (wegen)
to **achieve** *43* erreichen
achievement *111* Errungenschaft, Leistung
to **acknowledge** *37* bestätigen, anerkennen
to **acquire** *87* erwerben
to **act** *85* handeln, sich verhalten
to **activate** *31* aktivieren
activation *35* Aktivierung
activity *14T* Aktivität, Tätigkeit
addition, in ~ to *30* zusätzlich zu
additional *15* zusätzlich
to **address** *26* *(Problem etc.)* ansprechen, angehen, thematisieren
administration *109* Verwaltung
adult *66* Erwachsene/r
advance *60* Vorschuss; **in ~** *99* im Voraus
advance notice *45* Vorankündigung
advanced *54* entwickelt, fortgeschritten
advantage *25* Vorteil
to **advertise** *16* werben (für), anbieten
advertisement *58* Werbung, Reklame; **job ~** *109* Stellenanzeige, -ausschreibung
advice *10* Rat, Beratung; **Citizens A~ Bureau** *76* Bürgerbüro, Bürgerberatungsstelle
advisable *67* ratsam
to **advise** *45* (be)raten, empfehlen; *102* avisieren, ankündigen
adviser *6* Berater/in
to **affect** *43* beeinflussen, sich auswirken auf
to **afford** *7* (es) sich leisten (können)
affordability *15* Erschwinglichkeit, Bezahlbarkeit
affront *75* Affront, Beleidigung
afterwards *93* nachher, danach
agency *31* Agentur, Organisation
agent *(gramm)* *48* Agens, der/die Handelnde
agreement *7* Vereinbarung, Absprache, Zustimmung
ahead, straight ~ *10* geradeaus
to **aim to do sth** *86* bestrebt sein etw zu tun, etw tun wollen
aim *63* Ziel, Zweck, Absicht
aircraft, *pl* **aircraft** *96* Flugzeug
alike *6* gleichermaßen, in gleicher Weise
alimony *AE* *81T* Unterhalt, Alimente
allotment *97* Zuteilung
allowance, tax-free ~ *72* Steuerfreibetrag
all-time high *68* Allzeithoch
along with *38* zusammen mit
alongside *76* neben
to **alter** *44T* ändern, abändern
although *15* obwohl
altogether *59* insgesamt, zusammen
amid *63* inmitten, mitten unter
to **amount to** *39* betragen
to **amplify** *26* verstärken
to **analyse** *83* analysieren
analysis, *pl* **analyses** *8* Analyse
analyst *68* Analyst/in
angle *96* Winkel
angry *27* aufgebracht, ungehalten
to **announce** *15* ankündigen, bekanntgeben
announcement *63* Mitteilung, Bekanntgabe
annoying *19* ärgerlich, lästig, störend
annual *53* jährlich
annum, per ~ *109* pro Jahr
anonymity *52T* Anonymität
anonymous *52T* anonym
antique *85* Antiquität
anywhere, not … ~ *19* nirgends, nirgendwo(hin)
apart from *53* abgesehen von, außer
to **apologize (for)** *19* sich entschuldigen (für)
apology *18* Entschuldigung
appearance *6* Aussehen, Äußeres
appliance *39* Gerät, Haushaltsgerät
applicant *8* Bewerber/in
application *37* Antrag; **~ form** *54* Antragsformular; **~ for tax exemption** *72* Freistellungsantrag; **loan ~** *77* Kreditantrag, Darlehensantrag
to **apply (for)** *23* beantragen; sich bewerben (um)
appointment *10* Termin
to **appreciate** *15* würdigen, zu schätzen wissen
to **approach sb/sth** *18* an jdn/etw herantreten
approach *52T* Ansatz, Herangehensweise
appropriate *6* angemessen, passend, richtig
approval *38* Zustimmung
to **approve of sth** *75* etw gut finden
approximately *81* ungefähr, annähernd
APR (= annual percentage rate) *62* effektiver Jahreszins
area *14T* Gebiet, Bereich; **~ code** *AE* *21* Vorwahl
argument *116T* Argument, Streit
to **arise** *91* sich ergeben, entstehen, auftreten
around the corner *68* um die Ecke
to **arrange** *14T* arrangieren, vereinbaren

arrangement *12* Abmachung, Vereinbarung
arrangement fee *78* Bearbeitungsgebühr
art *85* Kunst; **fine ~** *85* schöne Künste, bildende Kunst
as of … *90* Stand …
asap (= as soon as possible) *68* so bald wie möglich
to **assess** *76* einschätzen, beurteilen, bewerten
assessment *116T* Beurteilung, Einstufung
asset, to **be an ~ (to)** *113* von Wert sein (für)
asset-building *64* vermögensbildend
assets *(pl)* *71* Aktiva, Vermögen(swerte)
to **assign** *85* abtreten
assignment *85* Abtretung; **~ by bill of sale** *85* Sicherungsübereignung
to **assist (with)** *8* assistieren, helfen (bei)
assistance *10* Hilfe, Unterstützung
assistent, managerial ~ *110F* Führungsassistent
associated *26* verbunden
association *19* Verband, Vereinigung
to **assume** *53* annehmen, davon ausgehen
assumption *24* Annahme
to **assure** *58* versichern, zusichern
assured *54* sicher
at present *43* momentan, derzeit, zurzeit
at hand *36* zur Hand
at your fingertips *21* zur Hand
ATM (= automated teller machine) *AE* *9* Geldautomat
atmosphere *7* Atmosphäre, Stimmung
to **attach** *29* anfügen, anhängen *(an ein E-Mail)*
attachment *68* Anhang *(E-Mail)*
attempt, failed ~ *48* fehlgeschlagener Versuch, Fehlversuch
to **attend** *39* besuchen
to **attend to sth** *14T* sich um etw kümmern
attention *7* Aufmerksamkeit, Beachtung; to **pay (close) ~ (to)** *7* (genau) aufpassen, achten (auf)
attitude (to/towards) *26* Einstellung, (Geistes-)Haltung (zu/gegenüber)
attorney, power of ~ *31* Handlungsvollmacht
to **attract** *39* anlocken, anziehen
attraction *52T* Anziehung(spunkt)
to **audit** *96* *(die Bücher)* prüfen
austerity *39* wirtschaftliche Einschränkung, Entbehrung
authority *63* Behörde
to **authorize** *30* autorisieren, ermächtigen
automated teller machine (ATM) *AE* *9* Geldautomat
automatic(ally) *37* automatisch
availability *114* Verfügbarkeit
available *17* verfügbar; zu sprechen *(Telefon)*
average, on ~ *39* im Durchschnitt
to **average sth** *81* etw durchschnittlich erreichen
to **await** *39* erwarten, abwarten
aware, to **be ~** *30* sich bewusst sein
awareness *8* Bewusstsein, Aufmerksamkeit
awkward *16* unangenehm, peinlich

B

backed *107* gedeckt
backslash *21* Schrägstrich nach links
baggage *53* Gepäck
bakery *51* Bäckerei
to **balance** *14T* ausgleichen, bilanzieren
balance *14T* Kontostand, Bilanz, Saldo; **credit ~** *90* Guthaben, Habensaldo
balance (sheet) *89* Bilanz
bank transfer *10* (Bank-)Überweisung
bank manager *10* Bankdirektor/in, Filialleiter/in
bank statement *9* Kontoauszug
bankrupt *94* bankrott
bargain *81T* Schnäppchen
base *15* Basis
…-based *39* in … stattfindend/ansässig
based on *33* basierend auf, auf der Grundlage von
basement *10* Keller, Untergeschoss
basically *69* grundsätzlich, im Grunde
basis, *pl* **bases** *15* Basis, Grundlage; **on a case-by-case ~** *15* durch/nach Einzelfallbetrachtung; **on a regular ~** *30* regelmäßig
to **bear** *51* tragen
to **beg** *96* flehen, eindringlich bitten
behalf, on sb's ~ *69* in jds Namen
to **behave** *70* sich benehmen, sich verhalten
behaviour *26* Benehmen, Verhalten
being, for the time ~ *31* vorläufig, für den Moment
belief (in) *7* Glaube (an), Vertrauen (in)
to **belong (to)** *66* gehören (zu)
to **bemoan** *15* beklagen, betrauern
beneficiary *104* Zahlungsempfänger/in
benefit *15* Nutzen, Vorteil, Pluspunkt
better off *53* besser dran, besser bedient
beyond *39* darüber hinaus, über etw hinaus
bill *24* Rechnung; **~ of exchange** *99* Wechsel; **~ of lading** *100* Konnossement
billing cycle *59* Abrechnungszeitraum
billion *51* Milliarde
billionaire *64* Milliardär/in
to **bind** *51* binden
to **blame sb** *27* jdm die Schuld geben
blame *27* Schuld; to **lay ~** *27* Schuld zuweisen
blessing *27* Segen; **be a ~ in disguise** *27* sich im Nachhinein als gut herausstellen, Glück im Unglück sein
bn (= billion) *63* Milliarde
board, on ~ *105* an Bord
boat, miss the ~ *51* den Anschluss verpassen
to **boil down to** *51* darauf hinauslaufen
to **bombard** *49* bombardieren
bond *65* Anleihe, Rentenpapier, Obligation; **government ~s** *(pl)* *73* Staatsanleihen
to **boom** *51* blühen, boomen
boring *16* langweilig
borrower *76* Kreditnehmer/in
borrowing *96* Darlehen, Kreditaufnahme
to **bother with** *51* sich kümmern um
to **bottle** *96* in Flaschen abfüllen
to **bounce** *(infml)* *52* platzen *(Scheck)*
bound to be *116T* zu erwarten sein, (dass)
boundary *26* Grenze, Begrenzung
to **brainstorm** *6* Ideen (ungeordnet) sammeln
branch *6* Zweig(stelle), Filiale
branch manager *13* Filialleiter/in
brand *25* Marke(nname)

break-in *85* Einbruch
brief *111* kurz, knapp
budget *60* Budget, Haushalt, Etat
building society *37* Bausparkasse
bulk *91* Masse, Menge
bullet point *115* Stichpunkt
burden of proof *51* Beweislast
bureau, *pl* **bureaus** *76* Büro; **Citizens Advice B~** *76* Bürgerbüro, Bürgerberatungsstelle
bus pass *40* Busticket *(Zeitkarte)*
business, to **get down to ~** *17* zur Sache kommen
business customer *8* Firmenkunde/-kundin, Geschäftskunde/-kundin
butcher *15* Metzger(ei), Fleischhauer(ei)
buyer, ultimate ~ *104* Endabnehmer, Endkäufer
by the way *10* übrigens, nebenbei (bemerkt)

C

to **calm sb down** *23* jdn beruhigen
calm *27* ruhig, gelassen
campaign *24* Kampagne, Aktion
camper van *81T* Wohnmobil
can *96* Dose
to **cancel** *20T* absagen, stornieren
candidate *110F* Bewerber/in
canned *96* in Dosen, Dosen-
capacity *94* Kapazität, Leistung
capital *10* Kapital
capital letter *21* Großbuchstabe
card, photographic membership ~ *38* Lichtbild-Mitgliedsausweis
cardholder *63* Inhaber/n einer Kreditkarte
to **care about sb/sth** *27* sich um jdn/etw kümmern, am Herzen liegen
care, Take ~. *8* Pass auf dich auf.
caring *27* fürsorglich, warmherzig
carrier *105* Spedition, Frachtführer *(Firma)*
to **carry out** *77* ausführen, durchführen
cartridge, ink ~ *14T* Tintenpatrone
case, in ~ *48* falls; **on a ~-by-~ basis** *15* durch/nach Einzelfallbetrachtung
cash *16T* Bargeld; **~ deposit** *74* Bareinlage; **~ dispenser** *16T* Bargeldautomat; **~ drawer** *14T* Kassenlade; **~ flow** *84T* Einnahmen, Geldzufluss; **~ machine** *9* Geldautomat
to **cash in** *(infml)* *81T* zu Geld machen
cashier *10* Kassierer/in
cashless *40* bargeldlos
cashpoint *9* Geldautomat
casual *6* leger, sportlich, Freizeit-
to **cause** *19* verursachen
cautious *73* vorsichtig
cell phone *AE* *21* Handy, Mobiltelefon
cellar *96* Keller
CEO, chief executive (officer), ~ *63* Geschäftsführer/in, Vorstandsvorsitzende/r
certain(ly) *15* sicher(lich), bestimmt
certificate *31* Zeugnis, Bescheinigung; **~ of origin** *100* Ursprungszeugnis
certification *8* Bestätigung, Zulassung
certified *14T* geprüft, diplomiert
chain *95T* Kette
to **chair (a discussion)** *99* (eine Diskussion) leiten
challenge *96* Herausforderung, (große/schwierige) Aufgabe
challenging *14T* anspruchsvoll, fordernd
chamber of commerce *118* Handelskammer
champion *78* Meister/in
channel *16* Kanal, Sender
character *36* Zeichen
characteristics *pl* *109* typische Merkmale, Eigenschaften
to **charge** *19* berechnen
charge *19* Gebühr; **free of ~** *18* gebührenfrei; **in ~ (of)** *11* verantwortlich (für), zuständig (für); **issuance ~** *104* Ausstellungsgebühr
charity *63* Wohltätigkeitsorganisation
chart *44* Diagramm, Tabelle
check *AE* *40* Scheck
chemistry *96* Chemie
cheque *10* Scheck; to **clear a ~** *30* einen Scheck gutschreiben (lassen)
chief executive (officer), CEO *63* Geschäftsführer/in, Vorstandsvorsitzende/r
chronological *111* chronologisch, zeitlich
circumstances *(pl)* *84T* Umstände
to **cite** *26* anführen, angeben
Citizens Advice Bureau *76* Bürgerbüro, Bürgerberatungsstelle
to **claim** *33* angeben, behaupten; *45* einziehen, verlangen
to **clarify** *99* klären, verdeutlichen
to **clear** *49* räumen; **~ a cheque** *30* einen Scheck gutschreiben (lassen)
client *14T* Kunde/Kundin
close, to **pay ~ attention (to)** *7* (genau) aufpassen, achten (auf)
closure *15* Schließung, Stilllegung
clue *44T* Hinweis, Anhaltspunkt
coach *116* Trainer/in
code, (dialling) ~ *21* Vorwahl; **area ~** *AE* *21* Vorwahl; **dress code** *6* Kleiderordnung
coin *22* Münze
cold *19* Kälte
collateral *85* Sicherheit(en)
collection of documents *100* Dokumenteninkasso
college *8* Fach(hoch)schule; **vocational ~** *112* Fachoberschule, Berufskolleg
to **combine** *73* verbinden, kombinieren
combined *30* kombiniert
to **come along** *116T* vorbeikommen
to **comment (on)** *51* kommentieren
commerce, chamber of ~ *118* Handelskammer
commercial *76* gewerblich, kommerziell; **~ invoice** *100* Handelsrechnung
commission, acceptance ~ *104* Akzeptprovision
commitment *63* Verpflichtung; **~ (to)** *109* Engagement (für), Bekenntnis (zu)
committed (to) *84T* engagiert (für)
common *37* verbreitet, üblich
commonly *85* häufig, üblicherweise
to **communicate** *94* sich verständigen, kommunizieren
communications *(pl)* *86* Kommunikationsnetz, Verbindung(en)
communicative *114* kommunikativ
communicator *110F* Kommunikator/in
community *15* Gemeinschaft, Gemeinde, Bevölkerungsgruppe
comparison *26* Vergleich
to **compete** *64* konkurrieren
competition *37* Wettbewerb
competitive *55* umkämpft, wettbewerbsintensiv; *77* konkurrenzfähig, günstig *(Preis)*
to **complain** *23* sich beschweren, sich beklagen
complaint *18* Beschwerde, Klage, Reklamation

to **complement** *108* ergänzen
complexity *63* Komplexität, Vielschichtigkeit
compliant *107* konform, verträglich
component *84T* Bestandteil, Komponente
to **comprise** *43* umfassen, bestehen aus
compromise *54* Kompromiss, (außergerichtlicher) Vergleich
computerized *109* Computer-
to **concentrate (on)** *93* sich konzentrieren (auf)
to **concern** *116T* betreffen, angehen, beunruhigen
concern *27* Befürchtung, Bedenken, Sorge
concerned *27* betroffen, besorgt
concert *39* Konzert
concession *94* Konzession, Zugeständnis
concise *115* kurzgefasst, prägnant
conclusion *99* Schlussfolgerung, Schluss
condition *94* Bedingung, Zustand
conditions, terms and ~ *(pl) 16T* Konditionen, (Allgemeine) Geschäftsbedingungen
to **conduct** *116T* leiten
conduct *63* Verhalten, Gebaren
conference *107* Konferenz, Tagung
confidence *27* (Selbst-)Vertrauen, Zuversicht
confident *108* (selbst)sicher
confidential *89* vertraulich
to **confirm** *29* bestätigen
confirmation *82* Bestätigung
to **conform (with)** *102* entsprechen, übereinstimmen (mit)
confrontation *103* Auseinandersetzung
conglomerate *96* Konzern
congratulations *09* herzlichen Glückwunsch
cons, pros and ~ *(pl) 33* Für und Wider, Pro und Contra
consecutive *48* in Folge, aufeinander folgend
consequence *83* Konsequenz, Folge
to **consider** *15* erwägen, in Betracht ziehen
considerable *33* erheblich, beträchtlich
consideration *26* Erwägung, Überlegung
consignee *102* (Waren-)Empfänger/in
consignment *103* Frachtgut, Lieferung, Sendung

to **consist of** *101* bestehen aus
to **consolidate** *77* konsolidieren
consternation *75* Bestürzung, Fassungslosigkeit
consulate *118* Konsulat
to **consult** *73* hinzuziehen, zu Rate ziehen
consultation *100* Beratung
to **consume** *96* verbrauchen, konsumieren
consumer *26* Verbraucher/in
consumption *96* Verbrauch, Konsum
contactless *40* kontaktlos
to **contain** *35* enthalten
content *26* Inhalt
continual *63* ständig, ununterbrochen, kontinuierlich
contract *69* Vertrag; **~ of sale** *105* Kaufvertrag
to **contrast (with sth)** *97* gegenüberstehen, im Gegensatz stehen (zu etw)
to **contribute** *66* beitragen
contribution *66* Beitrag
convenience *16* Bequemlichkeit, Annehmlichkeit, Komfort
convenient *23* passend, praktisch, angenehm
to **cooperate** *51* kooperieren, zusammenarbeiten
cooperation *89* Zusammenarbeit, Zusammenwirken
to **cope** *63* zurechtkommen
core *43* Basis(-), Kern(-), Schwerpunkt(-); *96* Kern-, Haupt-
corner, round the ~ *68* um die Ecke
corporate customer *20T* Firmenkunde/Firmenkundin, Geschäftskunde/Geschäftskundin
corporate business *89* Firmenkunden
corporate client *10* Firmenkunde/Firmenkundin, Geschäftskunde/Geschäftskundin
corporation *95* Konzern
correspondence *110F* Briefwechsel, Korrespondenz
corresponding (to) *23* entsprechend, passend (zu)
cosmetics *(pl) 96* Kosmetikprodukte, Kosmetika
cottage *85* kleines Haus, Hütte
council *43* Rat
counter *8* (Verkaufs-, Bank-) Schalter
counterpart *66* Gegenstück, Pendant
country code *21* Ländervorwahl
coupon *73* Zinsschein, Genussschein
courteous *7* höflich

to **cover** *37* (be-, ab-)decken
cover *38* Deckung
covering letter *108* Anschreiben, Begleitschreiben
co-worker *27* Arbeitskollege/-kollegin
crackly *20T* knisternd
to **crash** *45* abstürzen (lassen)
to **create** *7* (er)schaffen, erstellen
creativity *91* schöpferische Begabung, Kreativität
to **credit** *19* gutschreiben
credit *8* Kredit; **~ balance** *90* Guthaben, Habensaldo; **~ interest** *(no pl) 33* Guthabenzins(en); **~ record** *76* Bonitätsauskunft; **~ reference** *86* Kreditauskunft; **~ slip** *35* Einzahlungsschein; **~ transfer** *33* Überweisung; **~-scoring** *76* Kreditwürdigkeitsbewertung; **letter of ~** *99* Akkreditiv; **line of ~** *91* Kreditlinie, Kreditrahmen
creditor *46* Gläubiger/n
creditworthiness *58* Kreditwürdigkeit
creditworthy *59* kreditwürdig
to **crew** *15* besetzen
crisis, *pl* **crises** *107* Krise
criterion, *pl* **criteria** *85* Kriterium
critical *27* entscheidend
crofter *BE 15* Kleinbauer/-bäuerin *(in Schottland)*
cross-border *43* grenzüberschreitend
crucial *7* äußerst wichtig, entscheidend
cultural *118* kulturell
cup of tea, … is not my ~ *16* … ist nicht mein Fall. / nach meinem Geschmack.
currency *10* Währung
current *34* derzeitig, aktuell
current account *16T* Girokonto
current assets *(pl) 90* Umlaufvermögen, -kapital
currently *85* derzeit, zurzeit, aktuell
customer, corporate ~ *20T* Firmenkunde/Firmenkundin, Geschäftskunde/Geschäftskundin; **~ service officer** *16* Kundenberater/in
customer service *6* Kundenberatung
customer service representative *6* Kundenberater/in, Kundenservice-Vertreter/in
to **customize** *84T (individuell)* anpassen, zuschneiden, einrichten
CV (= curriculum vitae) *BE 108* Lebenslauf

cycle *91* Zyklus, Kreislauf

D

to **damage** *83* (be)schädigen, schaden
damage *26* Schaden
dash *20T* Gedankenstrich
database *113* Datenbank
date of expiry *104* Verfallsdatum, Ablaufdatum
daunting *27* einschüchternd, entmutigend, beängstigend
day-to-day *13* tagtäglich
to **deal, ~ in** *76* handeln mit; **~ with** *7* sich beschäftigen mit, sich kümmern um, umgehen mit
debenture *107* Obligation
to **debit** *19* belasten
debit *49* Lastschrift, Abbuchung; **~ card** *30* Bankkarte, ec-Karte
debt *54* Schuld(en); **in ~** *83* verschuldet
debtor *90* Schuldner/in
debut *97* Debüt
decade *33* Jahrzehnt
decision-maker *25* Entscheidungsträger
to **decline** *59* ablehnen; *70* zurückgehen, fallen, sinken
decline *70* Rückgang
to **decrease** *37* senken, reduzieren; sinken, abnehmen
to **deduct** *49* abbuchen; *81T* abziehen
to **default** *60* zahlungsunfähig werden
deficit, trade ~ *98* Handelsdefizit, Handelsbilanzdefizit
defined *66* festgelegt
definitely *54* bestimmt, sicher, definitiv
degree *8* Grad, Abschluss, Diplom
to **deliver** *26* überbringen, liefern
delivery *27* Zustellung, (Aus-) Lieferung
demand (for) *7* Forderung (nach), Bedarf (an), Nachfrage (an), Anforderung; **on ~** *38* auf Verlangen
to **demonstrate** *84T* vorstellen, vorführen
denominated in euros *43* in Euro ausgewiesen, auf Euro lautend
department *8* Abteilung
dependable *7* zuverlässig, verlässlich
to **depict** *39* darstellen, aufzeigen
to **deposit** *39* *(Geld)* einzahlen
deposit *9* Einzahlung; **cash ~** *74* Bareinlage; **time ~ account** *39* Festgeldkonto
derivative *107* Derivat
description *30* Beschreibung, Schilderung
to **designate** *31* benennen, bestimmen
despite *66* trotz
destination *103* Bestimmungsort
details *pl* *24* Angaben
to **determine** *27* ermitteln, feststellen
to **devastate** *96* zerstören, verwüsten
to **develop** *43* (sich) entwickeln
development *51* Entwicklung
to **dictate** *21* diktieren
differentiation *26* Differenzierung, Abgrenzung
to **diffuse** *27* zerstreuen
to **dig** *52* graben
digit *21* Ziffer
to **dilute** *95T* verdünnen, abschwächen
direct debit *30* Einzugsermächtigung, Lastschrift(verfahren)
directed, self-~ *26* selbstgesteuert
director *63* Geschäftsführer/in, Chef/in
disadvantage *25* Nachteil, Schaden
disappointed (with sb/sth) *18* enttäuscht (von jdm/etw)
disaster *69* Katastrophe, Unglück, Desaster
discharge *103* Entladung, Löschen
to **disclose** *48* offenlegen, mitteilen
discount *38* Rabatt, Skonto, Nachlass
discretion *109* Diskretion
disguise *27* Verkleidung, Tarnung
dish, satellite ~ *15* Satellitenschüssel
to **dislike** *101* nicht mögen
disorganized *91* chaotisch
to **dispatch** *99* versenden, (aus) liefern
disposable income *81T* verfügbares Einkommen
to **dispose of** *82* verfügen über
disruptive *26* (zer)störend, zerreißend
dissatisfied *18* unzufrieden
diversified *69* diversifiziert, gefächert, gestreut
to **divide up** *71* unterteilen
dividend *94* Dividende
documentary credit *87* Akkreditiv
domestic *105* Inlands-, inländisch
doorstep *15* Tür(schwelle)
dot *20T* Punkt, Pünktchen
to **double** *82* (sich) verdoppeln
to **doubt** *100* bezweifeln
down *45* außer Betrieb **ups and ~s** *63* Höhen und Tiefen; **to be ~ to sb** *37* jds Sache sein, jds Aufgabe sein; **to get ~ to business** *17* zur Sache kommen
down under *53* in/nach Australien
downtime *AE* *96* Freizeit, Auszeit
downturn *71* Kursrückgang
dozen *76* Dutzend
draft *104* Wechsel, Tratte
drastic *70* drastisch
to **draw** *46* einziehen
drawback *15* Nachteil
drawer, cash ~ *14T* Kassenlade
dreadful *17* schrecklich, furchtbar
dress code *6* Kleiderordnung
drive *109* Antrieb, Tatkraft, Energie
driving licence *32* Führerschein
to **drop** *49* fallen (lassen), verlieren
dual *8* Doppel-, doppelt, dual
due *45* fällig
due date *45* Fälligkeit(sdatum)
due to *26* wegen, aufgrund (von)
dumps, in the ~ *(infml)* *75* im Keller
duty *14T* Aufgabe, Pflicht
to **dwindle** *15* schwinden, nachlassen

E

to **earn** *62* verdienen, erwerben
earnings *(pl)* *66* Einkünfte, Verdienst
eco-friendly *70* umweltfreundlich
economic *43* wirtschaftlich, Wirtschafts-
economical *66* sparsam, wirtschaftlich
economics *(pl)* *59* (Volks-)Wirtschaft, Wirtschaftskunde
economies, emerging market ~ *(pl)* *98* Schwellenländer
economy *82* Wirtschaft, Volkswirtschaft
edition, limited ~ *39* limitierte Auflage/Serie
to **educate** *25* erziehen
education *83* Ausbildung
educational *108* Erziehungs-, Bildungs-
either, not ... ~ *16* auch nicht
electricity *43* Strom, Elektrizität
elevator *AE* *10* Lift, Aufzug
embarrassing *91* peinlich, unangenehm
embassy *118* Botschaft
to **embed** *51* integrieren, einbetten, einbauen
emergence *26* Entstehen, Aufkommen
emergency *48* Notfall, Not-

emerging market economies *(pl)* 98 Schwellenländer
emerging markets *(pl)* 69 Schwellenländer
to **empathize** 27 sich einfühlen
emphasis 88 Betonung, Schwerpunkt, Akzent
to **employ** 113 beschäftigen, einstellen *(Personal)*
employee 6 Angestellte/r, Arbeitnehmer/in
employer 7 Arbeitgeber/in
employment opportunities 14T Berufschancen
to **enable** 30 ermöglichen, befähigen
to **enclose** 29 beifügen, beilegen
enclosure, encl. 89 Anlage *(Brief)*
to **encounter sth** 15 auf etw stoßen/treffen
to **encourage** 64 ermuntern, fördern, unterstützen
encrypted 48 verschlüsselt
to **endorse** 105 indossieren
endowment insurance 77 Kapitalversicherung
energetic 91 energisch, kraftvoll
engaged 20T besetzt *(Telefon)*
engaging 26 fesselnd, spannend; verbindlich
to **enquire (about)** 100 fragen, sich erkundigen (nach/wegen)
enquiry 13 Anfrage
to **enrol** 36 (sich) eintragen, (sich) registrieren
enrolment 36 Registrierung
to **ensure** 63 sicherstellen
enterprise 91 Unternehmen, Unternehmung
entertainment 38 Unterhaltung
enthusiastic 109 begeistert
to **entice** 39 locken
entire 49 gesamte/r/s, ganz, vollständig
entrepreneur 95 Unternehmer/in
entry 8 Eintritt, Zutritt, Einstieg; 35 Buchung; **~-level** 14T Einstiegs-, Anfangs-; **(at) ~ level** 8 (auf) Einstiegsniveau
environmental 33 Umwelt-
equal 54 gleich
to **equip** 15 ausrüsten, ausstatten
equipment 78 Ausrüstung
equivalent 8 entsprechend; 27 Äquivalent, Gegenstück
era 39 Ära, Epoche
essence, in ~ 27 im Grunde genommen
essential 6 wesentlich
to **estimate** 51 schätzen
ethnic group 103 Volksgruppe
evaluation 116T Auswertung, Bewertung
event, in the ~ of 51 im Falle
eventuality 84T Möglichkeit, Eventualität
eventually 63 letztendlich, schließlich
to **evoke** 27 auslösen, hervorrufen
to **evolve** 26 sich weiter entwickeln
exam 112 Prüfung
to **exceed** 33 überschreiten
exception 70 Ausnahme
excess 75 Überschuss
to **exchange** 109 austauschen, eintauschen, umtauschen
exchange, bill of ~ 99 Wechsel
excited 39 (freudig) aufgeregt, begeistert
exclusive 110 exklusiv
excuse 15 Ausrede
executive 12 leitend, Vorstands-, Führungs-; **chief ~ (officer), CEO** 63 Geschäftsführer/in, Vorstandsvorsitzende/r
exemption, application for tax ~ 72 Freistellungsantrag
to **exercise** 97 ausüben
to **exist** 15 existieren
to **expand** 91 expandieren, (sich) erweitern, (sich) vergrößern
expansion 95T Ausweitung, Expansion
expat *(infml)* 87 Auswanderer/in
expectation 26 Erwartung; to **meet ~s** 97 Erwartungen erfüllen
expenditure 53 Ausgabe
expenses *(pl)* 29 Kosten, Auslagen
to **experience** 44T erleben, erfahren
experience 26 Erfahrung, Erlebnis
expiry, date of ~ 104 Verfallsdatum, Ablaufdatum
explanation 34 Erläuterung, Erklärung
exporter 99 Exporteur/in
to **expose** 26 aussetzen, zeigen
to **express** 17 ausdrücken, äußern, zum Ausdruck bringen
expression 8 Ausdruck
to **extend** 78 erweitern, ausdehnen
extension (number) 20T Durchwahl *(Telefon)*

F

to **face** 27 gegenüber stehen
face-to-face 14T persönlich
facilities *(pl)* 15 Einrichtungen
factory 96 Fabrik
factual 111 sachlich
to **fail** 60 (es) nicht schaffen, scheitern
failed attempt 48 fehlgeschlagener Versuch, Fehlversuch
faith 107 Glaube; **as a matter of ~** 107 aus Glaubensgründen
faithfully, Yours ~ 89 Mit freundlichen Grüßen
familiar 116F vertraut
to **fancy sth** 51 auf etw Lust haben
fantastic 39 fantastisch
to **fascinate** 10 faszinieren
fault 19 Fehler, Schuld; to **be at ~** 27 im Unrecht sein, schuldig sein
favour, in ~ of 102 zugunsten
favourable 23 günstig, vorteilhaft
feature 26 Merkmal, Eigenschaft, Kennzeichen
fee 18 Entgelt, Gebühr; **membership ~** 43 Mitgliedsbeitrag
feet, to **think on your ~** 109 schnell reagieren
fellow 83 Mit-, andere
fellow student 44 Mitschüler/in
female 51 Frau; weiblich
fighter pilot 96 Jagdflieger
file 78 Datei, Ordner, Akte
to **fill in** 10 eintragen, ausfüllen
final 44T endgültig, abschließend
to **finance** 87 finanzieren
financial 16T finanziell; **~ services provider** 26 Finanzdienstleister
findings *(pl)* 68 Ergebnisse
fine art 85 schöne Künste, bildende Kunst
finished 90 fertiggestellt
first floor 12 *(GB)* erste Etage, erster Stock, *(US)* Erdgeschoss
fiscal 75 finanzpolitisch, Steuer-
fit, to **throw a ~** 27 einen Anfall haben, durchdrehen
to **fix (a time / a date / an appointment)** 17 (eine Uhrzeit / ein Datum / einen Termin) festlegen, vereinbaren
fixed 13 fest, festgelegt, Fest-
to **fizzle** 97 im Sande verlaufen, missglücken
fizzy drink 96 Erfrischungsgetränk (mit Kohlensäure)
to **flag up sth** 63 auf etw aufmerksam machen
flatly 45 rundweg, entschieden
flaw 27 Schwachstelle, Fehler, Mangel
flawed 27 fehlerhaft, mangelhaft
fleet 15 Flotte
flexibility 30 Flexibilität
to **flog** *(infml)* 75 verscherbeln, verramschen
floor, first ~ 12 *(GB)* erste Etage, erster Stock, *(US)* Erdgeschoss;

~ **plan** *9* Grundriss, Lageplan; **ground ~** *9* Erdgeschoss
to **fluctuate** *68* fluktuieren, schwanken
fluctuation *69* Schwankung
fluent *70* fließend
flyer *41* Flugblatt, Flyer
to **focus (on)** *87* sich konzentrieren (auf)
follow-through *7* (konsequente) Durchführung
follow-up *17* Anschlusstermin
forbearance *63* Nachsicht, Geduld
to **forbid** *118* verbieten, untersagen
forecast *70* Vorhersage
foreign *8* ausländisch, Auslands-, fremd; ~ **trade** *98* Außenhandel
to **forge** *48* fälschen
forgery *49* Fälschung
formal *113* formell, förmlich
formality *82* Formalität
formula *86* Formel
fortune *78* Vermögen
to **forward** *102* senden, befördern, weiterleiten
forward, to **look ~ to (doing sth)** *8* sich darauf freuen (etw zu tun)
forwarding agent *105* Spediteur/in
to **found** *25* gründen
frame, time ~ *59* Zeitrahmen
framework *43* Rahmen, Rahmenbedingungen
fraud *49* Betrug
free of charge *18* gebührenfrei
freezing *19* eisig, eiskalt
freight forwarder *100* Spediteur/in, Spedition
frequent *53* häufig, oft
frequently asked questions (FAQ) *36* häufig gestellte Fragen
front-row *39* in vorderster Reihe
frustrating *18* frustrierend
to **fulfil** *85* erfüllen
fully *19* völlig, vollkommen
fund *13* Fonds, Fundus
fund of funds *69* Dachfonds
fundamental *91* wesentlich, grundsätzlich
futures *(pl)* *107* Termingeschäfte

G

to **gain** *27* erwerben, gewinnen, sammeln
gain *68* Gewinn, Vorteil
gambling *75* Glücksspiel
gap *84T* Lücke
GCSE (= General Certificate of Secondary Education) *110F* Prüfung für Schüler ab 15, mittlerer Schulabschluss
generalist *10* Generalist/in, Allrounder
generation *26* Generation
to **get sth** *10* etw verstehen, mitbekommen
to **get by** *83* auskommen *(mit Geld)*, über die Runden kommen
giant *51* Riese
gift *39* Geschenk
gimmick *52* Schnickschnack, Spielerei; (Werbe-)Trick
gist *75* das Wesentliche
to **give notice** *65* ankündigen; kündigen
to **give up** *97* aufgeben, abgeben
glad, to **be ~** *11* sich freuen, froh sein
glance, at a ~ *108* auf einen Blick
glue *100* Klebstoff, Leim
GMT (Greenwich Mean Time) *37* mittlere Greenwich-Zeit *(koordinierte Weltzeit)*
to **go on** *8* passieren, geschehen, los sein
to **go public** *97* an die Börse gehen
goal *116F* Ziel
Goodness no! *100* Um Himmels willen!
goods *(pl)* *30* Güter, Ware(n)
government *39* Regierung; ~ **bonds** *(pl)* *73* Staatsanleihen
to **grab** *49* packen, greifen, *sich* etw schnappen
grace period *38* Schonzeit, Karenzzeit
gradual *71* schrittweise, allmählich
to **graduate** *16* den Abschluss machen, sein Examen machen
graduate *84T* Absolvent/in
to **grant** *82* bewilligen
graph *51* Diagramm, Kurve
grateful *89* dankbar
gratification *39* Befriedigung, Genugtuung
groceries *(pl)* *59* Lebensmittel
gross *66* brutto
ground floor *9* Erdgeschoss
group, target ~ *51* Zielgruppe
growth *69* Wachstum
to **guarantee** *66* garantieren
guarantee *37* Garantie
guarantor loan *83* Bürgschaftskredit
guideline *6* Richtlinie

H

habit *116T* Gewohnheit
to **hack** *44T* hacken
hairy *39* haarig, brenzlig
hand, to **shake ~s** *116T* sich die Hand geben, die Hände schütteln
to **hand out** *14T* aushändigen, herausgeben
to **hand over** *39* übergeben, überantworten
to **handle** *7* umgehen mit, handhaben
handout *43* Flugblatt, Merkblatt
handshake *116T* Händedruck
handy, to **come in ~** *16* sich als nützlich erweisen, gelegen kommen
to **hang on** *10* warten, dranbleiben *(Telefon)*
hardly *70* kaum
hassle *49* Ungelegenheiten, Stress
hawkish *75* einen harten Kurs vertretend
to **head** *53* *(in Richtung von etw)* gehen, fahren
head *63* Leiter/in; ~ **office** *8* Zentrale, Hauptstelle
heading *6* Überschrift
headquarters, *pl* **headquarters** *10* Zentrale, Hauptsitz
hefty *30* satt, saftig *(Betrag)*
to **hesitate** *29* zögern
high *68* Hoch
high street bank *37* Großbank
to **highlight** *27* hervorheben, markieren
highly *8* höchst, äußerst
to **hire** *8* mieten, leihen
hire purchase *81T* Ratenkauf
history *58* Geschichte *(vergangene Zeiten)*
to **hold the line** *20T* am Apparat bleiben
holder, account ~ *31* Kontoinhaber/in
home, mobile ~ *81T* (großer) Wohnwagen, Wohnmobil
honest *7* ehrlich, aufrichtig
honesty *7* Ehrlichkeit
horrible *116T* fürchterlich
hospitality *87* Gastfreundschaft
household *39* Haushalt, Haushalts-
huge *63* gewaltig, riesig
Human Resources Manager *116* Personalleiter/in
to **hunt** *39* jagen
hyphen *21* Bindestrich, Trennstrich

I

i.e. *58* d.h.
ID card *38* Ausweis
identical *105* identisch
identification *20* Identifizierung, Nennung des Namens

identifier *45* Kennung, Identifikationsnummer
to **identify** *20* identifizieren, nennen
identity *54* Identität; **~ card** *16T* Personalausweis
to **ignore** *107* hinwegsehen über, ignorieren
ill, taken ~ *45* erkrankt
immediate *30* sofortig, sofort, umgehend
immigration *118* Einwanderung
impact (on) *6* (Aus-)Wirkung, Folge
impassive *96* unbewegt
implicit *103* implizit, stillschweigend
to **imply** *26* beinhalten, implizieren
importer *99* Importeur/in
to **impress** *6* beeindrucken
impression *6* Eindruck
improvement *23* Verbesserung
in full *60* in voller Höhe, vollständig
inaccurate *27* ungenau, unrichtig
inappropriate *6* ungeeignet, unpassend, unangemessen
Inc. (= incorporated) *68* (als Kapitalgesellschaft) eingetragen
incapacitated *31* arbeitsunfähig, außer Gefecht
incentive *39* Anreiz, Bonus
to **include** *6* einbeziehen, einschließen
income *39* Einkommen; **disposable ~** *81T* verfügbares Einkommen
incompetent *91* inkompetent, unfähig
inconvenience *19* Unannehmlichkeit(en)
Incoterm *98 Internationale Handelsklausel*
to **increase** *26* steigen, zunehmen; erhöhen
increasingly *26* zunehmend, in zunehmendem Maße
incremental *109* schrittweise
to **incur** *fml* *93* anfallen lassen *(Gebühren)*
incurred, to **be ~** *38* anfallen
indeed *15* in der Tat, wirklich
independent *26* unabhängig
in-depth *63* ausführlich
to **indicate** *31* anzeigen, angeben
indirect *103* indirekt
individual *64* einzeln, individuell; *76* Einzelne/r, Individuum
industrial *96* industriell, Industrie-
inequality *66* Ungleichheit
inevitable *75* unvermeidlich, unvermeidbar
inexperienced *73* unerfahren
infected *51* infiziert
influence *89* Einfluss
influencer *26* Einflussnehmer/in
to **inherit** *84T* erben
initial charge *69* Ausgabeaufschlag, Agio
initial(ly) *8* erste(r, s), Anfangs-, anfänglich
ink cartridge *14T* Tintenpatrone
innovation *26* Innovation, Neuerung
to **inquire (into)** *63* untersuchen, erkunden
inquiry *63* Untersuchung, Nachforschung
to **insert** *49* einführen, (hin) einstecken
insight (into) *118* Einblick (in), Verständnis (von)
to **insist** *15* darauf bestehen, beteuern
to **install** *85* einbauen, einrichten, aufbauen
instalment *43* Rate
instant *39* sofortig, unmittelbar
instead of *39* anstelle von, (an) statt
institution *43* Institution
institutional *97* institutionell
instructions *pl* *36* Anleitung, Anweisung(en)
insurance *8* Versicherung; **endowment ~** *77* Kapitalversicherung; **~ premium** *43* Versicherungsbeitrag, -prämie
to **insure** *22* versichern
to **integrate** *51* integrieren
to **intend** *73* beabsichtigen
intention *75* Absicht. Intention
interaction *26* Interaktion
interest *27* Interesse; *39* Zins; **~ rate** *34* Zinssatz; **credit ~** *(no pl)* *33* Guthaben-zins(en); **~-only loan** *77* endfälliges Darlehen
internship *35* Praktikum
interpersonal *8* zwischenmenschlich
to **interview** *86* befragen, interviewen
intrinsic *107* immanent, eigentlich
to **introduce sb to sb/sth** *9* jdm jdn/etw vorstellen
introduction *116* Einleitung, Einführung, Vorstellung
introductory offer *60* Einführungsangebot
invaluable *118* unbezahlbar, von unschätzbarem Wert
to **invent** *21* erfinden
to **invest** *10* anlegen, investieren
to **investigate** *63* untersuchen
investigation *63* Forschung, Untersuchung
investment *6* Anlage, Investition
investment bank *13* Anlagebank, Investitionsbank
investment fund *13* Investmentfonds
invitation *89* Einladung
to **invoice** *59* berechnen, in Rechnung stellen
invoice *50* Rechnung; **commercial ~** *100* Handelsrechnung
to **involve** *37* (mit) betreffen, (mit) einbeziehen
IPO (initial public offering) *97* Börsengang, Erstemission
irate *27* zornig, wütend
irreparable *26* irreparabel
irrevocable *102* unwiderruflich
IRS (= Internal Revenue Service) *39 US-Finanzbehörde*
Islamic *107* islamisch
issuance charge *104* Ausstellungsgebühr
to **issue** *46* ausgeben, ausstellen
issue *9* (Streit-)Frage, Thema
issuer, (card) ~ *76* Kartenunternehmen, (Karten-)Aussteller
italics, in ~ *101* kursiv (gedruckt)
item *29* Artikel, Gegenstand, Punkt

J

jewellery *6* Schmuck
job advertisement *109* Stellenanzeige, -ausschreibung
jobsite *118 Internetauftritt, auf dem Stellen angeboten werden*
joint *81* gemeinschaftlich, gemeinsam
joint account *30* Gemeinschaftskonto
jokingly *39* scherzhaft
journey *40* Fahrt, Reise
junior *78* Junioren-, Nachwuchs-
to **justify** *16* begründen, rechtfertigen

K

kayaking *78* Kajakfahren
keen *8* (sehr) interessiert, begeistert
to **keep track of** *61* verfolgen
to **keep up (with)** *59* Schritt halten (mit)
to **key in** *14T* eingeben, eintippen
key pad *48* Eingabefeld, Tastatur
keyboard *16* Tastatur, Keyboard
kick-off *97* Anstoß, Start
killer, a real ~ *59* mörderisch
kind (of) *10* Art
kit, welcome ~ *38* Begrüßungspaket

knee *16* Knie
to **knock, ~ (on)** *60* anklopfen (an); **~ sth into shape** *96* etw auf Vordermann bringen
knowledge *69* Wissen, Kenntnis(se)

L
lack (of) *15* Mangel (an), Fehlen (von)
lading, bill of ~ *100* Konnossement
land register *79* Grundbuch
land charge *85* Grundschuld
landline *21* Festnetz
largely *82* weitgehend, überwiegend
lately *70* neulich, in letzter Zeit
latterly *96* in letzter Zeit, am Ende
to **launch** *51* *(Produkt)* auf den Markt bringen, einführen
to **lay blame** *27* Schuld zuweisen
to **lead (to)** *14T* führen (zu), leiten
leaflet *48* Broschüre, Merkblatt
leak *51* Leck, undichte Stelle
to **leap** *68* springen
leather *96* Leder
to **leave a message** *20T* eine Nachricht hinterlassen
leave, maternity ~ *71* Mutterschaftsurlaub
legal *43* gesetzlich, juristisch, legal
lender *83* Kreditgeber/in
length *114* Länge, Dauer
letter, covering ~ *108* Anschreiben, Begleitschreiben; **~ of credit** *99* Akkreditiv
level, entry-~ *14T* Einstiegs-, Anfangs-
liabilities *(pl)* *90* Passiva, Verbindlichkeiten
liability *95* Haftung
liable *83* haftbar
life assurance *64* Lebensversicherung
lifetime, holiday of a ~ *77* einmaliger Urlaub
light, in the ~ of *51* angesichts
likely *33* wahrscheinlich, geeignet
limited *12* begrenzt, beschränkt; **~ edition** *39* limitierte Auflage/Serie; **Ltd (private ~ company)** *(UK)* *95* *entspricht* Gesellschaft mit beschränkter Haftung (GmbH)
line, ~ of credit *91* Kreditlinie, Kreditrahmen; to **hold the ~** *20T* am Apparat bleiben; **~ manager** *17* (direkte/r) Vorgesetzte/r; to **stand/wait in ~ (for)** *AE* *9* Schlange stehen, sich anstellen (für/nach)
link, navigation ~ *29* (Navigations-)Link, Hyperlink
liquid *75* flüssig, liquide
liquidity *86* Liquidität
living expenses *(pl)* *81T* Lebenshaltungskosten
LLP (= limited liability partnership) *95* Personengesellschaft
to **load** *105* verladen, laden, füllen
loading *103* Verladung; **port of ~** *103* Verladehafen
loan *7* Darlehen, Kredit; **guarantor ~** *83* Bürgschaftskredit; **interest-only ~** *77* endfälliges Darlehen; **~ application** *77* Kreditantrag, Darlehensantrag)
lobby *9* Eingangshalle, Vorraum
to **locate** *51* ausfindig machen, orten, lokalisieren
located *27* gelegen
location *109* Standort, Ort
to **lock** *48* sperren
to **lodge money** *38* Geld einlegen
to **log in** *35* sich einloggen
logbook loan *83* Pfandkredit *(bei dem ein Kfz das Pfand darstellt)*
logical order *17* logische Reihenfolge
lonely *16* einsam
long, a ~ way off *73* (noch) ein weiter Weg
long-standing *63* langjährig, schon lange bestehend
long-term *69* langfristig
to **look forward to (doing sth)** *8* sich darauf freuen (etw zu tun)
look, to **take a ~ (at sth)** *10* (sich) (etw) ansehen, betrachten
to **look after** *10* sich kümmern um, betreuen
loose *75* locker
loss *49* Verlust
lot *75* Menge, Haufen
lower case *21* kleingeschrieben
loyalty *7* Treue, Loyalität
Ltd (private limited company) *(UK)* *95* *entspricht* Gesellschaft mit beschränkter Haftung (GmbH)
luckily *16* glücklicherweise, zum Glück
lucrative *39* lukrativ
lump sum *69* Einmalzahlung, Pauschale; **~ repayment** *93* einmalige Rückzahlung
lure *63* Verlockung
luxury *59* Luxus

M
m (= million) *63* Million
machine, cash ~ *9* Geldautomat
machinery *90* Maschinen, Geräte
magnetic strip *49* Magnetstreifen
to **mail** *39* (zu)schicken, (zu) senden, mailen
mail, via regular ~ *33* auf dem Postweg
mailing shot *63* Werbesendung
mainly *81T* hauptsächlich, vor allem
mainstream *83* konventionell, regulär
to **maintain** *7* aufrecht erhalten
maintenance *14T* Wartung, Instandhaltung; **~ payment** *81T* Unterhaltungszahlung
major *51* bedeutend, wichtig
majority *15* größter Teil, Mehrheit
to **make sense** *55* sinnvoll sein
to **make an impact** *6* einen Eindruck hinterlassen
to **make ends meet** *83* über die Runden kommen
male *66* Mann; männlich
malicious *51* bösartig
to **manage** *16* (es) schaffen
management, personnel ~ *110F* Personalmanagement
management fee *69* Verwaltungsgebühr
managerial *14T* Management-, Führungs-; **~ assistant** *110F* Führungsassistent
mandate, (third party) ~ *31* Vollmacht
manifestation *15* Manifestation, Erscheinungsform
manner *27* Art (und Weise); *110F* Umgangsform(en)
to **manufacture** *96* herstellen, produzieren
map *42* Landkarte, Stadtplan
to **mark** *61* kennzeichnen, markieren, angeben
to **market** *63* vermarkten
market, emerging ~ economies *(pl)* *98* Schwellenländer; **stock ~** *64* (Wertpapier-)Börse
marketing *63* Marketing, Vermarktung
marketplace *91* Markt
masses *(pl)* *78* Massen, Mengen
maternity leave *71* Mutterschaftsurlaub
matter *7* Angelegenheit, Sache; **as a ~ of faith** *107* aus Glaubensgründen; **no ~ how** *7* (ganz) egal, wie
to **mature** *73* fällig werden
maturity *107* Fälligkeit
meager *AE*, **meagre** *BE* *97* mager, dürftig
meaningful *79* sinnvoll
meantime, in the ~ *49* in der Zwischenzeit

median 66 mittlere/r/s, durchschnittlich
medicine 96 Medikament(e), Medizin
medium-sized 87 mittelgroß
to **meet** 97 erfüllen
membership, ~ fee 43 Mitgliedsbeitrag; **photographic ~ card** 38 Lichtbild-Mitgliedsausweis
memorable 36 einprägsam
merger 87 Fusion
messing, no ~ (about ...) 61 locker (ohne ...)
meticulous 7 sorgfältig, gewissenhaft, gründlich
Middle Eastern 91 aus dem nahen Osten
mind, peace of ~ 77 Sicherheit, innere Ruhe; **would you ~ ...** 20T könnten Sie bitte ...
minimum payment 58 Mindestzahlung
minus 21 Minus(zeichen)
minuscule 75 unbedeutend, winzig
to **mirror** 75 (wider)spiegeln
to **miss a payment** 37 eine Zahlung versäumen
miss the boat 51 den Anschluss verpassen
to **miss off** 42 auslassen, nicht aufführen
to **mistrust** 75 misstrauen
misunderstanding 19 Missverständnis
to **misuse** 53 missbrauchen
misuse 40 Missbrauch
mobile 15 mobil, beweglich; **~ home** 81T Wohnmobil
mobility 26 Beweglichkeit, Mobilität
mode 105 Modus, Art
model 82 Muster-
monetary 14T finanziell, Geld-
money box 16 Spardose
monthly 33 monatlich
mortgage 43 Hypothek, Hypothekendarlehen
motivated 111 motiviert
motorhead 96 Autonarr
mouth, word of ~ 26 Mundpropaganda
move, on the ~ 25 auf Achse, in Bewegung
movie 39 Film
multi-modal transport 105 kombinierte Beförderung, multimodaler Transport
multiple 63 mehrere, vielfach
muscle 96 Muskel
Muslim 107 muslimisch; Moslem, Muslima
My pleasure. 116T Es ist mir ein Vergnügen. *(höfliche Erwiderung)*

N

nail varnish 6 Nagellack
nasty 60 Gemeinheit
native speaker 88 Muttersprachler/in
navigation link 29 (Navigations-) Link, Hyperlink
neat 6 ordentlich, elegant, adrett
necessary 7 nötig, erforderlich
necessity 38 Notwendigkeit
to **need to do sth** 7 etw tun müssen
negotiable 105 übertragbar
negotiation 87 Verhandlung, Vermittlung
net 63 Netz; 81T netto, Netto-
networker 118 Netzwerker/in
nevertheless 15 trotzdem, dennoch
new entrant 37 Neueinsteiger
no., *pl* **nos.** 50 Nr.
nominal value 107 Nominalwert
not at all 20T keine Ursache
not necessarily 69 nicht unbedingt
note 61 Geldschein, Banknote
notice account 65 Konto mit Kündigung(sfrist), Termingeldkonto
to **notify** 37 benachrichtigen, mitteilen
nowadays 9 heutzutage
to **nudge** 75 schubsen, anstoßen
to **number** 34 nummerieren
number, serial ~ 49 Seriennummer

O

obliged, to **be ~ to do sth** 39 etw tun müssen
observation 63 Beobachtung
to **obtain** 49 erhalten, bekommen
obvious 53 offensichtlich
to **occur** 116T vorfallen, geschehen
off you go! 61 los geht's!
to **offend sb** 103 jdn beleidigen, verletzen; jdm zu nahe treten
offer, introductory ~ 60 Einführungsangebot
office, head ~ 8 Zentrale, Hauptstelle
officer, customer service ~ 16 Kundenberater/in
official 63 offiziell
oh 21 Null *(im gesprochenen Englisch)*
olds, sixteen-year-~ *(pl)* 40 Sechzehnjährige
to **omit** 90 auslassen, weglassen
one-off 52T einmalig
ongoing 59 laufend
onwards 44T an
opening hours *(pl)* 82 Geschäftszeiten, Öffnungszeiten
to **operate** 63 arbeiten, in Betrieb sein, funktionieren
opportunities, employment ~ *(pl)* 14T Berufschancen
opportunity 27 Gelegenheit
oral 110F mündlich
to **order** 46 anweisen
order, logical ~ 17 logische Reihenfolge; to **place an ~** 100 eine Bestellung aufgeben
ordinary 75 gewöhnlich, normal
organizational 43 organisatorisch
orientated 111 orientiert, ausgerichtet
orientation 118 Orientierung
origin, certificate of ~ 100 Ursprungszeugnis
otherwise 15 ansonsten, andernfalls
outcome 27 Ergebnis, Resultat
to **outline** 63 skizzieren, beschreiben, darstellen
outlook 68 Zukunftsaussichten
outrageous 27 empörend, schockierend, unerhört
outstanding 59 ausstehend
overall 33 Gesamt-
overdraft 20T Kontoüberziehung
overdraft facility 30 Dispositionskredit
to **overdraw** 33 überziehen
overdrawn, go ~ 24 überziehen, ins Minus geraten
overdressed 6 zu elegant gekleidet
overnight 76 über Nacht, Nacht-
overseas 94 Auslands-
to **overstretch** 95T überfordern
overview 62 Überblick, Übersicht
to **owe** 54 schulden

P

packaging 96 Verpackung
packing list 100 Packliste, Packzettel
painful 37 schmerzhaft
painting 85 Bild, Gemälde
paltry 75 armselig, erbärmlich
panel 116T Gremium, Ausschuss
panic 49 Panik
paperless 33 papierlos
paperwork 15 Büroarbeit, Schreibarbeit
parallel, in ~ 26 nebeneinander
part, to **take ~ (in)** 37 teilnehmen (an)
partial shipment 104 Teillieferung
participant 43 Teilnehmer/in

to **participate (in)** *37* teilnehmen (an), sich beteiligen (an)
particular *69* besonders, speziell
particularly *16* besonders
partly *19* teils, teilweise
party, (third ~) mandate *31* Vollmacht
to **pass away** *77* sterben
patience *27* Geduld
patient *7* geduldig
to **pay (close) attention (to)** *7* (genau) aufpassen, achten (auf)
to **pay in** *14T* einzahlen, einlösen
to **pay off** *58* tilgen
pay slip *81T* Gehaltsabrechnung
payable *90* fällig
payday *63* Zahltag
payday loan *82* Kurzzeitkredit
payee *41* Zahlungsempfänger/in
payment *13* (Be-)Zahlung; **maintenance ~** *81T* Unterhaltungszahlung; **minimum ~** *58* Mindestzahlung; to **miss a ~** *37* eine Zahlung versäumen
peace of mind *77* Sicherheit, innere Ruhe
peer *26* Gleichaltrige/r, Altersgenosse
to **penalize** *23* bestrafen
penalized *16T* bestraft
penalty *16T* Strafe
pension *66* Rente
people skills *pl* *7* soziale Kompetenz
per *39* pro
per annum *109* pro Jahr
percentage *53* Anteil, Prozentsatz
to **perform** *70* abschneiden, Leistung bringen, Erträge erzielen
performance *70* Leistung; Abschneiden
period, grace ~ *38* Schonzeit, Karenzzeit
permanent *31* ständig, fest, dauerhaft
permission *33* Erlaubnis
permit, work ~ *118* Arbeitserlaubnis
permitted *107* erlaubt, gestattet
personal customer *8* Privatkunde/-kundin
personal loan *76* Kleinkredit, Privatkredit
personality *111* Persönlichkeit
to **personalize** *15* persönlich/individuell gestalten
personnel management *110F* Personalmanagement
perspective *27* Perspektive, Blickwinkel
to **persuade** *84T* überzeugen
pertinent *27* sachdienlich, relevant
pervasive *26* um sich greifend, durchdringend
photographic membership card *38* Lichtbild-Mitgliedsausweis
phrase *7* (Rede-)Wendung, Ausdruck
physical *107* materiell, konkret
to **place, ~ an order** *100* eine Bestellung aufgeben
place, to **put yourself in sb's ~** *27* sich in jds Lage versetzen; to **take ~** *14T* stattfinden
placement, work ~ *24* Praktikum
plan, floor ~ *9* Grundriss, Lageplan
plane spotter *96* Flugzeugbeobachter/in *(Hobby)*
plastics *(pl)* *96* Kunststoff(e)
PLC (= public limited company) *(UK)* *95* Aktiengesellschaft, AG
pleased *17* erfreut
pleasure, My ~. *116T* Es ist mir ein Vergnügen.
to **pledge** *85* pfänden
pledge *85* Pfand
to **plunge** *70* fallen, stürzen
point, bullet ~ *115* Stichpunkt
point of sale *48* Verkaufsstelle
police station *49* Polizeiwache, Polizeirevier
policy *64* (Versicherungs-)Police
poll *108* Umfrage
to **pool** *69* zusammenlegen, bündeln
to **pop out** *49* herauskommen, herausspringen
popularity *15* Beliebtheit, Popularität
pork *107* Schweinefleisch
port *103* Hafen; **~ of loading** *103* Verladehafen
portfolio *69* Depot, Wertpapierbestand, Portfolio
to **pose** *96* darstellen, posieren
to **possess** *33* besitzen
possession *90* Besitz, Besitztum
possibility *101* Möglichkeit
to **postpone** *23* verschieben
potential *51* potenziell, möglich, künftig
to **pour** *96* gießen, schütten
power of attorney *31* Handlungsvollmacht
power outage *AE* *33* Stromausfall
practical *15* praktisch, praxisbezogen
to **pre-approve** *63* vorab bestätigen, im Voraus genehmigen
precaution, (safety) ~ *48* Sicherheitsvorkehrung
precise *71* genau, präzise
to **predict** *71* voraussagen, vorhersagen
prediction *24* Voraussage
preferably *110F* vorzugsweise, am liebsten
preference *26* Präferenz, Vorliebe
premises *94* Geschäftsräume
premium *59* erstklassig; **insurance ~** *43* Versicherungsbeitrag, -prämie
prepaid *39* im Voraus bezahlt
preparation *116T* Vorbereitung
pre-printed *35* vorgedruckt
present, at ~ *43* momentan, derzeit, zurzeit
presentable *7* vorzeigbar, respektabel
to **preserve** *96* bewahren, erhalten
pressure *112* Druck
prestige *39* Prestige
prestigious *95T* renommiert, angesehen
presumably *75* vermutlich
to **prevent** *40* (ver)hindern, vorbeugen
previous *34* vorherig, früher
to **price sth** *97* für etw den Preis festsetzen
primary *26* Haupt-, hauptsächlich
principle *107* Grundsatz, Prinzip
printout *30* Ausdruck
procedure *35* Vorgang, Verfahren
to **process** *7* (weiter)verarbeiten
to **produce** *51* produzieren, herstellen
production *94* Produktion
productive *75* produktiv
profile *7* Profil, Porträt
profit and loss account *95T* Gewinn- und Verlustrechnung
to **progress** *116F* vorankommen, weiterkommen
prohibition *107* Verbot
to **promise** *60* versprechen
to **promote** *82* fördern, unterstützen
to **promote sb** *27* jdn befördern
promotion *8* Beförderung, (beruflicher) Aufstieg
to **prompt** *40* veranlassen
prompt *91* umgehend
to **pronounce** *51* aussprechen
proof *26* Beweis, Nachweis; **burden of ~** *51* Beweislast
proof of identity *49* Legitimation, Ausweis
proper *15* richtig
property *44T* (Grund-)Besitz, Immobilie
property loan *43* Baudarlehen
proposition *84T* Vorschlag
proprietor *95* Inhaber/in

pros and cons *(pl)* 33 Für und Wider, Pro und Contra
prospect 69 Aussicht
prospective 108 (zu)künftig, potenziell
prospectus 97 Emissionsprospekt
to **protect** 49 schützen
protection 46 Schutz
to **prove** 19 beweisen
to **provide** 14T (an)bieten, zur Verfügung stellen
provider 26 Anbieter/in; **financial services ~** 26 Finanzdienstleister
provision 26 Bereitstellung
to **publish** 63 veröffentlichen
punctual 46 pünktlich
punctuation 21 Interpunktion, Zeichensetzung
to **purchase** 30 kaufen
purchase 26 Einkauf, Kauf
purpose 53 Absicht, Zweck, Ziel
to **put sb through** 20T jdn durchstellen

Q

qualification 109 Qualifikation, Zeugnis, Fähigkeit
qualified 14T mit Abschluss, qualifiziert
quarterly 44T vierteljährlich
to **question** 37 befragen
to **queue** 10 sich *(in einer Warteschlage)* anstellen, Schlange stehen
quote 64 Zitat

R

race 96 Rennen
rack, roof ~ 78 Dachgepäckträger
to **rack up** 59 anhäufen, akkumulieren *(hier: Schulden bis zum Limit auf einem Kreditkartenkonto)*
RAF (= Royal Air Force) 96 *britische Luftwaffe*
to **raise** 26 erhöhen, (an)heben
to **raise capital** 73 Kapital aufbringen
to **rally** 71 sich erholen
range 14T Palette, Auswahl
to **rank** 108 einstufen, anordnen
rank 96 Dienstrang
rapid 26 schnell, rasch
rapport (with) 7 gutes Verhältnis (zu)
rarely 21 selten
rate 65 Rate, Quote
rather 16T ziemlich
rating 96 Bewertung, Beurteilung, Klassifizierung
raw material 90 Rohstoff

to **react (to)** 70 reagieren (auf)
real estate 13 Immobilien
realistic 84T realistisch
reality 60 Realität, Wirklichkeit
reassuring 54 beruhigend
to **rebound** 71 wieder steigen
to **recall** 96 sich erinnern
to **recap** 99 rekapitulieren, (kurz) zusammenfassen
receipt 49 Beleg
receivable, accounts ~ *(pl)* 90 Forderungen, Außenstände
receivables *(pl)* 91 Forderungen
to **receive** 31 erhalten, empfangen, bekommen
recent 51 jüngst, aktuell
recently 18 jüngst, kürzlich, neulich
reception 20T Empfang *(auch beim Telefon)*, Rezeption
recession 96 Rezession
recipient 39 Empfänger/in
to **reckon** 16 schätzen, glauben
to **recognise** 75 erkennen
to **recognize** 109 anerkennen
to **recommend** 17 empfehlen
recommendation 37 Empfehlung
record 68 Rekord; **credit ~** 76 Bonitätsauskunft
to **recover** 71 sich erholen
to **recruit sb** 96 jdn anwerben
to **recur** 45 sich wiederholen, wiederkehren
to **reduce** 51 senken, reduzieren, verringern
reduction 52T Nachlass, Rabatt
to **refer to** 9 sich beziehen auf
referee 111 Referenzgeber/in
reference 31 Auskunft, Referenz; 45 (Akten-)Zeichen, Referenznummer; **credit ~** 86 Kreditauskunft; **ref. no. (= ~ number)** 113 Referenznummer, Aktenzeichen
reform 75 Reform
refreshment 17 Erfrischung, Stärkung, Imbiss
to **refund** 23 erstatten
refund 46 Erstattung
to **refuse** 45 ablehnen, sich weigern
regard, as ~s 91 in puncto, hinsichtlich
regarding 25 bezüglich, betreffend
regardless of 27 ungeachtet
regards, Best ~ 29 Beste Grüße
to **register** 35 (sich) anmelden, (sich) registrieren, (sich) eintragen
register, land ~ 79 Grundbuch
registration, residence ~ 29 Meldebescheinigung
to **regret** 23 bedauern, bereuen

regular, on a ~ basis 30 regelmäßig; **~ (customer)** 15 Stammkunde/-in, Bestandskunde/-in; **via ~ mail** 33 auf dem Postweg
to **regulate** 43 regeln, regulieren
regulation 31 Vorschrift
regulator 63 Regulierungsbehörde
to **reinvest** 69 reinvestieren, neu investieren
reinvestment 90 Wiederanlage, Reinvestition
to **relate to sth** 116T sich auf etw beziehen
related 8 zugehörig, verbunden, verwandt
relating to 49 in Zusammenhang mit, bezüglich
relation 75 Beziehung, Verhältnis
to **relax** 49 (sich) entspannen
to **release** 45 freigeben, einlösen
reliability 109 Zuverlässigkeit, Verlässlichkeit
reliable 7 zuverlässig, verlässlich
to **rely on/upon** 26 sich stützen auf, sich verlassen auf
to **remain** 27 bleiben
to **remind (sb of sth)** 39 (jdn an etw) erinnern
reminder 39 (Zahlungs-)Erinnerung, Mahnung
to **remove** 14T entfernen
to **rent out** 81T vermieten
to **repair** 16T reparieren
to **repay** 54 zurückzahlen
repayable 38 rückzahlbar
repayment 43 Tilgung; **lump sum ~** 93 einmalige Rückzahlung
repayment loan 77 Annuitätsdarlehen
to **replace** 14T ersetzen
replacement 25 Ersatz
reply 58 Antwort
to **reply (to)** 23 antworten (auf)
to **repossess** 93 beschlagnahmen
to **represent** 39 ausmachen, darstellen
representative 62 repräsentativ
to **reprice** 63 den Preis neu festlegen
reputation 91 Ansehen, Ruf
request 7 Anfrage, Wunsch, Bitte
to **require** 7 benötigen, erfordern, verlangen
requirement 8 Voraussetzung, Bedingung, Anforderung
to **research** 116F recherchieren
research 26 Forschung, Recherche
to **resell** 107 weiterverkaufen

reservation *19* Reservierung, Buchung
to **reserve** *18* buchen, reservieren
residence registration *29* Meldebescheinigung
resident *118* Einwohner/in; **~s' registration office** *31* Einwohnermeldeamt
to **resist** *63* widerstehen
to **resolve** *103* lösen, auflösen
to **respond** *20* antworten, reagieren
responsibility *10* Verantwortung, Aufgabe(nbereich)
responsible (for) *11* verantwortlich, zuständig (für)
to **restrict** *45* beschränken, einschränken
restriction *31* Beschränkung, Einschränkung
restroom *AE* *12* Toilette *(in öffentlichen Gebäuden)*
résumé *AE* *108F* Lebenslauf
retail outlet *49* Ladengeschäft, Einzelhandelsgeschäft
retailer *96* Einzelhändler/in
retained profits *(pl)* *90* thesaurierte Gewinne
retention *68* Beibehaltung, Erhaltung
to **retire** *16* in den Ruhestand gehen, in Rente gehen
retirement *66* Pensionierung, Ruhestand
return *39* Rendite
to **reuse** *91* wiederverwenden
to **reveal** *63* enthüllen
revenue *27* Einkünfte, Einnahmen
reverse *111* umgekehrt, entgegengesetzt
to **revoke** *45* widerrufen
to **revolve** *58* rotieren, sich drehen
revolving credit *54* revolvierender Kredit *(Konto, das nur im Minus geführt wird)*
to **reward** *27* belohnen
rewarding *14T* lohnend, erfüllend
rifle *39* Gewehr
ring, to **give sb a ~** *16* jdn anrufen
to **rise** *66* (an)steigen
rise *26* Aufschwung, Anstieg; *26* Erhöhung, Anstieg
risky *55* riskant
robust *26* widerstandsfähig, robust
to **roll out** *15* einführen, ausbauen
roof rack *78* Dachgepäckträger
rough *81* grob, ungefähr
rounded *111* abgerundet
route *15* Route, Strecke; **off ~** *15* abseits
to **rule out** *107* ausschließen
to **rush** *49* eilen, sich beeilen

S
safe deposit box *10* Bankschließfach, Tresorfach
to **safeguard** *31* schützen
safety deposit box *10* Bankschließfach, Tresorfach
sage *96* klug, weise
sake, for the ~ of sth *116T* einer Sache zuliebe, einer Sache wegen
salary *8* Gehalt, Lohn
sale, contract of ~ *105* Kaufvertrag
sales *pl* *84T* Verkäufe
sample *100* Probe, Muster
satellite dish *15* Satellitenschüssel
satisfied *23* zufrieden
to **save up (for)** *12* (auf)sparen (für)
saver *64* Sparer/in
savings scheme *82* Sparplan; **~** *(pl)* *43* Ersparnisse
savings account *16T* Sparkonto
savings book *16T* Sparbuch
savings plan *43* Sparplan
savvy *26* versiert
say *10* zum Beispiel, beispielsweise
saying *115* Sprichwort, Redensart; **as the ~ goes** *115* wie man so sagt
scared, to **be ~** *44T* Angst haben
sceptical *75* skeptisch
scheme *37* Plan, Programm; **savings ~** *82* Sparplan
school, vocational ~ *112* Berufsschule, berufsbildende Schule
scope *63* Umfang
to **score** *78* bewerten
scoring, credit-~ *76* Kreditwürdigkeitsbewertung
season ticket *43* Zeit-, Jahreskarte; Abonnement
section *116T* Abteilung, Abschnitt
sector *63* Sektor, Bereich
to **secure** *79* sichern
secure *36* sicher
security *9* Sicherheit
security system *85* Sicherheitssystem
to **see sb (about)** *12* jdn aufsuchen (wegen)
to **seek** *8* suchen (nach), anstreben
to **seize** *91* ergreifen
selection *69* Auswahl
self-confessed *96* erklärt, nach eigener Aussage
self-service *9* Selbstbedienung(s-)
sense, to **make ~** *55* sinnvoll sein
sensible *55* vernünftig

separate *31* getrennt, separat
separately *21* einzeln
serial number *49* Seriennummer
serious *6* ernsthaft, seriös
service, customer ~ officer *16* Kundenberater/in
services, financial ~ provider *26* Finanzdienstleister
set *111* festgelegt, festgesetzt
to **set up** *31* einstellen, einrichten, eröffnen
settled, to **get ~** *31* sich einleben
severe *83* ernst, schwerwiegend
sexual *118* sexuell
to **shake hands** *116T* sich die Hand geben, die Hände schütteln
shameful *75* schändlich
to **shape** *26* formen
shape *15* Form
share *13* Aktie, Anteil
share price *70* Aktienkurs
shareholder *95* Aktionär/in, Teilhaber/in, Gesellschafter/in
to **ship** *78* verschicken, versenden
shipment *99* Sendung, Ladung, Lieferung; **partial ~** *104* Teillieferung
shipper *102* Versender/in, Spediteur/in
to **shirk** *75* umgehen, sich (vor etw) drücken
shopper *96* Käufer/in, Kunde/Kundin
short of time *15* in Zeitnot
shortlist *109* (engere) Auswahlliste
shortly *68* bald, in Kürze
short-term *20T* kurzfristig
shotgun *39* Schrotflinte
to **show sb (a)round** *9* jdn herumführen
to **shun** *75* scheuen, meiden
shy *26* schüchtern, scheu
side, (right/left-hand) ~ *36* (rechte/linke) Seite
sight, after ~ *99* nach Sicht
to **sign up** *39* sich anmelden
signature *48* Unterschrift
significant *83* bedeutend, wichtig
significant(ly) *48* deutlich, signifikant
silence *91* Stille, Schweigen
similar (to) *7* ähnlich, vergleichbar
similarity *9* Ähnlichkeit, Gemeinsamkeit
sincerely, Yours ~ *55* Mit freundlichen Grüßen
sixfold *107* sechsfach
sized, medium-~ *87* mittelgroß
skill *7* Fertigkeit, Fähigkeit
to **slash** *96* *(drastisch)* reduzieren, senken
slash *21* Schrägstrich

slice *51* Scheibe, Stück *(Kuchen)*
slightly *68* leicht, geringfügig
slip, credit ~ *35* Einzahlungsschein
to **slip by** *7* durchrutschen
slippery slope *60* Schlitterpfad, Weg nach unten
to **slump** *71* zurückgehen, fallen
smart *6* elegant, schick *(Kleidung)*; *38* intelligent, pfiffig, geschickt
smooth *91* glatt, reibungslos, problemlos
to **soar** *71* steigen
so-called *19* sogenannt
to **socialize** *111* sich treffen, unter Leute gehen
society, building ~ *37* Bausparkasse
sole *31* alleinig; **~ trader** *95* Einzelunternehmer/in
solution *43* Lösung
sooner or later *64* früher oder später, über kurz oder lang
sort code *37* Bankleitzahl
source *26* Quelle, Herkunft
speaker, native ~ *88* Muttersprachler/in
speaking *20T* am Apparat *(Telefon)*
to **specialize in** *101* sich spezialisieren auf
specialized *38* Spezial-
specific *92* bestimmt, speziell, spezifisch
specification *39* Spezifikation
to **specify** *35* angeben, spezifizieren
spectacular *39* sensationell, spektakulär
to **speculate** *75* spekulieren
speculation *107* Spekulation
spell *96* Abschnitt, Weile, kurze Zeit
to **sponsor** *86* finanziell unterstützen, fördern
spotter, plane ~ *96* Flugzeugbeobachter/in *(Hobby)*
to **spread** *26* (sich) ausbreiten, (sich) verbreiten; *69* verteilen
to **spur** *75* anspornen
stable *71* stabil, konstant
stage *116* Phase, Abschnitt
stand in line, to **stand/wait in line (for)** *AE 9* Schlange stehen, sich anstellen (für/nach)
to **standardize** *43* standardisieren
standing order *30* Dauerauftrag
to **stash** *75* bunkern
to **state** *82* erklären, angeben
statement, (bank) ~ *9* (Konto-)Auszug

statement printer *14T* Kontoauszugsdrucker
station, police ~ *49* Polizeiwache, Polizeirevier
statistics *(pl) 66* Statistik(en), statistische Angabe(n)
status *89* Status
steady *71* gleichmäßig, stetig
steep *70* steil
stepping stone *38* Sprungbrett
to **stick to sth** *16T* bei etw bleiben, sich an etw halten
to **stipulate** *107* festlegen
stock *13* Aktie, Anleihe; **~ exchange** *73* Börse; **~ market** *64* (Wertpapier-)Börse
stocks and shares *(pl) 13* Wertpapiere
stone, stepping ~ *38* Sprungbrett
to **stop payment (on)** *49* sperren
to **store** *48* speichern
straight ahead *10* geradeaus
straightaway *16T* sofort
straightforward *26* einfach, klar (ausgedrückt)
to **strain** *96* überlasten, zerren
strange *49* seltsam, merkwürdig
strength *115* Stärke
to **stress** *116F* betonen, hervorheben
strip, magnetic ~ *49* Magnetstreifen
strongroom *10* Banktresor, Tresor(raum)
structural *75* strukturell
to **structure** *17* strukturieren
to **struggle** *63* kämpfen, sich abmühen
stuck, to **get ~** *14T* sich festfahren, stecken bleiben, sich (auf) stauen
stuff *59* Zeug, Sache(n)
subject *90* Thema
subject to *38* vorbehaltlich
to **submit** *52T* einreichen, vorlegen, zusenden
to **subscribe to** *97* zeichnen
subsidiary *51* Tochterunternehmen, Filiale
subsidy *64* Subvention
substantial *95T* beträchtlich, ansehnlich
to **subtract** *58* abziehen, subtrahieren
to **suffer** *83* leiden, erleiden
to **suggest** *19* vorschlagen
suggestion *115* Vorschlag
to **suit sb** *23* jdm passen, jdm recht sein
suitable *55* geeignet, passend
sum, lump ~ repayment *93* einmalige Rückzahlung

to **summarize** *49* zusammenfassen
summary *111* Zusammenfassung
superb *109* ausgezeichnet
supervisor *27* Betreuer/in, Vorgesetzte/r
supplier *90* Lieferant, Zulieferer, Anbieter *(Firma)*
to **supply** *76* bereitstellen, zur Verfügung stellen, anbieten
to **support** *93* unterstützen, tragen, stützen
support *16T* Unterstützung
suppose, I ~ *16T* wohl
supposedly *15* angeblich
surge *97* Welle, starker Anstieg
surplus, trade ~ *98* Handelsüberschuss, Handelsbilanzüberschuss
surprising *51* überraschend, erstaunlich
survey *37* Umfrage
swap *107* Tauschgeschäft
to **sweep** *15* fegen
to **switch** *18* wechseln, umstellen
syllable *54* Silbe
syndicated loan *87* Konsortialkredit

T

tact *27* Takt(gefühl)
tail *96* Heck
tailored *77* maßgeschneidert
tailor-made *113* maßgeschneidert
to **take, ~ (your) time** *7* sich Zeit nehmen/lassen; **~ a look (at sth)** *10* (sich) (etw) ansehen, betrachten; **~ part (in)** *37* teilnehmen (an); **~ place** *14T* stattfinden
take, Take care. *8* Pass auf dich auf.
to **take in** *14T* einnehmen
to **take out (money)** *16T* (Geld) abheben
to **take out a mortgage** *85* Hypothek aufnehmen
takeover *87* Übernahme
to **tamper with** *33* manipulieren
tap *96* Wasserhahn
target group *51* Zielgruppe
targeted *63* gezielt
task *18* Aufgabe
tatters, in ~ *96* in Fetzen
tax *39* Steuer
tax-deductible *95T* steuerlich absetzbar
tax-free *66* steuerfrei; **~ allowance** *72* Steuerfreibetrag
taxman, the ~ *(infml) 39* das Finanzamt

tea, … is not my cup of ~. *16* … ist nicht mein Fall. / nach meinem Geschmack.
tech (= technology) *97* Technologie
technical *43* technisch
technique *108F* Methode, Technik
teens, in your ~ *83* im Teenageralter, zwischen 13 und 19
teller *AE* *6* Kassierer/in
temporary *45* vorübergehend, befristet
to **tempt** *39* in Versuchung führen, verleiten
tenant *43* Mieter/in
to **tend to** *66* dazu neigen
tendency *107* Neigung, Tendenz
term *14T* Begriff; *77* Laufzeit
terms *(pl)* *82* Bedingungen, Bestimmungen; **~s and conditions** *(pl)* *16T* Konditionen, (Allgemeine) Geschäftsbedingungen; **~s of payment** *(pl)* *99* Zahlungsbedingungen
terrible *20T* schrecklich, furchtbar
that, if …, ~ is. *39* wenn … überhaupt / auch wirklich …
theft *51* Diebstahl
thereby *89* dabei, dadurch
thief *49* Dieb/in
thin *15* dünn
to **think on your feet** *109* schnell reagieren
thorough *7* gründlich, sorgfältig
thrifty *75* sparsam, geizig
through, to **put sb ~** *20T* jdn durchstellen
throughout *51* überall (in), in ganz
to **throw a fit** *27* einen Anfall haben, durchdrehen
thus *75* so, somit, dadurch
to **tick** *31* ankreuzen
to **tie (to)** *59* verbinden (mit), anbinden (an), verknüpfen (mit)
to **tie up** *65* festmachen
till *10* Kasse
timber *89* (Nutz-)Holz
time, for the ~ being *31* vorläufig, für den Moment; **short of ~** *15* in Zeitnot; **~ deposit account** *39* Festgeldkonto; **~ frame** *59* Zeitrahmen; to **take (your) ~** *7* sich Zeit nehmen/lassen
tired, to **be ~ of sth** *52* etw satt haben
title document *105* Traditionspapier
to begin with *109* anfänglich
to **tolerate** *73* tolerieren
tool *36* Werkzeug, Tool
to **top, ~ up** *52T* aufladen
top, on ~ of that *52T* darüber hinaus, außerdem; to **go over the ~** *59* ausufern
topic *6* Punkt, Thema
to **total** *81T* sich summieren auf, sich belaufen auf
total *50* Gesamtbetrag, Summe
touch, to **get in ~ with** *61* (sich) in Verbindung setzen mit
tough *96* hart, grob, brutal
tour *35* Rundgang, Führung
track, to **keep ~ of** *61* verfolgen
to **trade** *37* handeln, Handel betreiben
trade, foreign ~ *98* Außenhandel; **~ deficit** *98* Handelsdefizit, Handelsbilanzdefizit; **~ surplus** *98* Handelsüberschuss, Handelsbilanzüberschuss; **volume of ~** *98* Handelsvolumen
trade body *63* Handelsinstitution
trader, sole ~ *95* Einzelunternehmer/in
tradesperson, *pl* **tradespeople** *30* Gewerbetreibende/r, Handwerker/in
traffic jam *24* (Verkehrs-)Stau
trainee *7* Auszubildende/r, Praktikant/in
traineeship *8* Ausbildung(sverhältnis), Praktikum
transaction *10* (Geschäfts-)Vorgang, Transaktion
to **transfer** *33* überweisen
transfer, (bank) ~ *10* (Bank-)Überweisung; **credit ~** *33* Überweisung
transferable *104* übertragbar, transferierbar
transition *40* Übergang, Umstellung
to **translate (as sth)** *39* sich (mit etw) übersetzen lassen
transparency *63* Transparenz
transportation *105* Beförderung, Transport(wesen)
transshipment *104* Umschlag, Umladung
trap *63* Falle
traveller *53* Reisende/r
treasury services *87* Treasury Services *Vermögensverwaltung und -dienstleistungen*
to **treat** *88* behandeln
treatment *75* Behandlung
tremendous *26* gewaltig
to **trick** *60* täuschen, hereinlegen
trillion *75* Billion
triple *19* dreimalig, dreifach
trust *7* Vertrauen
trustworthy *7* zuverlässig, vertrauenswürdig
turn, in ~ *14T* wiederum
turnover *87* Umsatz, Absatz
twenty-four seven (24/7) *25* rund um die Uhr
typical *14T* typisch, charakteristisch
typically *75* typischerweise

U

ultimate buyer *104* Endabnehmer, Endkäufer
unable *48* nicht in der Lage
unacceptable *6* unannehmbar, inakzeptabel
unaffordable *63* unerschwinglich
unchanged *71* unverändert
unclean *105* unsauber
underdressed *6* zu lässig/leger gekleidet
underinvestment *75* Unterinvestition(en)
underneath *41* darunter; unterhalb
underscore *20T* Unterstrich
underwriter *97* Anleger/in, Zeichner/in
unemployed *77* arbeitslos
unfamiliar *21* unbekannt, ungewohnt
unfinished *7* unerledigt, unvollendet
unfortunately *16* leider
unit price *50* Stückpreis
units *(pl)* *69* Investmentanteile
unlike *48* anders als, im Gegensatz zu
unmet *84T* unerfüllt, unbefriedigt
unpaid *49* unbezahlt
ups and downs *63* Höhen und Tiefen
up to *83* bis zu
to **update** *15* auf den neusten Stand bringen, aktualisieren
to **upload** *52T* hochladen, aufladen
upper case *21* großgeschrieben
upset *27* verstimmt, verärgert
upsetting *27* ärgerlich
upside down *91* umgekehrt, auf den Kopf gestellt
upturn *71* Kursanstieg
urban-dwelling *15* städtisch
urgent *44T* dringend
user ID *35* Nutzerkennung
usual *59* üblich, normal
utility bill *43* Betriebskostenabrechnung

V

vacancy *110F* offene Stelle
vacation *AE* *59* Urlaub
valid *52T* gültig
validity *52T* Gültigkeit, Echtheit

Banking word list

Die folgende Liste enthält ca. 650 Fachbegriffe aus dem Bankwesen.

(haftendes) Eigenkapital equity capital
abbuchen debit
Abbuchung debit (entry)
abheben withdraw
Abhebung withdrawal
Ablaufdatum date of expiry, expiry date
Abrechnung(stag) settlement (day)
Abteilung department
abtreten assign
Abtretung assignment
abzahlen pay off
abziehen deduct
Abzug deduction
Akkreditiv letter of credit, documentary credit
Aktie share, stock (AE)
Aktiengesellschaft (AG) public limited company (plc)
Aktienkurs share price
Aktionär/in shareholder
Aktiva assets
Akzeptanzstelle point of sale
Allgemeine Geschäftsbedingungen General Business Conditions
an der Börse notiert listed on the stock exchange
an die Börse gehen go public
Anfrage inquiry
Angebot offer
Angebot und Nachfrage supply and demand
Angestellte/r clerk, employee
Anlage investment
Anlageberater/in investment consultant
Anlagevermögen non-current assets
anlegen invest
Anleger/in investor
Anleihe(papier) bond
Annuitätsdarlehen repayment loan
Anteil share
Antragsformular application form
Antragsteller/in applicant
Arbeitgeber/in employer
Arbeitnehmer/in employee
auf eigene Rechnung handeln act on one's own account
Aufenthaltserlaubnis residence permit
Aufenthaltsnachweis proof of legal residence
Aufschwung upturn, rise
Ausbildung(sverhältnis) traineeship
Ausführung transaction
Ausgabe issue
Ausgabe(n) expenditure (pl. only)
Ausgabeaufschlag initial charge
ausgeben issue
ausgeübter Beruf occupation
Auslagen costs
Außenhandel foreign trade
ausspähen spy on
Aussteller issuer
Ausstellungsdatum date of issue
Ausstellungsort place of issue
Auszubildende/r trainee
Baisse bear market
Bankleitzahl bank sort code
bankrott bankrupt
Banktresor strongroom
Bargeld cash
Bargeldautomat cash dispenser
bargeldlos cash-free, cashless
Barscheck open cheque
Baudarlehen property loan
Bausparkasse building society
Bausparvertrag building society policy
beantragen apply (for)
Bearbeitungsgebühr handling, arrangement fee
Begleichung settlement
Beitrag contribution
belasten debit
Beleg receipt
Berater/in adviser
Beratungsgespräch consultation
berechnen charge
Beruf profession
Berufsschule vocational school
bestätigen confirm, endorse
besteuert werden be taxed
Bestimmungsort destination
Betrag amount
betragen amount to
betriebliche Altersversorgung company pension
Betriebskosten running costs, overheads
Betrug fraud
Betrüger/in cheat
betrügerisch fraudulent
beurteilen assess
bevollmächtigen authorize
Bewertungspunkt valuation point
bewilligen grant
bezahlen pay, honour
Bezahlung payment, settlement
Bezugsrechtsemission rights issue
Bilanz balance (sheet)
Billion (BE) thousand billion, (AE) trillion
Börse stock exchange, stock market
Börseneinführung listing
Börsengang flotation, IPO (initial public offering)
Broschüre brochure
brutto gross
Bruttoinlandsprodukt (BIP) GDP (gross domestic product)
Buchung entry
Bürge guarantor
Bürgschaft guarantee
Dachfonds fund of funds
Darlehen loan
Dauerauftrag standing order
Deckung cover
Deckungslücke shortfall
Depot portfolio
Depot (im ~ der Bank) in the custody of the bank
Depotkonto safe custody account
Devisen foreign exchange
Diebstahl theft
Dienst(leistung) service
Disagio discount
Dispositionskredit overdraft facility
Dividende dividend
Dokumente gegen bar/Zahlung documents against payment
Dokumenteninkasso collection of documents
ec-Karte debit card
effektiver Jahreszins APR (annual percentage rate), true APR
Eigenkapital equity (capital)
eine Hypothek aufnehmen take out a mortgage
eingeben key in
Einkommen income
Einkünfte income
Einlagensicherungsfonds financial services compensation scheme
Einmalanlage lump sum investment
Einrichtung setting-up
einschätzen assess

Banking word list

Eintrag entry
Einwohnermeldeamt residents' registration office
einzahlen pay in, pay into
Einzahler/in payer
Einzahlung deposit
einziehen claim
Einzugsermächtigung direct debit
Einzugsverfahren direct debit
Emission flotation, issue
Emissionsbank issuing house
Emittent issuer
emittieren issue
Empfänger/in recipient
endfälliges Darlehen interest-only loan
Entgelt fee
Entsprechung equivalent
erben inherit
ermächtigen authorize
Ersatz replacement
ersetzen replace
Ersparnisse savings
erstatten reimburse, refund
Erstattung refund
Erstnotierung first listing
Ertrag yield
Erwerb acquisition
erwirtschaften yield, make
erzielen yield
Europäische Zentralbank European
fällig werden fall due, mature
Fälligkeit maturity
Fälligkeit(sdatum) redemption date, maturity date, due date
fälschen forge
Familienname surname
Familienstand marital status
Festgeldkonto term deposit account, notice account
Filiale branch
Filialleiter/in branch manager
Finanzamt tax authority
Finanzierung financing
Firmendarlehen corporate loan
Firmenkunde corporate client
Firmenkunden corporate business
Fonds fund
Forderungen provisions for receivables, trade debts
Frachtgut consignment, freight (no plural)
Freiberufler self-employed person
Freigabe release
Freistellungsantrag application for tax exemption
Fremdkapital creditors
Fremdwährung(en) forex = foreign exchange
führen (Konten) keep (accounts)
Fusion merger
Gebühr charge, fee
gebührenfrei free of charge
Geburtsdatum date of birth
Geburtsname name at birth
Geburtsort place of birth
Gegenwert equivalent
gegenzeichnen countersign
Gehalt salary
Gehaltskonto current account,
Geheimnummer code number, PIN
Geldautomat ATM, cash dispenser
Geldwäschegesetz Money Laundering Act
Gemeinschaftskonto joint account
genehmigen approve
Geschäftskunde/in corporate client
Geschäftszeiten opening hours
Gesellschaft mit beschränkter Haftung (GmbH) private limited company (Ltd)
gewähren grant
Gewinn profit
Gewinn- und Verlustrechnung profit and loss account
Girokonto checking account (AE), current account
Großbank high street bank
Grundschuld eintragen register a land-charge
gültig valid
günstig favourable
Güterstand system of marital property
Guthaben credit balance
Guthabenzinsen credit interest
gutheißen approve
gutschreiben credit
Gutschrift credit (entry)
Habensaldo credit balance
haftbar liable
halbjährlich half-yearly
Handelsrechnung commercial invoice
Handelsvolumen volume of trade
Handlungsvollmacht power of attorney
Hauptgeschäftsführer/in chief executive (officer)
Hauptstelle head office
Hausse bull market
Höhe amount
Hypothek aufnehmen take out a mortgage
Hypothekenbank mortgage bank
im Rückstand in arrears
immaterielle(s) Vermögen(swerte) intangible assets
Immobilien real estate
in Umlauf in circulation
Indossament endorsement
indossieren endorse
Inkassoauftrag erteilen place a collection order
Insolvenz insolvency
institutionelle/r Fonds-manager/in institutional fund manager
Inventar inventory
investieren invest
Investition investment
Investmentanteile units
Investmentfonds unit trust, investment fund
Investor/in investor
Jahreshauptversammlung annual general meeting (AGM)
jährlich annual(ly)
Kai quay
Kapital aufbringen raise capital
Kapitalanleger/in investor
Kapitalversicherung (als Rente auszahlbar) annuity assurance
Kapitalversicherung life assurance, endowment insurance
Karteneinzug slot (for inserting cards)
Kassa gegen Dokumente documents against payment
Kasse till
Kassierer/in cashier
Kaufpreis purchase price
Kaufvertrag contract of sale
Kleinanleger/in retail investor
Kleinkredit personal loan
Kollege/Kollegin colleague
Konkurs bankruptcy
Konkurs (in ~ gehen) go bankrupt
Konnossement bill of lading
Konsortialführer lead manager
Konsortialkredit syndicated loan
Konsortium syndicate
Konto account
Konto mit Kündigung(sfrist) notice account
Kontoauszug bank statement
Kontoauszugsdrucker statement printer
Kontoinhaber/in account holder
Kontokorrentkonto current account

Banking word list

Kontokorrentschuldner trade debtors
Kontosperrung blocking an account
Kontostand balance
Kontoüberziehung overdraft
kostenlos free of charge
Kredit loan, credit (no plural)
Kreditgeber/in lender
Kreditinstitut bank
Kreditkarte credit card
Kreditnehmer/in borrower
kreditwürdig creditworthy
Kreditwürdigkeit creditworthiness
Kunde/Kundin customer
Kundenberater/in customer service officer
Kundenberatung customer service
kündigen give notice
Kündigungsfrist period of notice
Kurs-Gewinn-Verhältnis price-earnings ratio
kurzfristig short-term
Ladung shipment
Lager(bestand) stocks
Lager(haus) warehouse
Lagerbestände inventory
Lagerschein warrant
langfristig long-term
Lastschrift debit, direct debit
Lebenshaltungskosten living expenses
Lebensversicherung life assurance, life insurance
Legitimation proof of identity
Leitzins base rate
Lieferung consignment, shipment, delivery
Lohn wage
löschen cancel
Mahnung reminder
Miete; mieten rent
Milliarde (BE) thousand million, (AE) billion
Mindeszahlung minimum payment
Missbrauch misuse
Misstrauen mistrust
Mitantragsteller/in co-applicant
mittelfristig medium-term
mitunterzeichnen co-sign
Münze coin
Nachfrage demand
Nennwert denomination, nominal value
netto net
nichtselbständige Arbeit employment
Nichtveranlagungsbescheinigung certificate of exemption
Obligation bond, debenture
Orderscheck order cheque
Packliste packing list
Passiva liabilities
Pension pension
Pensionierung retirement
Personal staff
Personalausweis proof of identity, identity card
Pfand pledge
pfänden pledge
Pfandrecht lien
plündern plunder, raid
Portefeuille portfolio
Praktikant/in trainee, work experience student
Praktikum period of work experience
Präsentation presentation
Preisfindung bookbuilding
Privatkundengeschäft retail banking
Provision commission
prüfen examine
Quellensteuer withholding tax
Quittung receipt
Rate instalment
Ratenkauf hire purchase
realisieren realize
Rechnung invoice, bill
reingezeichnet clean on board
Reisescheck traveller's cheque
Rekordhoch record high
Rendite return, yield
Rente pension
Rentenpapier bond
Rentner/in pensioner
Reserven reserves
Rezession recession
risikobereit risk-tolerant
Risikobereitschaft risk tolerance
Risikokapital venture capital
rückgängig machen revoke
Rückkaufswert surrender value
Rücklagen reserves, retained earnings
Rückstellungen für Verbindlichkeiten und Forderungen provisions for liabilities and charges
Rückzahlung repayment, redemption
Ruhestand retirement
Sach(anlage)vermögen tangible assets
Saldo balance
Schalter counter
Scheck cheque
Schiff vessel
Schiffsladung shipment
schriftlich in writing
SCHUFA German banks' credit reference agency
SCHUFA-Klausel SCHUFA declaration
Schuld(en) debt
schulden owe
Schuldner debtor
Schuldverschreibung debenture
schwanken fluctuate
Schwankung fluctuation
Schwellenländer emerging markets
selbstständig self-employed
selbstständige Tätigkeit self-employment
Selbstauskunft voluntary disclosure
Sendung consignment, shipment
Seriennummer serial number
Sicherheit(en) collateral, security
Sicherheitsvorkehrung safety precaution
Sicherungsübereignung assignment by bill of sale
Solidaritätszuschlag solidarity tax
Soll debit
Soll(saldo) debit balance
Sorten foreign currency
sparen save
Sparkasse savings bank
Sparkonto deposit account, savings account
Sparplan savings scheme, plan
Sparschwein piggy bank
Spediteur/in freight forwarder, forwarding agent
spekulativ speculative
sperren stop (payment on)
staatliche Förderungen government support/incentives
Staatsanleihen government bonds
Stahlkammer strongroom
Stammaktie equity, ordinary share
Stammaktien equities, ordinary shares
Standardwert blue chip
Steuer tax
steuerfrei tax-free
Steuerfreibetrag tax-free allowance
Steuerhinterziehung tax evasion
Steuerklärung tax return

Strafgebühr penalty fee
Strafzinsen penalty interest
Stückelung denominations
subventionieren subsidize
Summe amount, total
Tätigkeit occupation
Teilrückzahlung partial repayment, instalment
Termin appointment
Termingeldkonto notice account
tilgen pay back, pay off, repay
Tilgung repayment
Traditionspapier title document
Tresor(raum) strongroom
Überbringerscheck bearer cheque
Übernahme takeover
überschreiten exceed
übersteigen exceed
übertragbar negotiable
übertragen assign
überweisen transfer
Überweisung credit transfer, remittance
überziehen overdraw
Überziehungskredit overdraft
Umlaufvermögen, -kapital current assets
Umsatz turnover
umtauschen change
Umtauschkurs exchange rate
unbefugt unauthorized
unbeständig volatile
ungesicherte Schuldverschreibungen junk bonds
Unterhaltskosten running costs
Unterhaltungszahlungen maintenance (payments)
Unternehmer/in entrepreneur
unterschätzen underestimate
unterschreiben sign
Unterschrift signature
Unterschriftsprobe specimen signature
Untersuchung inquiry
unwiderruflich irrevocable
Ursprungszeugnis certificate of origin
Verbindlichkeiten liabilities
Verfallsdatum expiry date
verfügbar available
verfügbares Einkommen disposable income
Verfügbarkeit availability
verfügen über dispose of
Verladehafen port of loading
Verladung loading
Verlust loss
Vermögen(swerte) assets
Vermögensberater/in investment consultant
Vermögensverteilung wealth distribution
Vermögensverwaltung asset management
vermögenswirksam asset-building
verpfänden pledge
Verrechnungsscheck crossed cheque
Versand dispatch
Verschiffer shipper
Verschiffung shipment
verschlüsselt encrypted
verschuldet in debt
versichern insure
Versicherung(spolice) insurance (policy)
Versicherungsbeitrag insurance premium
Vertrag contract
vertraulich confidential
Verwendungszweck purpose
verzinsen pay interest on
vierteljährlich quarterly
Vollmacht authority for per pro signatory, third party mandate
vorausgesetzt subject to
Vorlage presentation
vorlegen present
Vorname first name, given name
vorrätig in stock
Vorsorge treffen für make provision for
vorsorgen provide for the future
Vorstand board of directors
Vorzugsaktien preference shares
Währung currency
Warenausfuhr exports, exported goods
Wechsel bill of exchange
Wechselkurs exchange rate, rate of exchange
wechseln change
Werktag working day
Wertbezeichnung denomination
Wertpapierbestand Portfolio
Wertpapierbörse stock market, stock exchange
Wertpapiere securities (pl. only), stocks and shares
Wertstellung value
wertvoll valuable
widerrufen revoke
wohlhabend affluent, wealthy
Wohnverhältnisse residential status
Zahlung settlement, payment
Zahlung gegen Rechnung (mit offenem Zahlungsziel) payment on open account
Zahlungsbedingungen terms of payment
Zahlungsempfänger/in beneficiary, payee
Zahlungsmittel means of payment
zahlungsunfähig werden default
Zahlungsunfähigkeit insolvency, default
Zahlungsweise method of payment
zeichnen subscribe to
Zeichnungsfrist subscription period
Zentrale head office
Zins(en) interest (no plural)
Zinsabschlagsteuer tax on investment earnings
Zinssatz rate of interest, interest rate
zu pari at par
zugunsten von in favour of
Zulassung listing
zurückverfolgen trace
zurückzahlen pay back, pay off, repay
Zusammenschluss merger
Zweck purpose, reason
Zweig(stelle) branch

Irregular verbs

be – was/were – been	sein
beat – beat – beaten	schlagen, besiegen
become – became – become	werden
begin – began – begun	anfangen, beginnen
break – broke – broken	brechen
bring – brought – brought	bringen
build – built – built	bauen
burn – burnt/burned – burnt/burned	(ver)brennen
buy – bought – bought	kaufen
catch – caught – caught	fangen
choose – chose – chosen	wählen
come – came – come	kommen
cost – cost – cost	kosten
cut – cut – cut	schneiden
deal (with) – dealt (with) – dealt (with)	sich kümmern um, umgehen mit
do – did – done	tun, machen
draw – drew – drawn	zeichnen
dream – dreamt/dreamed – dreamt/dreamed	träumen
drink – drank – drunk	trinken
drive – drove – driven	fahren
eat – ate – eaten	essen
fall – fell – fallen	fallen
feed – fed – fed	füttern, ernähren
feel – felt – felt	(sich) fühlen, empfinden
fight – fought – fought	kämpfen
find – found – found	finden
fit – fit/fitted – fit/fitted	passen
fly – flew – flown	fliegen
forget – forgot – forgotten	vergessen
freeze – froze – frozen	frieren
get – got – got (*AE* gotten)	bekommen
give – gave – given	geben
go – went – gone	gehen, fahren
grow – grew – grown	wachsen
hang – hung – hung	hängen
have – had – had	haben
hear – heard – heard	hören
hide – hid – hidden	(sich) verstecken
hit – hit – hit	schlagen
hold – held – held	halten, festhalten
keep – kept – kept	behalten
know – knew – known	kennen, wissen
lay – laid – laid	legen
lead – led – led	führen
learn – learnt/learned – learnt/learned	lernen
leave – left – left	abfahren, verlassen, weggehen
let – let – let	lassen
lie – lay – lain	liegen
light – lit – lit	anzünden, beleuchten, anmachen
lose – lost – lost	verlieren
make – made – made	machen
mean – meant – meant	meinen, bedeuten
meet – met – met	treffen
pay – paid – paid	bezahlen
prove – proved – proved/proven	nachweisen, beweisen
put – put – put	setzen, stellen, legen
read – read – read	lesen
ride – rode – ridden	reiten, fahren
ring – rang – rung	klingeln, anrufen
rise – rose – risen	(an)steigen
run – ran – run	laufen, rennen
say – said – said	sagen
see – saw – seen	sehen
seek – sought – sought	suchen
sell – sold – sold	verkaufen
send – sent – sent	senden, schicken
set – set – set	setzen, stellen
show – showed – shown	zeigen
shrink – shrank/shrunk – shrunk	schrümpfen, zurückgehen
shut – shut – shut	schließen
sing – sang – sung	singen
sit – sat – sat	sitzen
sleep – slept – slept	schlafen
smell – smelt/smelled – smelt/smelled	riechen
speak – spoke – spoken	sprechen
spell – spelt/spelled – spelt/spelled	buchstabieren
spend – spent – spent	ausgeben, verbringen
stand – stood – stood	stehen
steal – stole – stolen	stehlen
stick – stuck – stuck	kleben
swim – swam – swum	schwimmen
take – took – taken	nehmen
teach – taught – taught	unterrichten, beibringen
tell – told – told	sagen, erzählen
think – thought – thought	denken
throw – threw – thrown	werfen
understand – understood – understood	verstehen
wake – woke – woken	wecken
wear – wore – worn	tragen (Kleidung)
win – won – won	gewinnen
write – wrote – written	schreiben

Acknowledgements

Bildquellen
Titelfoto Shutterstock – Image Wizard | **p. 6** v. o. l.: Fotolia – nyul, fotodrobik; Shutterstock - Paul Matthew Photography, danilobiancalana, Kiselev Andrey Valerevich, Elena Dijour, Luba V Nel | **p. 9** Shutterstock – wavebreakmedia | **p. 17** Fotolia – Volker Witt | **p. 18** Shutterstock – Pressmaster | **p. 25** Jonathan Nicholson/Demotix/Corbis (RM) | **p. 26** PricewaterhouseCoopers (de.pwc) | **p. 28** Deutsche Postbank AG | **p. 39** INVESTOPEDIA Fincance & Investing | **p. 40** Shutterstock – Chris Jenner | **p. 41** Shutterstock – AC Manley | **p. 51** F.A.Z.-Grafik Walter| **p. 52** v. l.: cartoonstock - Edgar Argo, Mike Flanagan | **p. 53** Shutterstock – NotarYES | **p. 56** Commerzbank AG | **p. 59** Fotolia – Boggy | **p. 62** Shutterstock – jesadaphorn | **p. 66** Corbis/Eric Audras/PhotoAlto | **p 76** Fotolia – Klaus Eppele | **p. 81** Shutterstock – racorn | **p. 83** Shutterstock – vlad.georgescu | **p. 86** v. o. l.: Reuters/mecom (RM); Mauritius Images/Alamy (RM); Mauritius Images/Alamy (RM); imago/GEPA-pictures | **p. 91** Wells Fargo | **p. 95** Clip Dealer – Sean Prior | **p. 96** Shutterstock – Paul Matthew Photography | **p. 97** Statista GmbH – Zalando | **p. 98** v. o. l.: Fotolia – CROSS DESIGN; © Jim Austin; Shutterstock – E.G. Pors | **p. 98** u.: © 2015 United Nations | **p. 106** Mauritius Images/Alamy (RM) | **p. 107** Shutterstock – Vladislav Gajic | **p. 108** 1: Shutterstock – Hans Kim, 2: Bevan Goldswain, 3: mimagephotography, 4: Olga Sapegina, 5: Minerva Studio | **p. 115** v. l.: Fotolia – olly; Shutterstock – Syda Productions | **p. 118** Shutterstock – Steven Coburn.
Maps: C. Borrell p. 42, inside covers
Cartoons/Illustrations: Oxford Designers & Illustrators: p. 9, p. 61, p. 64, p. 87, p. 102, p. 103, p. 125

Videoquellen (Screenshots):
p. 24 The Royal Bank of Scotland Group plc | **p. 29** Nationwide Building Society | **p. 44** Money Advice Service | **p. 65** Moneywise Publishing Limited.

Textquellen:
p. 15 http://www.bbc.com/news/business-26993637, by Brian Milligan, 22. April 2014 | **p. 27** http://www.investopedia.com/financial-edge/0512/wild-incentives-for-opening-a-bank-account.aspx, by John Tschohl, 9. Januar 2012 | **p. 37** http://www.bbc.com/news/business-23633788, 11. September 2014 | **p. 39** http://www.investopedia.com/financial-edge/0512/wild-incentives-for-opening-a-bank-account.aspx, by Rachel Brown, 13. Mai 2014 | **p. 40** http://www.theguardian.com/uk-news/2014/jul/06/london-buses-cashless, 6. Juli 2014 | **p. 63** http://www.theguardian.com/business/2014/nov/25/credit-card-market-city-watchdog-investigate, by Jennifer Rankin, 25. November 2014 | **p. 66** http://www.telegraph.co.uk/finance/personalfinance/savings/9446989/Women-open-more-savings-accounts-but-men-deposit-more-cash.html, by Lara May, 2. August 2012 | **p. 74 o.:** iBonds, by Christian Siedenbiedel, Frankfurter Allgemeine Sonntagszeitung, 2. November 2014 | **p. 74 u.:** http://www.manager-magazin.de/finanzen/artikel/bild-994323-756609.html, by Christoph Rottwilm, 29. September 2014 | **p. 75** http://www.economist.com/news/finance-and-economics/21631140-interest-rates-turn-negative-some-worse-nothing?fsrc=rss%7Cfec, by Jennifer Batchelor, 8. November 2014 | **p. 83** http://www.theguardian.com/money/2014/oct/16/young-people-debt-payday-loan-bank, byLisa Bachelor, 16. Oktober 2014 | **p. 96** http://www.thesundaytimes.co.uk/sto/business/business_interviews/article1452828.ece, by John Collingridge, 31. August 2014 | **p. 97** http://www.forbes.com/sites/ryanmac/2014/09/29/zalando-worth-6-8-billion-after-pricing-ipo-at-more-than-27-a-share/, by Ryan Mac/Forbes Staff, 29. September 2014 | **p. 129** http://www.bbc.co.uk/news/business-16596949, by David Black, 18. Januar 2012

Danksagung
Wir bedanken uns bei folgenden Banken und Firmen/Institutionen, die uns freundlicherweise Material für dieses Lehrwerk zur Verfügung gestellt haben:
Commerzbank AG
HSBC Trinkaus & Burkhardt AG
Deutsche Postbank AG
Raiffeisenbank Burgenland / Raiffeisen Zentralbank Wien
The Royal Bank of Scotland (RBS)
Saxo Bank A/S
United Nations (UNCTAD)
Wells Fargo & Company

2023